DAVID BOWIE
THE MUSIC AND THE CHANGES

1947

8 January
Born David Robert Jones in Brixton, London.

1963

Leaves school to work in advertising.

1964

5 June
Releases first single 'Lisa Jane' credited to Davie Jones with the King Bees for the Vocalion Pop label, an imprint of Decca Records. Les Conn becomes his first manager.

DAVID BOWIE
THE MUSIC AND THE CHANGES

1969

'Space Oddity' single is given its first important public airing at Hyde Park as it is played through the PA immediately before the Rolling Stones take to the stage.

David's father, Haywood Stenton Jones, dies of pneumoni.

'Space Oddity', released on Mercury Records becomes Bowie's first hit single in the UK, reaching number five.

David Bowie (later renamed *Space Oddity* in the UK and *Man Of Words, Man Of Music* in the US) released.

1970

Bowie marries Angela Barnett and moves into Haddon Hall along with producer Tony Visconti and other musical colleagues.

1970

January
Bowie plays arguably the world's first glam rock concert with his new band Hype at the Roundhouse.

1973

Bowie's *Aladdin Sane* reaches number one in the UK with 100,000 advance orders, the highest number for any album in the seventies thus far. It would be the first Bowie album to reach the US Top 20.

1972

Under pressure from RCA who are concerned about the lack of hit material on the new album, Bowie writes and records 'Starman' which is added to the changed tracklisting of the *Ziggy Stardust* album.

The Rise And Fall Of Ziggy Stardust And The Spiders From Mars released in June. It eventually reached number five in the UK and number 72 in the USA. It would become, along with *Hunky Dory*, Bowie's biggest-selling back catalogue album.

1977

January
Low is released to a mixed critical reception but is still a substantial hit reaching number two in the UK.

Bowie records the *"Heroes"* album at Hansaton Studios, Berlin, again with Visconti and Eno with the addition of King Crimson's Robert Fripp on lead guitar.

"Heroes" reaches number three in the UK and is *Melody Maker's* album of the year.

1974

Diamond Dogs becomes Bowie's third consecutive UK number one album, and the first of Bowie's albums to make the US Top Five. Again, the album is credited to 'Bowie'.

1975

A re-released 'Space Oddity', backed with 'Changes' and the unreleased 'Velvet Goldmine' reaches number one in the UK.

1976

Bowie's world tour, entitled, *Isolar*, introduces a new alter ego, the Thin White Duke.

1979

The new album, entitled *Lodger*, is completed in New York.

1982

Now out of contract, Bowie records *Let's Dance* at the Power Station in New York in December with new producer, Nile Rodgers (Chic, Sister Sledge, and Diana Ross).

1981

Bowie wins Best Male Singer in the *Rock And Pop Awards* (forerunner of *The Brits*).

1983

'Let's Dance' single reaches number one in the UK and US.

July
Ten Bowie albums can be found in the UK Top 100, the first time one artist had dominated the charts to such an extent since the death of Elvis Presley in 1977.

1985

July 13
Bowie's set is a highlight at Live Aid, Wembley Stadium. A video made with Mick Jagger, a cover of 'Dancing In The Street', is premiered. It would later become a UK number one.

1987

January 8
Bowie turns 40.

Dates for Bowie's first world tour in four years, *Glass Spider*, are announced.

1989

Bowie returns as one-quarter of a band by forming Tin Machine with Gabrels and Iggy Pop's old rhythm section of Hunt and Tony Sales. *Tin Machine* reaches number three in the UK, and Top 30 in the USA garnering, contrary to popular myth, mostly favourable reviews.

Bowie tours with Tin Machine in intimate venues playing a set list with no solo material.

1991

Tin Machine score their one and only UK Top 40 hit with 'You Belong In Rock And Roll'.

1995

Bowie tours USA with Nine Inch Nails. Bowie tours with Morrissey in the UK until the singer leaves the tour midway through.

1992

Bowie marries model Iman Abdulmajid.

1996

The Outside Festival Tour sees Bowie reintroduce a small selection of well-known songs such as '"Heroes"'. 'Hallo Spaceboy' a re-recording of the *Outside* track with the Pet Shop Boys reaches UK number 12.

Bowie receives Lifetime Achievement Award at the Brits from future Prime Minister Tony Blair.

2003

Bowie declines Knighthood.

Reality, Bowie's 24th solo studio album, reaches UK number three.

2013

'Where Are We Now?', the first new solo Bowie material for a decade is released on January 8, his 66th birthday. It reaches number six in the UK Charts.

The Next Day album is number one in 17 countries including the UK and Germany, and is kept off the US top spot by Bon Jovi.

2006

Bowie receives a Lifetime Achievement Award at *The Grammys*.

DAVID
BOWIE
THE MU
SIC AND
THE CH
ANGES

ISBN: 978-1-78038-988-2
Order No: OP55231

Exclusive Distributors
Music Sales Limited,
14-15 Berners Street,
London, W1T 3LJ.

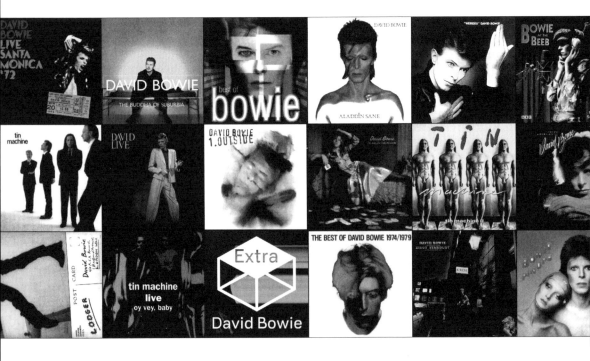

Music Sales Corporation
180 Madison Avenue, 24th Floor,
New York,NY 10016, USA.

Macmillan Distribution Services,
56 Parkwest Drive
Derrimut, Vic 3030, Australia.

To the Music Trade only:
Music Sales Limited,
14-15 Berners Street,
London, W1T 3LJ.

Visit Omnibus Press on the web at
www.omnibuspress.com

DAVID BOWIE
THE MUSIC AND
THE CHANGES
DAVID BUCKLEY

OMNIBUS PRESS

LONDON / NEW YORK / PARIS / SYDNEY / COPENHAGEN / BERLIN / MADRID / TOKYO

1947

8 January. Born David Robert Jones in Brixton, London.

1953

The family move to Bromley in Kent.

1962

Hospitalised after a fight over a girl with friend George Underwood. He is left with permanently dilated pupil in his left eye after corrective surgery fails to fully cure the injury. Forms his first band, the Konrads.

1964

5 June. Releases first single 'Lisa Jane' credited to Davie Jones with the King Bees for the Vocalion Pop label, an imprint of Decca Records. Les Conn becomes his first manager.

1968

Continues to record and release unsuccessful singles; learns mime under the tutelage of Lindsay Kemp. First film, *The Mask*. First prominent appearance, *Pierot In Turquoise*.

1965

5 March. Releases a cover of Bobby Bland's 'I Pity The Fool'. B-side, 'Take My Tip' is Bowie's first songwriting credit (as Davie Jones).

1963

Leaves school to work in advertising.

1967

1 June. Bowie releases eponymous debut, produced by Mike Vernon, on Deram imprint of Decca Records.

1966

Ken Pitt becomes Bowie's manager and friend and encourages him to move into areas outside of popular music – film, mime, dance. Crucially, Pitt would introduce Bowie to the music of the Velvet Underground.

1958

Attends Bromley Technical High School.

1972

'Changes' is the first single off *Hunky Dory*; again, another flop.

Bowie, now with new spiky, short hair, tells journalist Michael Watts from *Melody Maker* that he is gay.

Under pressure from RCA who are concerned about the lack of hit material on the new album, Bowie writes and records 'Starman' which is added to the changed tracklisting of the *Ziggy Stardust* album.

David Bowie and The Spiders From Mars (Ronson on lead, Trevor Bolder on bass, and Mick 'Woody' Woodmandsey on drums) embark on a heavy touring schedule. An appearance at Frairs, Aylesbury marks a significant breakthrough.

'Starman' is released in April and eventually reaches number 10 in the UK charts in August after two notable TV appearances on *Lift Off With Ayesha* and *Top Of The Pops*.

The Rise And Fall Of Ziggy Stardust And The Spiders From Mars released in June. It eventually reached number five in the UK and number 72 in the USA. It would become, along with *Hunky Dory*, Bowie's biggest-selling back catalogue album.

Bowie's 'All The Young Dudes' becomes a UK number three hit for Mott The Hoople.

Bowie co-produces Lou Reed's most successful album, *Transformer,* for RCA.

A special 'David Bowie is Ziggy Stardust' event takes place in August 1972. Backed by the Lindsay Kemp mime group, it is Bowie's most theatrical performance to date.

'John, I'm Only Dancing', a non-album single, peaks at number 12 in the UK charts. A promotional film, made by Mick Rock, is rejected by *Top Of The Pops*.

Iggy Pop and the Stooges, with Bowie's help, are signed to RCA. Bowie co-produces their comeback album, *Raw Power*.

Bowie tours the US in the autumn of 1972. An iconic live show at Santa Monica is much bootlegged.

'The Jean Genie' single is released and enters the UK chart before Christmas. Sessions start for Bowie's sixth studio album in America.

1970

In January Bowie plays arguably the world's first glam rock concert with his new band Hype at the Roundhouse. Mick Ronson, on lead guitar, would remain with Bowie until late 1973.

Bowie splits with Ken Pitt. British lawyer Tony Defries and his Mainman company would manage Bowie for the next five years.

Bowie marries Angela Barnett and moves into Haddon Hall along with producer Tony Visconti and other musical colleagues.

Records *The Man Who Sold The World*, his first major album, although unsuccessful at the time.

1969

Supports Tyrannosaurus Rex as mime act.

'Space Oddity' single is given its first important public airing at Hyde Park as it is played through the PA immediately before the Rolling Stones take to the stage.

David's father, Haywood Stenton Jones, dies of pneumoni

'Space Oddity', released on Mercury Records becomes Bowie's first hit single in the UK, reaching number five.

David Bowie (later renamed *Space Oddity* in the UK and *Man Of Words, Man Of Music* in the US) released.

1971

Bowie's son, then called Zowie, born in April.

Peter Noone scores a UK number 12 hit with Bowie's 'Oh! You Pretty Things'.

Bowie records *Hunky Dory* at Trident Studios with Ken Scott as co-producer.

Bowie signs to RCA records. During the trip to New York, Bowie meets a distinctly unimpressed Andy Warhol.

Bowie records *Ziggy Stardust*, also at Trident.

December: *Hunky Dory* released on RCA records but fails to chart initially. It would subsequently reach number three in the UK chart after the success of *Ziggy Stardust*.

1973

Bowie performs 'The Jean Genie' on *Top Of The Pops*, January 4. The single reaches number two in the UK charts, Bowie's highest placing to date.

Bowie's *Aladdin Sane* reaches number one in the UK with 100,000 advance orders, the highest number for any album in the seventies thus far. It would be the first Bowie album to reach the US Top 20.

The *Aladdin Sane* tour begins and takes in America, Japan, and the UK.

The British press coin a new phrase, 'Bowiemania'. Bowie's success reaches the mainstream when early-evening news programme *Nationwide* carries a mildly disapproving feature on Bowie and his deviant persona.

'Drive-In Saturday' reaches number three in the UK.

'Life On Mars?' from *Hunky Dory* reaches number three in the UK.

July 3: At the Hammersmith Odeon Bowie announces his retirement from live touring.

Bowie begins work immediately on his seventh album, a collection of covers, *Pin-Ups*. This would be the last record to be co-produced by Ken Scott and to feature The Spiders From Mars.

Pin-Ups reaches number one in the UK chart and the single, 'Sorrow', number three. The album was the credited to 'Bowie'.

Bowie begins work on a concept album based on George Orwell's novel *1984*. When Orwell's widow refuses to grant Bowie the rights to the novel, Bowie changes direction and recasts the music as *Diamond Dogs*. Bowie works with engineer Keith Harwood at Olympic Studios in London. Bowie's drug use escalates.

1974

'Rebel Rebel' reaches number five in the UK charts.

The first major David Bowie biography, *The David Bowie Story* by George Tremlett, is published by Futura, priced 40p.

Bowie performs 'Rebel Rebel' on the Dutch programme, *Top Pop*.

April: Bowie leaves for the USA.

Diamond Dogs becomes Bowie's third consecutive UK number one album, and the first of Bowie's albums to make the US Top Five. Again, the album is credited to 'Bowie'.

June: *The Diamond Dogs Revue*, one of the most lavish rock spectacles of all-time, opens its sixth-month run in Toronto, Canada. A 22-year-old New Yorker, Earl Slick, is Bowie's new lead guitarist while pianist Mike Garson is the only musician to be retained from the *Aladdin Sane* tour.

Recording sessions for Bowie's ninth studio album begin at Sigma Sound Studios, Philadelphia with Tony Visconti as producer. The band includes recent recruit Carlos Alomar along with soon-to-be-famous Luther Vandross.

The *Diamond Dogs* tour continues, later to be called the *Philly Dogs* tour as Bowie strips away much of the theatricality to incorporate his new soul approach.

Bowie's first album, *David Live*, preceded by the single, 'Knock On Wood', reach number two and number 10 in the UK respectively.

1975

Alan Yentob's Bowie documentary *Cracked Actor* airs on BBC.

Young Americans album reaches number two in the UK, number nine in the USA.

Bowie begins filming for his first major film role, Nicolas Roeg's *The Man Who Fell To Earth*.

Bowie splits with manager Tony Defries and Mainman.

'Fame', co-written with John Lennon and Carlos Alomar becomes Bowie's first US number one single.

Bowie begins work on his 10th album, *Station To Station* in Los Angeles.

A re-released 'Space Oddity', backed with 'Changes' and the unreleased 'Velvet Goldmine' reaches number one in the UK.

Sessions with Paul Buckmaster for the soundtrack of *The Man Who Fell To Earth* take place but the music is never finished and remains unreleased.

Bowie announces world tour. New single 'Golden Years' is Bowie's first single to reach the top 10 in both UK and US.

1977

January – *Low* is released to a mixed critical reception but is still a substantial hit reaching number two in the UK. 'Sound And Vision' reaches number three in the UK without any promotion from Bowie.

Bowie tours as keyboard player with Iggy Pop to promote *The Idiot* album, co-produced and co-written by Bowie himself.

Bowie records the *"Heroes"* album at Hansaton Studios, Berlin, again with Visconti and Eno with the addition of King Crimson's Robert Fripp on lead guitar.

Iggy Pop's *Lust For Life*, again featuring songwriting contributions from Bowie, reaches the UK Top 30.

'"Heroes"' single becomes a moderate hit, reaching number 24 in the UK, though charting for an impressive ten weeks.

Bowie sings '"Heroes"' and a duet 'Peace On Earth Little/Drummer Boy' with Bing Crosby for the show *Bing Crosby's Merrie Olde Christmas*. Crosby died five weeks later.

Bowie appears with Marc Bolan on the *Marc* TV show just days before his friend's death in a car crash. Bowie is visibly distressed at Bolan's funeral.

"Heroes" reaches number three in the UK and is *Melody Maker's* album of the year.

Bowie films the David Hemming's-directed, *Just A Gigolo*.

1976

Station To Station reaches number three in the US, number five in the UK.

Bowie's world tour, entitled, *Isolar*, introduces a new alter ego, the Thin White Duke.

Bowie arrested and charged with a misdemeanour for possession of cannabis.

Changesonebowie, Bowie's first greatest hits compilation: number two in the UK, number 10 in US.

Work begins on Bowie's 11th album with producer Tony Visconti and collaborator, Brain Eno in Paris.

The tabloid press report Bowie as having a 'heart scare'.

The new album is completed in West Berlin where Bowie is now based with Iggy Pop.

1978

Bowie again tours the world with Frank Zappa's then guitarist Adrian Belew on lead guitar and Simon House on electric violin. A section of the set list is devoted to the *Ziggy Stardust* album.

In a mid-tour break, work begins in Switzerland on Bowie's 13th studio album, again with Eno and Visconti in tow.

A double-live album, *Stage*, reaches number five in the UK.

The world tour ends in Japan in December. It would be Bowie's last concert performance for five years.

1979

The new album, entitled *Lodger*, is completed in New York.

'Boys Keep Swinging', backed with a controversial drag video made in collaboration with David Mallet, reaches number seven in the UK. Bowie also promotes the single with a memorable appearance on the *Kenny Everett Video Show*.

Bowie plays two hours of his favourite music on Radio 1's *Star Special*.

Lodger reaches number four in the UK but garners mixed reviews – a five-star review in *Record Mirror* is balanced by Jon Savage in *Sounds* who calls the album 'Avant AOR'.

The second single, 'DJ' reaches UK number 29.

'John I'm Only Dancing (again)'/'John I'm Only Dancing', pairs the then unreleased soul version of the song with the 1972 version and reaches number 12 in the UK.

Bowie ends the seventies by filming two TV appearances. For *The Kenny Everett Video Show*, Bowie recreates 'Space Oddity' and for *Saturday Night Live*, Bowie performs 'The Man Who Sold The World', 'TVC15' and 'Boys Keep Swinging' with performance artists Klaus Nomi and Joey Arias.

1982

Baal EP charts inside the UK Top 30, possibly the least commercial release by Bowie so to do.

'Cat People (Putting Out Fire)' a collaboration with Giorgio Moroder, and the theme song from the *Cat People* movie, reaches UK number 26, but number one in Norway and Sweden.

Bowie films the vampire movie, *The Hunger*, with Tony Scott directing, before starring in Nagasi Oshima's POW-film, *Merry Christmas Mr Lawrence*. Both films would be released the following year.

Bowie demos tracks for his 14th album in Switzerland.

Now out of contract, Bowie records *Let's Dance* at the Power Station in New York in December with new producer, Nile Rodgers (Chic, Sister Sledge, and Diana Ross).

1980

Sessions begin for *Scary Monsters (And Super Creeps)* in New York.

'Ashes To Ashes' backed with a stunning video co-directed by Bowie and David Mallet becomes Bowie's second UK number one.

Scary Monsters is Bowie's first UK number one since *Diamond Dogs* and receives glowing critical reviews.

'Fashion' reaches UK number five.

Bowie stars in the lead role on Broadway in *The Elephant Man*, directed by Jack Hoffsiss.

1981

Bowie wins Best Male Singer in the *Rock And Pop Awards* (forerunner of *The Brits*).

K-Tel's *The Best Of David Bowie* reaches UK number three.

Bowie is cast as the lead in the BBC's adaptation of Berthold Brecht's *Baal*, and records the *Baal EP* with Tony Visconti back at Hansaton Studios. After a major falling out, it would be 17 years before they would work together in the studio again.

Omnibus Press's year-by-year chronology, *Bowie: Black Book* sells in excess of 100,000 copies in the UK.

'Under Pressure' a one-off collaboration with Queen reaches UK number one.

'Wild Is The Wind' is chosen as a single to promote Bowie's *Changestwobowie*.

1983

Now signed to EMI-America, Bowie announces dates for the Serious Moonlight tour.
'Let's Dance' single reaches number one in the UK and US.
The Serious Moonlight tour debuts in Brussels. Massively oversubscribed, more dates are added to the tour including three concerts at UK's Milton Keynes Bowl in July.
'China Girl' reaches number two in the UK, number 10 in the US.
In July, ten Bowie albums can be found in the UK Top 100, the first time one artist had dominated the charts to such an extent since the death of Elvis Presley in 1977.
'Modern Love' peaks at UK number two.
Ziggy Stardust: The Motion Picture, the soundtrack to the 1973 DA Pennebaker film of the last date of the *Aladdin Sane* tour, reaches UK number 17.

1987

January 8, Bowie turns 40
Dates for Bowie's first world tour in four years, *Glass Spider*, are announced.
New single, 'Day-In-Day-Out' reaches number 17 (UK), number 21 (US).
June: Bowie plays consecutive nights at Wembley Stadium.
Bowie is romantically linked with tour dancer Melissa Hurley.
November: the focal point of the stage presentation, the spider itself, is ceremonially burnt after the last gig in Auckland, New Zealand.

1986

'Absolute Beginners' reaches number two in the UK and is Top 10 in seven other European countries. It is Bowie's last major hit single to date.
Bowie is interviewed for BBC 2's *Video Jukebox*.
Bowie plays Jareth, the Goblin King, in Jim Henson's *Labyrinth*. The film met with poor reviews on release but has now become a cult classic. 'Magic Dance' from the film's soundtrack is one of Bowie's most successful tracks on I-Tunes.

1984

May – Bowie begins work on the *Tonight* album in Canada.
The first part of the *Serious Moonlight Tour* video reaches number one in the UK Video charts.
Single 'Blue Jean', backed by long-form video directed by Julian Temple reaches UK number six and US number eight.
Tonight becomes Bowie's third number one album of the eighties although receives a lukewarm critical reception.
Although unavailable for the recording of the song, Bowie introduces the first TV airing of Band Aid's 'Do They Know It's Christmas?' on BBC TV.

1985

'This Is Not America', a collaboration with the Pat Metheny Group, reaches number 14 in the UK, number five in Germany, and number one in Holland.
'Loving The Alien', promoted with a stunning video co-directed again by David Mallet, reaches number 19 in the UK.
July 13: Bowie's set is a highlight at Live Aid, Wembley Stadium. A video made with Mick Jagger, a cover of 'Dancing In The Street', is premiered. It would later become a UK number one.
Alias David Bowie, a biography by Peter and Leni Gillman, published amidst some controversy, asserting as it did that Bowie's family was riven with histories of mental illness.
Bowie films a role in Julian Temple's musical adaption off Colin MacInnes' *Absolute Beginners*.

1988

July: Bowie performs with avant-garde dance troop La La La Human Steps at the Institute Of Contemporary Arts (ICA), London.
Bowie plays Pontius Pilate in *The Last Temptation Of Christ*.
Promoters contact Bowie with the idea of a greatest hits-only tour.
Bowie begins collaboration with American guitarist, Reeves Gabrels.

1992

Bowie plays The Freddie Mercury Tribute Concert for AIDS Awareness at Wembley Stadium, duetting with Annie Lennox on 'Under Pressure'.
Bowie marries model Iman Abdulmajid.
Sessions begin for Bowie's first solo album since 1987 with Nile Rodgers back producing.

1990

The *Sound + Vision* world tour contains a set list partially chosen by Bowie fans through a phone hotline. A campaign by *NME*, 'Just Say Gnome' to get 'The Laughing Gnome' included on the set list is unsuccessful. Bowie vows never to play his greatest hits again.
Compilation *Changesbowie* reaches UK number one.
Ryko begin a reissue programme of Bowie's back catalogue on CD with bonus tracks and unreleased material.

1993

'Jump They Say' reaches number nine in the UK charts, and *Black Tie White Noise* becomes Bowie's eighth UK number one album.
November: Bowie releases *The Buddha Of Suburbia*, a critical success but a commercial flop.

1991

Tin Machine score their one and only UK Top 40 hit with 'You Belong In Rock And Roll'.
Tin Machine 2 reaches UK number 23.

1989

Bowie returns as one-quarter of a band by forming Tin Machine with Gabrels and Iggy Pop's old rhythm section of Hunt and Tony Sales. *Tin Machine* reaches number three in the UK, and Top 30 in the USA garnering, contrary to popular myth, mostly favourable reviews.
Bowie tours with Tin Machine in intimate venues playing a set list with no solo material.

1994

The first, and to date only, exhibition of Bowie's art, *New Afro Pagan And Work*.
Bowie is asked to play Andy Warhol in the film, *Basquiat*.

1995

Outside 1, a collaboration with Brain Eno and featuring Mike Garson and Reeves Gabrels, reaches UK number eight. It would go on to become a firm fan favourite.
Bowie tours USA with Nine Inch Nails.
Bowie tours with Morrissey in the UK until the singer leaves the tour midway through.

1998

Bowie launches his own subscription website, *Bowienet*.

2003

Bowie declines Knighthood.
Reality, Bowie's 24th solo studio album, reaches UK number three.
Bowie begins the *A Reality* world tour.

1999

hours..., the final album to feature Gabrels, is a number five UK hit, number four in Germany, and provides Bowie with the Top 20 single, 'Thursday's Child'.

1996

The Outside Festival Tour sees Bowie reintroduce a small selection of well-known songs such as '"Heroes"'.
'Hallo Spaceboy' a re-recording of the *Outside* track with the Pet Shop Boys reaches UK number 12.
Bowie receives Lifetime Achievement Award at the Brits from future Prime Minister Tony Blair.

2002

Heathen, the first Tony Visconti co-production since *Scary Monsters* reaches UK number five and is a critical success, being nominated for the Mercury Music Prize. Bowie tours the album.
EMI's *Best Of Bowie* reaches UK number 11 and would remain a regular chart feature for over a decade.

2001

Toy, a collection of new songs and re-workings of many rare and unreleased Bowie songs from the sixties and early seventies, falls foul of 'scheduling issues' at Virgin and remains officially unreleased.

1997

Bowie celebrates his 50th birthday with a special gig at Madison Square Garden featuring pop and rock celebrities such as Lou Reed, Billy Corgan, Robert Smith and Frank Black.
Bowie Bonds scheme launched.
'Little Wonder' single is a UK number 14 hit, while album, *Earthling*, influenced by drum'n'bass, industrial and techno music, reaches UK number six.

2000

Bowie plays a memorable gig on the Pyramid Stage, Glastonbury.
Alexandria Zahra Jones, Bowie's daughter, is born on 15 August.
Bowie At The Beeb reaches UK number seven.
Bowie declines a CBE.

2004

June: Bowie suffers heart problems at the Hurricane Festival in Scheeßel, Germany and the rest of the tour is cancelled.

2008

Bowie provides backing vocals on Scarlett Johansson's *Anywhere I Lay My Head*. Releases *I-Select*, a collection of Bowie's own favourite songs from his back catalogue. Provides a voice-over for *Spongebob Squarepants*.

2013

'Where Are We Now?', the first new solo Bowie material for a decade is released on January 8, his 66th birthday. It reaches number six in the UK Charts. *The Next Day* album is number one in 17 countries including the UK and Germany, and is kept off the US top spot by Bon Jovi. The V&A Bowie exhibition, *Bowie Is*, opens in London. Francis Wheatley's *Five Years* documentary airs on BBC 2.

2006

Bowie receives a Lifetime Achievement Award at *The Grammys*.
Plays Nikola Tesla in the film, *The Prestige*.
Appears with David Gilmour at Royal Albert Hall.
Plays alongside Alicia Keys at *The Black Ball*, to date, his final stage performance.

2009

VH1 Storytellers, originally recorded a decade earlier, is released. With no new studio material for six years, speculation mounts that Bowie is in poor health.

2007

Curates the High Line Festival in New York.

2014

Wins Best British Male Solo Artist at the Brit Awards, 30 years after his first triumph. Bowie promises, 'More music soon.' Releases career-spanning best–of, *Nothing Has Changed*.

2010

The *A Reality* double live album is released.

2012

Bowie's studio album is completed and readied for release.

2005

Bowie performs with Arcade Fire at *Fashion Rocks*.

2011

The *Toy* album is leaked online. May: Bowie begins work on demos for new album in New York.

INTRODUCT

This is the second revised edition of a book originally commissioned 20 years ago. In 1995, CD was king, Britpop and Trip-hop ruled popular music in the UK, while rap, grunge and R&B took over most of the planet. There were relatively few pop video channels, no Internet presence for music and no digital radio. Heritage acts such as Bowie, the Stones, the Beatles and the Who, had such extensive back catalogues that short consumer guides seemed a good way to steer the potential punter through the good, bad and ugly of a musician's oeuvre at a time when most major acts of the sixties and seventies were suffering 'death by compilation', endless reissues of past glories with bonus tracks or non-stop greatest hits packages tending to obscure the depth of their catalogue and often vital new product from acts then well into the forties and, sometimes, fifties.

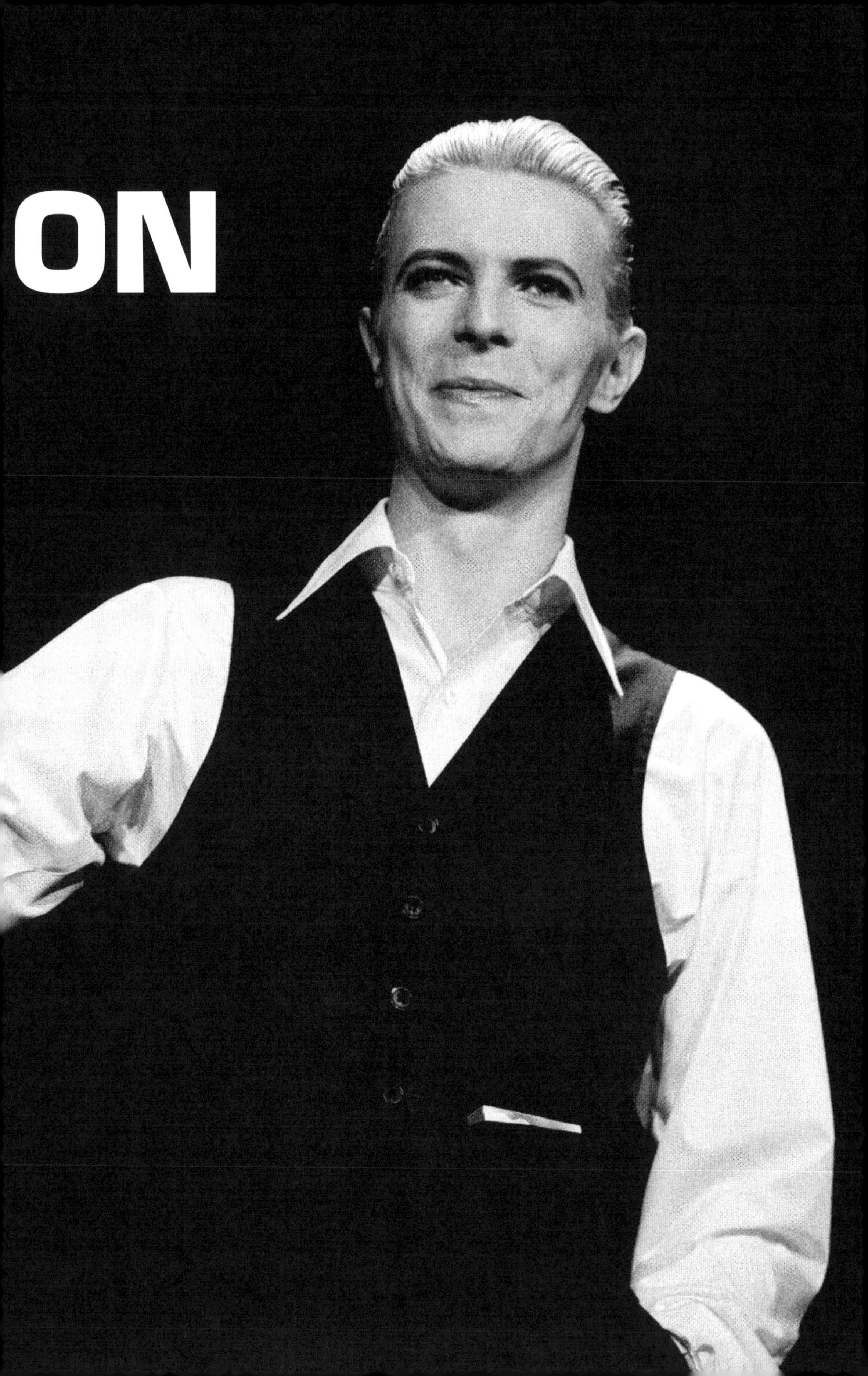
ON

Twenty years on and the way we listen to and buy music has been revolutionised, along with how we construct our musical tastes. David Bowie, the first major pop artists to make an album available as a download way back in 1999, saw it all coming. "Music itself is going to become like running water or electricity," he told Jon Parales of *The New York Times* in 2002. "So it's like, just take advantage of these last few years because none of this is ever going to happen again. You'd better be prepared for doing a lot of touring because that's really the only unique situation that's going to be left."

So music in developed western society has become as quotidian as running water. Some still hang on to the ugly compact disc, and in the last five years sales of vinyl have increased substantially, but for most of us it's a mouse click or two and bingo, a stream or a download of new music is on our computer within a minute of having the idea in the first place. And what of live performance, according to Bowie himself, the "only unique situation" left? Bowie has not toured since 2004 when he underwent heart surgery after being taken ill backstage on the *A Reality* tour, and has not performed live since performing with Alicia Keys at *Black Ball* two years later.

His absence from the music world was almost total, or so it appeared, and, not least, one suspects, from Bowie himself, totally unexpected. In 2002, on being asked if his appearance on Moby's *Area 2* tour would see him end live work for good, he said in a webchat: "Absolutely not so. I shall be touring for many more years." Yet we are used to Bowie changing his mind. Three years earlier, Bowie had also told BBC's Jeremy Paxman that coming back to live in the UK was "a given", with the complete conviction he had told journalists in 1990 that he was retiring his old songs.

January 8, 2013 was promising to be another gloomy mid-winter's day in the northern hemisphere. With psychologists predicting January 25 as the gloomiest day of the year, we were just over a fortnight away from the year's most dispiriting period; Christmas bills to pay, three months before the next public holiday, no sign of spring and a distinct lack of vim and vigour. But for Bowie fans, it turned out to be a perfect day; seemingly out of nowhere arrived a fully-formed late Christmas present. No build up, no hype, no pre-orders, 'Where Are We Now?' was Bowie's first new song for a decade, appearing on David's 66th birthday. It arrived as an interlocutor; it spoke to us only. Bowie himself was completely silent. We would know him now only as one of his fictional creations. No press, no comment, just art. Almost no one saw it coming, and those that knew kept "schtum".

David Hepworth aside, the song was greeted by universal critical praise, its slow-paced melancholia perfect for the January mood. For the next few weeks, it seemed that everybody was a David Bowie fan. Just the fact that he was back, totally unexpectedly and so completely out of the blue, was news enough, guaranteeing him the kind of coverage that lesser 'stars' would kill for, the complete absence of pre-planned promotional build-up a big story in itself. As ever, Bowie proved a master at manipulating the media. Affording a whole new generation of TV presenters the opportunity to mispronounce his name, many in the media who had previously ignored, dismissed or mocked him professed their undying love; callow journalists with no track record of ever having heard a Bowie album, let alone being Bowieheads, suddenly appeared in print like a rash, or popped up as venerable talking heads.

For Bowie followers with longer memories, the media explosion recalled other massive moments from years earlier. In 1972, Bowie made headlines by announcing he was gay, and the jury is still out on whether this was fact or fiction. The following year, with Bowiemania firmly established in the UK, the *Aladdin Sane* tour played to mesmerised fans in intimate halls, culminating in his famous 'retirement' at London's Hammersmith Odeon. In 1983, the *Serious Moonlight* tour took on the world as Bowie went viral, ten albums in the UK charts simultaneously and, in *Let's Dance*, the biggest-selling album of his career.

It helped that *The Next Day*, his 25th solo album, was so strong, and, perhaps more significantly, Bowie made half-a-dozen brand new promotional films for the album. Bowie 'the artful lodger' was back as a multimedia event. Two other major Bowie-related events occurred that year. Firstly, *Five Years*, the Beeb's first serious Bowie documentary film since *Cracked Actor* appeared. Secondly, London's Victoria & Albert Museum staged the *Bowie Is* exhibition, a mesmerising explosion of comment, sound and much vision for which more than 42,000 advance tickets were sold, more than double the advance for any previous V&A exhibition.

Despite this recent critical renaissance, and the excellence of much of his later material, it was the seventies and early eighties when Bowie was truly at his peak, and anyone yet to explore these peerless albums is in for a real treat. It wasn't just that the music was exceptional; it was the fact that Bowie made his mark at a time when rock music was still in its growth stage, still forming and re-forming and setting agendas. Those early albums made with Ken Scott as co-producer – *Hunky Dory*, *Ziggy Stardust*, *Aladdin Sane* – remain not only among Bowie's biggest sellers, but those generally most admired by the public. They work completely on every level: beautiful melodies, fantastically played and sung, and wonderfully produced. They may lack the experimental edge of some of Bowie's later works, but seldom has pop been crafted so perfectly. Hardcore fans, however, gravitated towards the more obviously theatrical *The Man Who Sold The World*, *Diamond Dogs*, *Scary Monsters*, even *1.Outside*, though it is his mid-to-late seventies output, particularly *Station To Station* and *Low*, which many critics regard as his greatest work. Some of us admit to an undying love for *Let's Dance*, his most crowd-pleasing album and the biggest-seller of his career, while *Lodger*, dismissed by many at the time, seems now like the sound of tomorrow. Bowie himself has a soft spot for 1993's *The Buddha Of Suburbia*, while

there is also a doughty band of aficionados who love every minute of his relatively obscure work in the sixties. It's surely a testimony to his astonishing creative talent that no real consensus has been established concerning what makes a great David Bowie album, or even a defining Bowie era. Was his peak in 1971, 1973, 1977, 1980, or even 1983? And I haven't even mentioned his ground-breaking 'plastic soul' album *Young Americans*, his doomy but brilliant Berlin album, *"Heroes"*, the title song of which is probably the most famous and most loved Bowie ever recorded, or 2002's *Heathen*, a sombre and often chilling collection with genuine gravitas, written as New York burnt.

Bowie is now nearing his 70th birthday. Arguably, he is the only superstar from his generation to be making music which is valid, challenging and relevant and, at the time of writing, a new album is promised. Whether we see him back on stage, even for a one-off performance, remains in doubt, and Bowie himself has not given an interview of note for ten years. The mythogenic Bowie is back, limiting his engagement with the media and his fans to gnomic messages to be read out at award ceremonies. As long time Bowie-watcher Charles Shaar Murray said in 2013, "We don't know who David Bowie is any more." So many questions remain unanswered about his health, his views, his music, his relationship to the outside world and to his incredible legacy.

The original edition of this book, published in 1996, was republished twice at David Bowie's behest, as a promotional gift for the media at the time of the release of *Earthling* and *hours...* It was a genuine thrill to be asked to update the book with new reviews of his subsequent albums. This new commercial edition carries completely different reviews of those two albums, and takes the story right up to the present day with coverage of his latest studio album, *The Next Day*. I have also taken the opportunity to update all of the entries as new information is brought to light and as my own preferences and likes and dislikes change over time. Not every aspect of Bowie's recorded output is covered in great depth, and indeed, some material is left out altogether, which may disappoint his hardcore following. But there is method in the madness. This book is designed to provide a

quick guide for the enduring fan, and also (and more importantly) to reawaken the interest of the lapsed Bowie fan, or those coming to Bowie afresh. As such, it is a short, partial guide to Bowie's records, highlighting what's really worth listening to and buying rather than detailing the minutiae of every recording session and every rare release.

For this edition, I'd like to say a big thank you once again to my editor, Chris Charlesworth. Chris commissioned the original book back in 1995 and is in fact the author of a Bowie book himself, *David Bowie: Profile* (Proteus, 1981). Chris met Bowie on numerous occasions as a writer for *Melody Maker* in the seventies and later when he became Bowie's press officer at RCA Records, so he's a man who knows his Bowie better than most. Finally, thank you to David Bowie himself for providing the soundtrack to my life, from the age of eight to the age of, ahem, 49. May he never wave bye bye.

David Buckley, July 2014

Unless otherwise stated, all reviews relate to the latest CD versions available. All songs are by David Bowie unless otherwise stated. All lyrics are quoted for the purpose of criticism only.

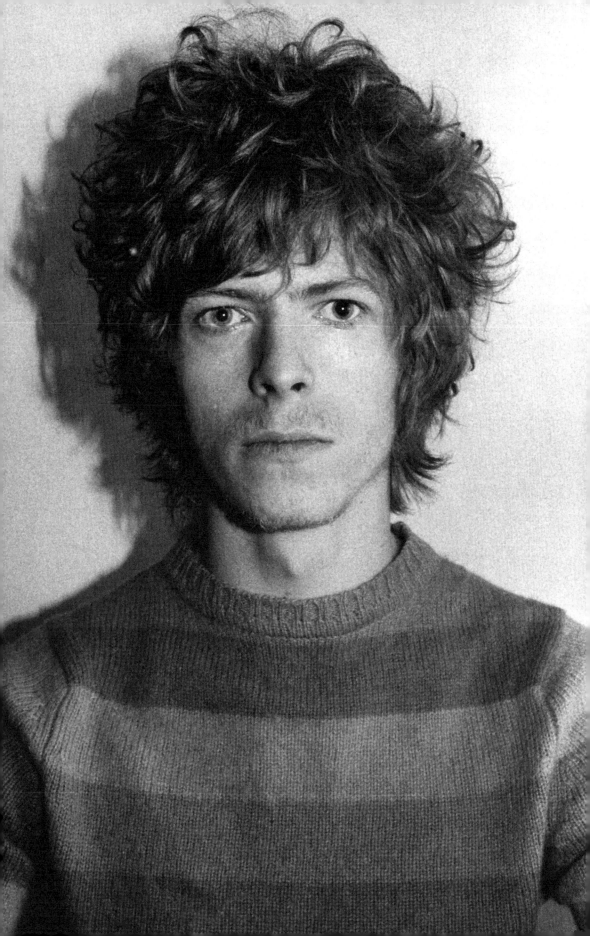

PART I
ALBUMS

DAVID BOWIE

(Original UK issue: Deram DML 1007, released 1 June 1967; UK CD: Deram 800 087 2; did not chart. Reissued Deluxe Edition, 1 February 2010, Deram 531 792-5)

Bowie's eponymously-titled début album was released by the progressive label Deram at the high-water mark of Britain's counter-culture. It was not Bowie's first appearance on vinyl however. He had written songs and performed for a succession of short-lived beat and rhythm and blues outfits since 1964 (The Konrads, The King Bees, The Mannish Boys and The Lower Third) as David/Davey Jones with little artistic or commercial success. There was, in truth, nothing in his mid-sixties musical beginnings to suggest the innovative work to come. For those interested in Bowie's earliest work, see the compilations listed in the appendix at the end of the book.

His first album, produced by Mike Vernon, consists of 14 short narrative vignettes delivered in a mannered cockney indebted to Anthony Newley. Newley's 1960 ATV surrealist comedy programme, *The Strange World of Gurney Slade*, had been a prime influence on the young soon-to be musician, a world within a world in which inanimate objects speak, and poster girls come to life. Manager Ken Pitt, who directed Bowie away from rock'n'roll and early on recognised his innate sense of theatre, encouraged the young Bowie's wildly eclectic tastes, and an unashamedly bizarre range of topics found

their way on to the album. The album's engineer, Gus Dudgeon, producer of Bowie's first hit 'Space Oddity' and producer of many of Elton John's platinum-selling albums, reminisced: "Listening to it now I can't believe that it was actually released because it must have been about the weirdest thing Deram had ever put out. In fact it must be about the weirdest thing any record company have ever put out."

And Dudgeon is absolutely right. There is no lead guitar and almost no attachment sonically to blues or rock music at all. The album has an English music-hall demeanour with the use of the waltz on 'Little Bombardier' and 'Maid Of Bond Street', and the overall impression is of a style of music located well outside the pop mainstream. The strings, bassoon and trumpet dove-tail with the dreaded neo-classicism heralded by The Beatles on *Sgt Pepper* (their eighth studio album, coincidentally, released on the same day as this, Bowie's first) which was also released that year, but Bowie's use of classical music is grafted not on to rock or pop music but on to an odd pantomime ballad style. Almost throughout, his mini-London Town dramas require the listener to be of charitable good humour, teetering as they do on the fine line between absurdist good fun and the equivalent of aural Chinese water torture (one suspects, felt most keenly, by Bowie himself).

Bowie was, however, beginning to explore some of the themes he would later develop with far greater clarity on future albums. 'She's Got Medals' gives a foretaste of the cross-dressing gender-confusion themes of many of his early seventies songs. 'London Boys' deals with drug abuse and alienation (but without the sense of near glorification found on *Aladdin Sane* or *Diamond Dogs*). 'We Are Hungry Men' depicts a world so overpopulated that mass abortion is legalised and a blind eye is turned to infanticide. The central character of 'Little Bombardier', a lonely, war-broken man, is chased out of town for appearing to spend too much time spoiling children with treats. The lyrical weight of the songs is counterbalanced by the often charming, if twee, melodies. "The one thing he did have," said producer Mike Vernon in my Bowie biography *Strange Fascination*, "was hooky little songs." Catchy tunes, and, of course, the beginnings, despite the obvious comparisons with Newley, of a distinctive voice: "I love unique voices," said Dudgeon. "That's one thing Bowie has got going for him, he does have a very unique voice, no question, and funnily enough you can hear it on that first album."

Perhaps the clearest indication of Bowie's future direction comes on 'Join The Gang' and 'Please Mr Gravedigger'. The first contains a jaundiced view of hippy culture: for Bowie, the idea of communality and shared love, which the counter-culture reputedly cherished, would prove anathema to his narcissism, sense of alienation and hard-headed commerciality. 'Please Mr Gravedigger' is arguably the most bizarre moment on any of his albums, with Bowie as a soliloquising child-murderer. The song itself comes on like a macabre parody of the bonhomie of a song such as 'Oh Mr Porter'. Delivered without instrumental backing, the lyrics are supplemented by a number of special effects (thunderclaps, raindrops, a bell tolling), creating a pop equivalent of a radio play. Bowie even convincingly fakes a sneeze or two, showing an early predilection for the sort of theatricality which would become his trademark. Producer Mike Vernon was completely bamboozled by it all. "Occasionally he got into things where I thought, what the bloody hell is this? I don't understand this! 'Gravedigger' was something I didn't understand at the time. I had no concept of what the hell it was!"

Interestingly, *David Bowie* was not included in the Rykodisc/EMI set of CD re-mastered re-issues in the early nineties, as Bowie presumably wanted to keep this piece of juvenilia locked away in the vaults. However, for all those with a high enough embarrassment threshold, there is now a new, and excellently-produced reissue by Universal Music, using the original Deram label .

The reissue, with excellent sleeve notes by Bowie expert Kevin Cann, contains the original stereo and the original mono mix of the album on CD 1, full track listing: 'Uncle Arthur', 'Sell Me A Coat', 'Rubber Band', 'Love You Till Tuesday', 'There Is A Happy Land', 'We Are Hungry Men', 'When I Live My Dream', 'Little Bombardier', 'Silly Boy Blue', 'Come And Buy My Toys', 'Join The Gang', 'She's Got Medals', 'Maid Of Bond Street', 'Please Mr Gravedigger'.

The two are, in places, quite different, and although the stereo mix is kinder on the ears, the mono mix is more faithful to the spirit of the times, when most listeners tuned in on mono radios and for whom a mono mix would sound more powerful.

Disc 2 is a real treat for the dedicated fan. There is Bowie's first great song, 'Let Me Sleep Beside You', and 'Karma Man', not far behind in quality. 'When I'm Five', is a rather charming children's' song while 'Ching-A-Ling', recorded in 1968 by Bowie's ensemble Feathers (including his musical collaborator John Hutchinson, and then girlfriend Hermione Farthingale), is a folksy ditto, catchy, yet almost excruciatingly so, with a vocal backing melody Bowie would reuse two-and-a-half years later for 'Saviour Machine'. Concluding with five live tracks for Radio One's *Top Gear*, side two takes the Bowie story up to the end of 1968. And, what's even better, there's the welcome appearance of the perversely endearing 'The Laughing Gnome', a UK number six hit in 1973 and a seventies children's favourite (lovingly introduced on the *Tony Blackburn Show* as 'a song from Uncle David Bowie'!). Its punky little beat, and punning lyric, make this one of Bowie's oddest, and best, songs from the sixties.

Disc 2 track listing: 'Rubber Band' (single version), 'The London Boys', 'The Laughing Gnome', 'The Gospel According To Tony Day', 'Love You Till Tuesday' (single version), 'Did You Ever Have A Dream', 'When I Live My Dream' (single version), 'Let Me Sleep Beside You', 'Karma Man', 'London Bye Ta-Ta (previously unreleased), 'In The Heat Of The Morning' (previously unreleased mono vocal version), 'The Laughing Gnome' (previously unreleased stereo mix), 'The Gospel According To Tony Day' (previously unreleased stereo mix), 'Did You Ever Have A Dream' (previously unreleased stereo mix), 'Let Me Sleep Beside You' (previously unreleased stereo mix), 'Karma Man' (previously unreleased stereo mix), 'In The Heat Of The Morning', 'When I'm Five', 'Ching A-Ling' (previously unreleased stereo mix), 'Sell Me A Coat' (remix). BBC Radio One's *Top Gear*: 'Love You Till Tuesday', 'When I live My Dream', 'Little Bombardier', 'Silly Boy Blue', 'In The Heat Of The Morning'.

DAVID BOWIE

(Original UK issue: Philips SBL 7912, released 4 November 1969. Re-issued entitled Space Oddity, RCA Victor LSP 4813, released November 1972; UK CD: EMI 521 8980; US CD: Virgin 21898)
UK chart: No. 17 [total weeks in chart: 39]; US chart: 16 [36 in the Billboard Top 200 – all subsequent US chart positions are for the Top 200])

Bowie's second album was a vast improvement on his first, but is arguably not an essential purchase for those coming to his music for the first time. 'Space Oddity' aside, there's nothing on the album to match his very best seventies writing. That said, there are glimpses of the quality to come – 'Cygnet Committee' is a decorous folly with a stream-of-consciousness lyric assessing the violent demise of the counterculture over a musical backdrop showing all the twists and turns of structure so beloved of progressive rock at the time. Bowie broods: 'We can force you to be free/ We can force you to believe', in an eerie echo of Rousseau's quasi-totalitarianism of the Enlightenment, while the ending, with Bowie literally screaming: 'We want to live. I want to live' is, as *The Guardian*'s Mark Rice-Oxley puts it, 'a visceral scream that even 40 years later makes the hairs on the neck stand up.' The moral seems to be that all revolutions in the end eat their young. 'The Wild Eyed Boy From Freecloud' is a beautifully poetic song with an acute observational sensibility. 'Unwashed And Somewhat Slightly Dazed' is a tumble of arrogant, self-regarding spite: 'I'm a phallus in pigtails/And there's blood on my nose/And my tissue is rotting/Where the rats chew my bones', all paced very much in the style of Bob Dylan's declamatory *Sprechgesang*. Lyrically, however, the most important song is also the most direct – 'Janine'. When he sings 'But if you took an axe to me /You'd kill another man not me at all' the idea of Bowie at a distance from his real self (the theme which would dominate the whole of his work in the first half of the seventies) comes across loud and clear. 'An Occasional Dream' and 'Letter To Hermione' show Bowie in weepy mood and concern his first real love, Hermione Farthingale, a member of Bowie's mime troop Feathers.

But it was 'Space Oddity' itself which rightly won all the plaudits. The album's producer Tony Visconti refused to have anything to do with it, seeing it as a cheap cash-in on the recent Apollo moon landing, and the session was produced by Gus Dudgeon. Dudgeon, together with classically-trained musician and arranger Paul Buckmaster, created a sonic masterpiece for the times, detailed, spacey, the music massively improved from the original demo. It's still a wonderful, if dated, epic of alienation, undoubtedly influenced by Stanley Kubrik's *2001: A Space Odyssey*, telling the tale of astronaut Major Tom, destined to roam the universe forever: 'planet earth is blue/and there's nothing I can do'. The entire song was also a metaphor for drug-taking, the countdown sequence intended to mirror the lag between an injection of heroin and the hit. It became Bowie's first big success, reaching number five in the autumn of 1969 (it later reached number 15 in the States and number one in the UK in 1975), but it failed to break him into the big time as more flop singles soon followed. After an unsuccessful solo tour Bowie 'retired' to his multi-media Arts Lab in Beckenham and waited for the future.

What Bowie needed was a plan, and competition. The latter came from his friend Marc Bolan, whose career was about to take off with 'Ride A White Swan'. The strategy came from Bowie's decision to really dress up pop performance (undoubtedly aided by mime artist Lindsay Kemp whom Bowie had befriended), to play characters on stage in order to hide his real self from the sort of hostility he encountered on a recent tour. In fact, Bowie's tour in support of *Space Oddity* in 1969 was one of his most demoralising experiences ever. The shell-shocked singer-songwriter with the bad perm was given an often harrowing reception by the assembled skinheads in the audience. Never the most confident of performers, Bowie resolved that next time he took to the stage it would be in character to create a barrier between his 'real' self and the audience. In February 1970 at the Roundhouse, Bowie and his band The Hype performed in costume – Bowie as 'Rainbowman', Tony Visconti as 'Hypeman', Mick Ronson as 'Gangsterman' and drummer John Cambridge as 'Cowboyman'. The Hype bombed but Glam Rock was born. Foxy, folky Marc Bolan was in the audience, mentally taking notes. The future of pop had taken an irrevocable new direction.

Full *Space Oddity* track listing: 'Unwashed And Somewhat Slightly Dazed', 'Don't Sit Down', 'Letter To Hermione', 'Cygnet Committee', 'Janine', 'An Occasional Dream', 'Wild Eyed Boy From Freecloud', 'God Knows I'm Good', 'Memory Of A Free Festival'.

In 2009, the album was given the fortieth anniversary treatment, sleeve-notes from the most knowledgeable writer on Bowie during this period, Kevin Cann, and a second CD of bonus material (although many hardcore Bowie fans will already own many of these tracks as they are featured on previous reissues). The stand-out is 'Conversation Piece', in 1970 the B-side to the original version of 'The Prettiest Star'. 'Conversation Piece' marks the end of Bowie's whimsical, observational phase, but it does so with such poignancy. The song is a study in solitude and, along with 'Space Oddity', is the blueprint for the future examinations of a world in which people (and Bowie himself) struggle to fit in. The central character in the song is beaten by his own shyness, his own awkwardness, and his sense of disconnection from the world around in which people 'walk in twos or threes or more', while he '… a thinker, not a talker', has 'no-one to talk to, anyway'.

Also of note in the 15-strong bonus CD is the superior version of 'Wild Eyed Boy From Freecloud', sans orchestral arrangement and with Paul Buckmaster playing the coy melody on cello, and the single that manager Ken Pitt hoped would succeed 'Space Odity', 'London Bye, Ta Ta'. Finally, the fantastic sing-song of 'Memory Of A Festival', Parts 1 and 2, re-recorded for single release as two separate tracks and souped-up impressively with a Moog synth and harder rock attack. It is the first recording to feature the talents of musicians Mick Ronson and Mick 'Woody' Woodmansey, and may just may have invented rave music: 'The Sun Machine Is Coming Down, And We're Gonna Have A Party' – a classic, almost-forgotten, Bowie track.

40th Anniversary 2-CD Limited Edition tracklisting: CD 1: The Original Album. CD 2: The Bonus Material 1. 'Space Oddity' (Demo version) 2. 'An Occasional Dream' (Demo version) 3. 'Wild Eyed Boy From Freecloud' (B-side of 'Space Oddity') 4. Brian Matthew interviews David / 'Let Me Sleep Beside You' (BBC Radio session D.L.T. [Dave Lee Travis Show]) 5. 'Unwashed And Somewhat Slightly Dazed' (BBC Radio session D.L.T. Show) 6. Janine (BBC Radio session D.L.T. Show) 7. 'London Bye Ta–Ta' (Stereo version) 8. 'The Prettiest Star' (Stereo version) 9. 'Conversation Piece' (Stereo version) 10. 'Memory Of A Free Festival (Part 1)' (Single A-side) 11. 'Memory Of A Free Festival (Part 2)' (Single B-side) 12. 'Wild Eyed Boy From Freecloud' (Alternate album mix) 13. 'Memory Of A Free Festival' (Alternate album mix) 14. 'London Bye Ta–Ta' (Alternate stereo mix) 15. 'Ragazzo Solo, Ragazza Sola' (Bowie [music], Ivan Mogul [lyric]) (Full-length stereo version).

THE MAN WHO SOLD THE WORLD

(Original UK issue: Mercury 6338041, released April 1971 (UK) November 1970 (US), re-issued: RCA Victor LSP 4816, released November 1972; UK CD: EMI 521 9010, US CD: Virgin 21901 UK chart: 26 [total weeks in chart: 31]; US chart: 105 [23])

This is the first of Bowie's truly essential albums. Its futuristic vision of a technologically mediated hell, snapshots of almost Bosch-like perversions and fixation with madness and paranoia make this one of his most harrowing albums to date. It is also his most personal. In their book *Alias David Bowie* (Hodder & Stoughton, 1986), Peter and Leni Gillman unearthed a history of mental illness in the Jones family which has obviously had a direct influence on his writing. Forced to exorcise or transcend this legacy through dealing with it in fictionalised form, Bowie, on this album, in fact makes the plight of the mentally ill (particularly that of step-brother Terry, eight years his senior) more real.

The Man Who Sold The World was, up until the first *Tin Machine* album, Bowie's most hard-rock oriented album. Although Mick Ronson's solos do dominate, the music, courtesy of the Moog synthesizer, also has a forbidding futuristic feel, harsh and unrelenting on 'Saviour Machine', macabre and child-like on the merry-go-round pop of 'After All'.

Recorded in April and May 1970, the successful realisation of the project owes much to the arranging skills of Mick Ronson and the production of Tony Visconti (who also played bass on the record). At the time, Visconti was much interested in the possibilities afforded by the synth, not so much for making spacey sounds, but for creating a larger-than-life Wagnerian experience. Visconti scored the parts with Ralph Mace. The overall sound is one of the most majestic and eerie on any Bowie record. According to Visconti, the unsung hero of the project was whiz-kid engineer Gerald Chevin, who 'was able to go wherever our imaginations took us'.

Bowie himself was leaving it late, very often writing crucial parts of the song at the very last minute, and taking what seemed to Visconti to be a less than rigorous approach to the recording process (Bowie and Angie were apparently honeymooning in the lobby during studio time), and this was one factor behind his decision to leave Bowie's employ to concentrate on Marc Bolan. Apparently, the title song's vocal, one of the most impressive melodies in Bowie's career, was tracked on the very final day of mixing the album. So began a phase when Bowie could hardly put a foot wrong; melodies, ideas, concepts seemed to spill forth almost fully-formed, while in Mick Ronson he had the perfect foil. Bowie's golden years had begun...

WIDTH OF A CIRCLE

Clocking in at over eight minutes, this is one of Bowie's most important early seventies songs and is the album's pivotal track. A neat, infectious Ronson riff introduces a song which builds into a tale of Kafkaesque proportions. Bowie begins in picaresque mood before the killer couplet, 'then I ran across a monster who was sleeping by a tree/ And I looked and frowned 'cos the monster was me', re-introduces the central theme of split personalities. What then ensues is no less than an account of a homoerotic encounter with God in the Devil's lair, before a Ronson

guitar solo and timpani roll draw this quite remarkable piece of music to a breathless halt. Not heard live since 1974, it's a Bowie classic awaiting re-discovery.

ALL THE MADMEN

Descant recorders give this tale of madness a child-like intensity. The lyrics, a comment on Terry's own stay at the Cane Hill mental asylum, tell the tale of how the disturbed are interned in 'mansions cold and grey'. The track was successfully updated for the 1987 Glass Spider tour.

BLACK COUNTRY ROCK

The mood is temporarily lightened with this catchy piece of rock. In the early seventies Bowie and Bolan, although sometime friends, emerged as media rivals, and this track is notable for Bowie's quite accurate Marc Bolan take-off towards the end.

AFTER ALL

Bowie was beginning to self-consciously target a following of blighted, disillusioned hippies, and this song speaks to them, melding the warped music-hall of his earlier work with a queasy fairground-ride melody. Although never a single, its use in Alan Yentob's 1975 BBC Omnibus documentary *Cracked Actor* as the background music to a camera sweep along a line of war-painted American Bowie fans has provided an image as powerful as any video.

RUNNING GUN BLUES

This pop-rocker is truly bizarre. The lyric is a puckish commentary (and deliberate trivialisation) on war-time atrocities in an era when pictures from Vietnam were flooding the media daily. Bowie's gung-ho, proto-Rambo figure is a product of diseased contemporary mores, and the throwaway nature of the song merely makes the effect more telling.

SAVIOUR MACHINE

From a contemporary and real dystopia to an imagined one. 'Saviour Machine' deals with a future society dominated by technology which has outstripped the human intellect. The bleakly insistent synth is this track's stand-out feature.

Incidentally, the song's instrumental passage was based on an earlier song recorded with Feathers, 'The Ching-a-ling Song'.

SHE SHOOK ME COLD

Groups such as Led Zeppelin and Black Sabbath were beginning to make what was later termed heavy metal *de rigueur*. It's easy to forget that this song arguably, if only fleetingly, puts Bowie (or perhaps more accurately Ronson) in the vanguard of the development of the style.

THE MAN WHO SOLD THE WORLD

With the album's finest melody, this continues the favourite theme of ego-stratification, as Bowie and *alter ego* meet on the stair. Nirvana's cover of the song on their *Unplugged* album helped to re-acquaint the American public with Bowie's work after a low-profile period. Indeed Cobain's tortured, uncertain rendition of the song as he stumbles to find the correct chords has some claim to be its defining version, certainly for those under 30. Others will recall that the track was also successfully covered by Lulu in 1974, becoming a UK top three hit with

Bowie co-producing and providing backing vocals and sax. However, the best version was given by a mannequin-like Bowie himself late in 1979 on *Saturday Night Live*, with Blondie's Jimmy Destri on keyboards and Klaus Nomi on backing vocals.

THE SUPERMEN

This reveals Bowie with a head full of Nietzsche. Bowie was to draw on the idea of the superhuman potentialities of mankind later in 1971 when framing his omnipotent Ziggy Stardust character. The overwrought and hysterical singing and grandiose guitar lines proved an idea so potent that Queen appear to have based an entire career on it.

Footnote: Although a slow seller on release, the album has attained cult classic status. Bowie himself has performed songs from the album only very rarely since the early seventies. Perhaps as a corrective, in September 2014, the band Holy Holy performed the album in full for the very first time. Holy Holy included Tony Visconti on bass, with Woody Wodmansey replacing John Cambridge, the original drummer. Mick Ronson's legacy would be represented on stage by the presence of daughter Lisa on vocals, his sister Maggi on vocals and recorder and niece Hannah on vocals, recorder and keyboards, while other guest slots included Heaven 17 singer Glenn Gregory, Spandau Ballet's Steve Norman and Erdal Kizilcay who played with Bowie in the eighties and nineties.

HUNKY DORY

(Original UK issue: RCA Victor SF8244, released 17 December 1971; UK CD: EMI 521 8990; US CD: Virgin 21899; UK chart: 3 [total weeks in chart: 122]; US chart: 93 [16])

1971 was a spectacularly productive year for David Bowie. Now signed to a major label, RCA, and with manager Tony Defries and his Mainman company building up public expectations that Bowie was the next big thing, he wrote an enormous amount of material which would later be featured on both *Hunky Dory* and *Ziggy Stardust*. These two albums are, for many, still Bowie's finest-ever contribution, and remain essential purchases. He now also had in place the musicians who would soon become The Spiders From Mars, with Ronson and drummer Mick 'Woody' Woodmansey, retained from *The Man Who Sold The World* sessions, joined by Trevor Bolder on bass guitar.

Hunky Dory, recorded in three months over the summer at Trident Studios in London and produced by Ken Scott (assisted by 'the actor', i.e. Mr Bowie), shows Bowie's music acquiring a whimsical melodic sheen after the hard rock of *The Man Who Sold The World*. *Hunky Dory* is, in fact, one of his most conventional albums in purely musical terms – Rick Wakeman's piano and Ronson and Bowie's acoustic guitar dominate, with Ronson's string arrangements on 'Life On Mars?' and 'Changes' giving the music a

stirring and dramatic edge. However, its comparative easy-listening status has drawn attention away from the disturbing imagery found on songs such as 'Oh You Pretty Things!', and particularly the epic 'The Bewlay Brothers', undoubtedly one of Bowie's finest songs.

Released in the week before Christmas 1971, the album and lead-off single 'Changes' both sold poorly. It wasn't until its lofty successor had bitten hard into the nation's consciousness that the undoubted charms of *Hunky Dory* were given their rightful status. However, by January 1972, there was no doubt Bowie's star was in the ascendant: a live performance revealed Bowie's new puckish short hair and also a newly completed song, 'Five Years', a taster for a new album already in the can. The album also marked the beginning of Bowie's 'Classic Album Cover Phase'; with the pastel shade of the colourised black-and-white shot for *Hunky Dory*, it is Bowie at his most dreamily androgynous.

An additional achievement of this album was to help popularise the American slang term (albeit with a hyphen) in the UK.

 CHANGES

This song, more than any other in the Bowie canon, has an almost manifesto-like quality. For Bowie, whether we like it or not, it would always be (sing along now!) Ch-ch-ch-Changes. Bowie also neatly restates his position as poseur: 'Look out all you rock and rollers'. For him, if it had to be rock, it had to be rock done as an outsider, as a thespian, commenting on rock, never becoming a rocker in reality. It is a great tune too, and, amazingly, despite its appearance in almost every Bowie greatest hits compilation, never a hit single. The song became a live favourite once more, and in 2004 it found its way onto the soundtrack for *Shrek 2* (Geffen 9862698), covered by Butterfly Boucher featuring someone called David Bowie, no less.

OH! YOU PRETTY THINGS

This song had already been covered by Peter Noone (ex-Herman's Hermits) and had reached number 12 in the UK charts. The music here is almost 'McCartneyesque' but the lyric, dealing as it does with cracks in the sky and other manifestations of split personality, reveal a man with a very troubled mind. Unperformed live since 1973, it is probably fair to say that it is not one of Mr Bowie's personal favourites.

EIGHT LINE POEM

A simple piano part and Ronson's light, country-style guitar is the backdrop for Bowie's parodic cod-Yankee drawl. It must come as no surprise that – unlike Rod, Elton or Mick – Bowie, since he was born in England, sang with a sarf-London accent as opposed to being Kentucky-Fried like most of his contemporaries. The theory went that if you sounded American you were closer to the blues masterprint and thus more 'authentic' and honest. Bowie, quite properly, thought all this was rubbish, thus helping to pave the way for the caterwauling cockney of Johnny Rotten five years down the line. No longer did Deptford have to sound like Dallas.

LIFE ON MARS?

With one of pop's most stirring melodies, this has gone on to become one of Bowie's best-loved songs, and was a number three hit in the UK at the height of Ziggy-mania in July 1973. In fact, Bowie was conducting a little-known musical vendetta. He had been asked to write a set of lyrics to a French melody, 'Comme D'habitude', but they were rejected and Paul Anka was asked to submit a different set. The result was 'My Way', endless Sinatra comebacks and the Karaoke evening down the pub. 'Life On Mars?' is therefore a pretty neat parody of 'My Way', utilising a very similar four-bar melody. Bowie was not only settling an old musical score (no pun intended!) but was also signalling that he too could now be counted among the greats of popular music. Resurrected as a poignant opener for 2002's *Heathen* tour, with Bowie

taking the stage to Mike Garson's stately piano accompaniment, it remains a classic Bowie single. In 2005, post-heart surgery, Bowie performed a uniquely vulnerable rendition for *Fashion Rocks*. In 2006, it gave the title for the BBC's crime-fantasy-drama, *Life On Mars*, staring John Simm and Philip Glenister (the track is played over season two's brilliant finale). As of April 2013, it was Bowie's best-selling download.

KOOKS

This is a fey, twee, but very popular, paean to his newborn son Zowie. 'Kooks' is all pretty strings and cod precautionary lyrics: 'Don't pick fights with the bullies or the cads/'Cos I'm not much cop at punching other people's dads'. Not silly enough to be likeable and not camp enough to be kitsch, this is the album's only weak spot and is notable only for the fact that a decade and a half later Morrissey cribbed the line about throwing your homework onto the fire for the fab Smiths' song 'Sheila Take A Bow'.

QUICKSAND

After the candyfloss of 'Kooks' the mood is immediately darkened with the arrival of this piece of philosophising about the futility of the human condition. A rag-bag of name-dropping and highbrow referencing (there's an allusion to Aleister Crowley, a diabolist and self-styled 'wickedest man in the world'), it works because of one of the most moving melodies of any Bowie song. And Bowie, 'playing in a silent film', is setting himself up as the bit-part actor waiting for the starring role.

FILL YOUR HEART

(Rose/Williams)

This cover version of a song by American singer-songwriter Biff Rose is another example of *Hunky Dory*'s rather forced jollity. Lyrically almost hippy-like with its talk of 'happiness is here today' and lovers with minds free of 'thoughts unkind', it is downright weird in view of Bowie's own writing, which glorifies individualism and self-absorption. A good pop tune, though, with the strings and piano dominating as usual.

ANDY WARHOL

Never one to hide his influences, Bowie paid homage to three pivotal figures on *Hunky Dory*. Andy Warhol, by making non-talents into celebrities, showed up the artificiality of image creation, and this idea had an enormous influence on Bowie. The song has some positively vicious Spanish-styled guitar, whip cracks and the kind of effective riff Bowie could rifle off at will during the early seventies. In 1995, Bowie, clad in Andy's leather jacket and platinum fright-wig, actually got to play the man himself in the film *Basquiat (Build A Fort, Set It On Fire)* and included the song on the Outside tour set-list. Warhol apparently hated the song.

SONG FOR BOB DYLAN

This doesn't really work. Bowie seems unsure whether to go for an outright parody of Dylan or not, but again, like everything on *Hunky Dory*, has a catchy melody and a winning chorus.

QUEEN BITCH

Bowie's scrawly sleeve notes say 'Some V.U. white light returned with thanks', and The Velvet Underground influence is marked on this song, a rollicking, knock-about tale of cross-dressing and gay love set against the *crème de la crème* of campy guitar riffs from Ronno. These were the days when Bowie could relegate songs such as this to mere B-sides. The ever public-fleecing RCA tagged this on to the 'Rebel Rebel' single over two years later.

THE BEWLAY BROTHERS

One of Bowie's most important songs, and undoubtedly the best closure to any Bowie album, this song deals in fictionalised form with the relationship between Bowie and step-brother Terry. The lyrics are full of imagery centered yet again on the malleability and deceptive qualities of the individual: 'Now my brother lays upon the Rocks/He could be dead. He could be not; he could be You', and a homosexual relationship is also implied with the lines: 'In the Crutch-hungry Dark/Was where we flayed our mark'. A remarkable song, it was finally performed live on Bowie's *Heathen* tour of 2002, thirty-one years after it was first written.

THE RISE AND FALL OF ZIGGY STARDUST AND THE SPIDERS FROM MARS

(Original UK issue: RCA Victor R SF 8287, released 6 June 1972; UK CD: EMI 521 9000, UK Super Audio CD 521 9002, Thirtieth Anniversary Edition 8 June 2002 EMI 5398262; US CD: Virgin 21900 UK chart: 5 [Total weeks in chart: 181]; US chart: 75 [72])

The album that changed our perception of what rock as a medium could be was recorded almost immediately after *Hunky Dory* in 1971. In many ways *Ziggy Stardust*, again co-produced by Ken Scott, and recorded at Trident Studios, London, now seems like the 'son of' *Hunky Dory*.

Musically, it may be slightly conservative by comparison with the astonishingly eccentric do-wop meets sci-fi movie music of 1972's other crucial album, Roxy Music's eponymous debut, also released in the summer of that year. But together, the two records torched flower-power for good, replacing it with a confused agenda of post-modern irony and theatricality which became the roots of British art rock.

By the time of *Ziggy*, Bowie had hit top form as a songwriter, and the album is a genuine classic. All of Bowie's self-penned songs are truly astonishing. Co-producer Ken Scott gives the album a more hard-hitting rock sound without departing too far from the acoustic timbres of the previous album, and the sound is sparkling, clear and detailed, if lacking in the sonic weirdness of the later *Aladdin Sane*. Incidentally (and for many, inexplicably) in a recent interview Ken Scott has talked down the whole piece claiming *Ziggy* was, 'a good rock album, nothing extraordinary in my opinion'.

Ziggy Stardust remained an almost constant feature in the UK Top 50 until well into 1974 and indeed reached its highest chart position of number five on February 10, 1973, having already been in the charts for eight months. Its initial success saw first *Space Oddity* and then *Hunky Dory* enter the UK charts. Bowie was almost constantly either playing live or recording during 1972. He played the Rainbow, London, with the Lindsay Kemp Mime Troupe in August. However, before then, he was out in the provinces. A Bowie gig at Newcastle City Hall that June would have set you back the princely sum of 40p for a seat in the stalls. In July, he played the gig that all but made him, on July 15 at Friars Aylesbury, in front of dozens of American journalists flown in specially for the show.

Although *Ziggy* is regularly touted as one of pop's great concept albums, telling the tale of the rise and fall of the fictional rocker Ziggy Stardust, there is, in fact, no consistent plot development or narrative structure beyond an opener, which temporally places the events five years from

the apocalypse, and an ending which neatly wraps up things with a suicide. An elaborate Ziggy stage show was planned by Bowie in late 1973, with a more developed narrative sketched in, but it never came to fruition.

What Bowie actually did was to collect a portfolio of songs which dealt with stardom and how it is manufactured within the entertainment business. Read like this, the album makes far more sense. 'Star' for example then becomes a shameless exercise in destroying the myth of art for art's sake and reveals the grasping self-promotion that is at the centre of most popular music. 'Starman' loses the comic book sci-fi trappings and becomes a statement about the Messianic quality of our rock idols.

Ziggy Stardust is also heavily laden with images of rock's past, with Hendrix and Bolan making guest appearances. This sense of history, taken together with the album's self-referentiality – a rock star making an album about a rock star – makes *Ziggy Stardust*, as writer Jon Savage pointed out, pop's first postmodern record. Fact/fiction, past/present are deliberately being played around with in a way new to pop. It is Bowie's second-best seller globally with sales of around 7.5 million.

 FIVE YEARS
The inspiration behind this song has been the cause of some discussion among Bowieologists for several years. Various theories have been put forward, including a take on a Roger McGough poem, a rewrite of a Wordsworth sonnet, and a dream Bowie had in which his dead father returned to warn him of the perils of flying. That heartbeat of a drum figure introduces what is arguably the strongest cut on the album, as the narrative locates the action five years from the end of the world. The music moves with Bowie the narrator at a walking pace, and Bowie is once again treading the boards in an imagined real life: 'It was cold and it rained so I felt like an actor'. There's still a shrill, almost hysterical feel to many of the performances on the album, and 'Five Years'

is a masterpiece of the overwrought. Swirling violins, impassioned cries, and this pop song, so full of danger and drama, is over. The song was reportedly scheduled to be performed at Live Aid, but was dropped at the last minute when Bowie discovered that there was no room in the schedule to show a short film made by CBC TV of starving children in Addis Ababa, a film which would spur millions to donate on the day.

SOUL LOVE

Only the most tortuous piece of hypothesising could actually fit this particular song into any sort of complete narrative concept. It's still a very fine song indeed, full of remonstrations about the link between secular and non-secular love, and the infectious rhythm, neat pop guitar solo, and sing-a-long-a-Bowie coda make it.

MOONAGE DAYDREAM

This is one of Bowie's best-ever songs, beautifully paced, beautifully played. The religiosity of the opening two tracks again resurfaces: 'The church of man-love/ Is such a holy place to be' and Bowie is still playing the sci-fi card for all it's worth ('Put your ray-gun to my head'). It's also noticeable, as journalist Chris Brazier pointed out in a 1976 prize-winning essay, how much Bowie, in an attempt to comment on rock history, utilised slangy, hip Americanisms. 'Moonage Daydream' is a good example of this, filled as it is with lines such as 'Mama-papa', 'freak out', 'lay it [the real thing] on me', and 'rock and rolling-bitch'. Ziggy Stardust, despite being regarded as the embodiment of the English obsession with style, is also, at least lyrically, peculiarly Americanised. The closing guitar freak out is Ronno's greatest moment on a Bowie record.

STARMAN

Bowie's second UK Top 10 hit (and the single which really broke him big-time) finally came with this cartoonesque slab of highly contagious pop with its unforgettable chorus. Bowie's fascination with all things galactic tapped into an area of public fascination with sci-fi hitherto unexplored within popular music, although undoubtedly part of the national psyche, as the success of TV programmes such as *Dr Who* proved. Here the arrival of the Ziggy figure, who, in another bout of Americanism, thinks he'll 'blow your minds', is equated with the second coming of Christ, and Bowie neatly draws attention to the Messianic qualities of superstardom. Anyone around in the seventies will never forget Bowie's appearance on *Top Of The Pops*, crimson of hair, pallid of complexion and pally of demeanour, a lovingly limp wrist dangling over Mick Ronson's shoulder. The instantly decodable melody, courtesy in part of a cheeky and nifty rewrite of 'Somewhere Over The Rainbow', is glam rock's finest show-tune.

IT AIN'T EASY
(Davies)

This pleasant enough cover of a little-known Ron Davies song just doesn't fit in and its inclusion on the album is doubly puzzling given the stock-pile of excellence Bowie had at the time.

LADY STARDUST

Another effective piano part dominates this undemanding piece of pop. 'Lady Stardust' takes Marc Bolan and his myth as subject matter and thus continues the idea of the album as a sort of self-referential universe dominated by fictionalised accounts of rock's real-life history.

STAR

Backing vocals like air-raid sirens, a hammering piano and the best lyric on the album make this a pivotal song in the Bowie canon. Here Bowie's lyric embodies his obsession with notoriety ('So inviting – so enticing to play the part'), and the hard-headed commercialism ('I could do with the money') behind pop's façade of integrity and authenticity.

HANG ON TO YOURSELF

Again the acoustic, rather than lead, guitar hogs the limelight in this out-and-out rocker. It's as if Bowie can't sonically distance himself from the singer-songwriting pretensions of the previous *Hunky Dory* version of Bowie. That said, it is a fabulous song with another fine guitar break from Ronson. The 'Come on' exhortation at the end is almost coital in its repeated delivery. Live, it has always been a winner. It was a superb opener to many Spiders' shows, a reworked tour-de-force on the '78 tour with Adrian Belew's guitar duelling with Simon House's violin, and even a surprise addition to several dates on the 2003-2004 *Reality* tour.

ZIGGY STARDUST

During the early seventies Bowie was so adroit at writing instantly recognisable and skilful pop/rock riffs, and nowhere is there a better example than on this, the title track of the album. Like Jimi Hendrix, Ziggy 'played it left hand/But made it too far' and, in what many take to be a reference to the fans who helped provide Hendrix with the drugs that would eventually kill him, Bowie sings 'When the kids had killed the man/I had to break up the band'. There is also a powerful sense of drama at the song's dénouement, when the band cuts off before the final 'Ziggy played guitar' salvo. Performed as a brilliant final song on both the *Heathen* and *Reality* concert tours, that show-stopping final line, 'Ziggy played guitar', has an almost epitaph-like quality to it.

SUFFRAGETTE CITY

This is another 'lost' Bowie single, which was coupled with 'Stay' and released in Britain to promote the hits compilation *ChangesoneBowie* in 1976. It was a complete flop, not even denting the lower reaches of the Top 75. That said, this tale of a hot and bothered Bowie fending off his male lover while his female one 'said she had to squeeze it but she... and then she' remained a live favourite over three decades and the 'Wham bam thank you mam' is still naughty, but nice. Incidentally, 'Wham Bam Thank You Man' (a song) is the B-side of a 1969 single by the Small Faces, 'Afterglow Of Your Love'.

ROCK'N'ROLL SUICIDE

Not content to wait for the *Diamond Dogs* material to be completed, RCA turned this, perhaps Bowie's

most dramatic moment ever, into a minor hit single (UK number 22) and thus once again short-changed Bowie fans, many of whom would literally buy an EP of his selected sneezing at this stage. (Remember, 'The Laughing Gnome' had just sold well over a quarter of a million copies in the UK alone.) 'Rock And Roll Suicide' is an effective parody of the sort of Las Vegas show business schmaltz Bowie found so execrable. Pounding away at the 'Gimme your hands 'cos you're wonderful' line, he lashes out at the light entertainment 'you were a lovely audience' rhetoric to great effect. According to producer Ken Scott, Bowie's vocal was just two live takes: the first, quieter section, and then the second, belted-out finale. As perfectly as 'Five Years' sets the agenda, so 'Rock 'n' Roll Suicide' ends the album with unbridled power and desolation. The final little orchestral flourish at the end closes the curtain on a piece of genuine rock theatre.

THE THIRTIETH ANNIVERSARY EDITION

In 2002, *Ziggy Stardust* was again reissued, with a bonus CD (details below) and came newly refurbished with a booklet, timeline, exclusive photographs and, most importantly, an excellently clear digital remastering. Those cross-speaker phasing strings at the end of 'Moonage Daydream' really have never sounded so good.

CD 2 includes 'John, I'm Only dancing', one of Bowie's few overtly gay songs, and a number 12 in the autumn of 1972. Bowie assures his male lover that he is only flirting with the opposite sex. Bowie had famously admitted to being gay (although bisexual would have been more accurate) in an interview with *Melody Maker*'s Michael Watts in January 1972. This admission not only secured him the tabloid publicity to make him a star, but also, very importantly, as the first instance of a male pop star being open about the gay side of his sexuality, helped others who felt themselves to be on the margins to take centre stage and admit their true orientation. Also included in this Thirtieth Anniversary edition is the great early Bowie pop song 'Velvet Goldmine' which, of course, would later provide the title to one of the few glam rock movies of our time. The film itself, although undoubtedly amusing, was basically one long homo-erotic romp, which is particularly ironic since the song itself discusses in coded terms the pleasures of the (heterosexually) fleshly. 'Holy Holy' is, of course, a well-known (and great) Bowie rocker, 'Amsterdam' and 'Round And Round' are inessential, while 'Sweet Head', an average Bowie tune, is another sex-obsessed Bowie rocker.

CD 2: 'Moonage Daydream (Arnold Corns version)', 'Hang On To Yourself (Arnold Corns version)', 'Lady Stardust (Demo)', 'Ziggy Stardust (Demo)', 'John I'm Only Dancing', 'Velvet Goldmine', 'Holy Holy', 'Amsterdam' (Jacques Bel/Mort Shuman), 'The Supermen', 'Round And Round' (AKA 'Around And Around') (Chuck Berry), 'Sweet Head (Take 4)', 'Moonage Daydream (New Mix)'

THE FORTIETH ANNIVERSARY EDITION

On June 4, 2012, EMI re-released *Ziggy* again. On CD the original was remastered by original Trident Studios' engineer Ray Staff (at London's Air Studios, Trident having long since closed down). For the hardcore collector there was an impressive vinyl re-issue with a bonus DVD containing a variety of mixes by original producer Ken Scott as well as the bonus tracks 'Moonage Daydream' (instrumental), The Spiders' version of 'The Supermen', 'Velvet Goldmine' and 'Sweet Head'.

ALADDIN SANE

(Original UK issue: RCA Victor RS 1001, released 13 April 1973; UK CD: 521 9020; US CD: Virgin 21902 ; Thirtieth Anniversary Edition 27 May 2003; Fortieth Anniversary Edition 14 April 2013, UK chart: 1 [Total weeks in chart: 74]; US chart: 17 [22])

Regarded at the time as something of a let-down after *Ziggy* ('superficially stunning and ultimately frustrating', moaned *Melody Maker*), *Aladdin Sane*, although conceptually weaker and perhaps not as consistent in terms of overall quality, might now be regarded as the definitive glam-rock Bowie album. The band are altogether more daring: Ronson's guitar is prominent and high in the mix and Mike Garson's manically jazzy piano further broadens the musical canvas. Bowie's songs are bolder and more eccentric, particularly on the epically-fractured title track and the gorgeously melodramatic 'Time'. Again it's co-produced by Bowie and Ken Scott (who was becoming, as Bowie later commented, his George Martin figure).

The album is also more informed, as Bowie was later to comment, by the spirit of rock'n'roll, thus making the more experimental sections even more audacious in comparison. Mostly written during the latter half of 1972 on tour in America, much of the material has a more strident R&B sensibility, not least the album's biggest hit 'The Jean Genie'. *Aladdin Sane* was, after all, as Bowie claimed, 'Ziggy goes to America'.

Although in many ways the playful theatricality of his work makes him the product of a typically English sensibility, Bowie had long been influenced by American rockers, and on this album he took the traditions of Americana and gave them a peculiarly parochial spin.

Aladdin Sane was released during a period when Bowie's commercial and artistic stock, at least on the home front, had never been higher. He had already earned a reputation as pop-resuscitator by helping to produce albums for the ailing Mott The Hoople (*All The Young Dudes*), Lou Reed (the really excellent *Transformer*) and Iggy & The Stooges (*Raw Power*) and, after almost ten years of trying, had finally won mainstream acceptance. Looking back at the version of Bowie at the time – a war-painted sex-change harlequin with a fast-growing repertoire of songs concerning galactic apocalypse, mind-warp, suicide and 'try-sexuality' – one might reasonably wonder how on earth he became the biggest mainstream commercial success of 1973. In fact it's not so difficult to see why. Musically, Bowie had a locker-full of soaring, catchy melodies still conventional enough for your Dad to whistle along to. And, perhaps more importantly, his work was at the very core of English pop sensibility, re-articulating, in an admittedly extreme manner, the British love for theatricality and make-up. *Aladdin Sane* is the album in which these stylisations work the best.

Throughout the first half of 1973, Bowie and the Spiders were almost continually on the road. He told BBC's *Nationwide*, 'Yeah... I believe in my part... all the way down the line... right the way down... but I do play it for what it's worth because that's the way I do my stage thing – that's part of what "Bowie" is supposedly all about... I'm an actor...' David Jones played 'Bowie' with tireless aplomb. Soon neither he nor his audience were really sure whether this Kabuki-styled androgyne was his real self or not. Bowie showed that everyone's personality could indeed be a 'sack of things', and the idea that pop could not only comment on, but enable, these changes became central to how pop would develop from that day on.

By the summer of '73, Bowie had a top three hit with 'Life On Mars?' and five albums in the chart simultaneously. The first rush of success took him by surprise and he felt a little out of control. Panicked, he looked for a route out. An exhausted Bowie brought matters to a head on July 3, the final date of the *Aladdin Sane* tour. At the Hammersmith Odeon, with only a very few in the know (*NME*'s Charles Shaar Murray was one), he announced to the audience before playing, fittingly, the show's closing number, 'Rock 'n' Roll Suicide', that it would be 'the last show we'll ever do'. His management company MainMan issued a statement confirming that Bowie was 'leaving the concert stage forever'. There has been so much after-the-fact post-rationalisation of this announcement (not least by Bowie himself) that the gig has been assigned quasi-mythical status; it was, as many claim, the 'death of Ziggy Stardust', the real-life rocker was ending his career in the same way as the fictional character. However, this was the *Aladdin Sane* tour, and the costuming and song selection reflected this. Many subsequent articles and books about Ziggy use the *Aladdin Sane* look and era as the template, a fact further confused by Bowie's own book, *Moonage Daydream: The Life And Times of Ziggy Stardust* which also merges the two characters. What seems to be more accurate is the idea that Bowie had simply outgrown his musical skin. *Aladdin Sane* was already, as Ken Scott argued, almost too big a musical leap for Bowie's fans to digest. Bowie, however, was tumbling over himself with new ideas, ideas which his then current band set-up was perhaps not the right musicians for. 'Killing Ziggy' was, in fact, perhaps more a cover for sacking the band, stripping back to build again.

Aladdin Sane has yet another classic album cover; shot by Duffy, it's Bowie at his most alien – a red (lipstick) and blue thunderbolt splits the face (and thus the psyche) in two, and an ellipsoid teardrop oozes from the collar bone of his preternaturally white skin, the latter a surrealistic touch from Duffy himself. This was *the* rock image of 1973.

WATCH THAT MAN

Musically, this is a superb, high-octane glam stomper, with Ronson's lead guitar so high in the mix that Bowie's vocals are drowned out. However, this was the intention as Ken Scott's original mix which features on the album was preferred to a second mix which he completed which brought the vocal and the instrumentation into a more conventional balance, but which lacked the bleeding edge of the original noisy version. Another killer chorus makes this one of his finest rock songs, and pianist Mike Garson again adds that special touch. Sadly, unperformed live for decades.

ALADDIN SANE (1913-1938-197?)

This is arguably the album's most outstanding track, with Bowie's vocals beautifully poised and Garson's truly manic piano showing how effective a soloist he can be. The title is, of course, a pun – A Lad Insane - while also alluding to the pantomime aspect of Aladdin, and the cross-dressing theatricality of such performances. Mike Garson reckons he has been asked about this one solo on an almost weekly basis from 1973 to the present day. It has a good claim to be the most powerful piano solo in modern recorded music. Bowie's decision to ask Garson to play an avant-garde jazz part on a pop song was, in terms of 1973, as wonderfully inventive as any moment in his career.

The dates in brackets after the song title were, of course, meant to add a general air of apocalyptic doom to the proceedings, predicting, as they do, World War Three, while Bowie himself later said that one inspiration for the entire work was to reinvent Evelyn Waugh's decadent 'Bright Young Things' from his novel *Vile Bodies* for a rock audience. Whatever, the resultant song is one of Bowie's very finest.

DRIVE-IN SATURDAY

Bowie has always been interested in fracturing time, in looking at the future in terms of the past. On 'Drive In Saturday' the future is one in which sex has to be re-learned through watching old films: 'When people stared in Jagger's eyes and scored/Like the video films we saw'. It's one of Bowie's all-time catchiest melodies, suitably melding fifties doo-wop with seventies pop, and the single justifiably soared to number three in the UK during the spring of 1973.

PANIC IN DETROIT

Bowie's seventies music was all about alien states, and, in America, Bowie had found one just across the pond. In 1993, Bowie commented: 'Here was this alternative world that I'd been talking about and it had all the violence and all the strangeness and bizarreness and it was really happening. Suddenly my songs didn't look out of place'. Ronson's guitar is even more blues-influenced and the soon-to-be-famous backing singer Linda Lewis providing a hint of what was to come on *Young Americans*.

CRACKED ACTOR

A devilish track. Bowie's obsession with stardom is brilliantly captured on this grungy blues cut replete with 'authentic' harmonica and a cod daddy-o blues progression from Ronson. Bowie's muse projects him twenty-five years into the future as a redundant, fucked-up, ex-movie star, bloated and gloating, enmeshed in the trappings of his own washed-out stardom. The line 'forget that I'm fifty 'cos you just got paid' now has a most bizarre ring to it.

TIME

Not only is this one of the few pop songs to include the word 'wanking' and get away with it, it is another highly inventive track. Musically this is simply soaring, with Garson's piano and Ronson's guitar again dominating, and Bowie's overwrought vocal again perfect for the melodrama. Ronson's little appropriation of Beethoven's Ninth, Bowie's signature tune

for the *Aladdin Sane* tour in the Walter/Wendy Carlos guise, is the album's best musical moment. The 'Billy Doll' mentioned in the lyric is the late Billy Murcia, original drummer with The New York Dolls who overdosed in London in November 1972. Sadly, unperformed live since the *Glass Spider* Tour, this, once again, is a classic Bowie song whose absence from any Bowie Best Of is, as David Coleman's old *Spitting Image* puppet would have said, 'quite remarkable'.

THE PRETTIEST STAR

Bowie had originally released this, reputedly about his soon-to-be wife Angie, as a single in 1970 with Marc Bolan on guitar. That rather limp version was beefed up for this album cut, and again Bowie injects a dose of fifties doo-wop into the mix. Pretty, but probably the album's least interesting moment, although as a companion piece to 'Cracked Actor', this time casting his beloved in the wholesome role of a glittering Lilian Gish-like starlet, it's effective enough.

LET'S SPEND THE NIGHT TOGETHER

(Jagger/Richards)

Bowie's zapped-up and arguably superior version of the 1966 Stones single was a staple on the Spiders' 1973 tour. Again, Garson excels: "I was pretty much on the fringe there," he later said, "just banging away!" This cover no doubt strengthened Bowie's friendship with Mick Jagger which had been developing all year but which would be sorely tested when both commissioned the then-trendy Belgian artist Guy Peelaert to design the sleeves for their forthcoming albums. The Stones found Peelaert first but David got his album out before them.

THE JEAN GENIE

A perfect rock/pop artefact, this is the song that stole the riff – Muddy Waters' 'I'm A Man', played by The Yardbirds in the sixties, and rewritten (slightly) by Bowie in 1972. Gallingly, Bowie's single reached number two in January 1973, while just a few weeks later Sweet's 'Blockbuster', with an almost identical riff, reached number one. Still, Bowie's song is culturally significant in that not only is its title a shamanistic pun on the genie of the lamp, and is in keeping with the Aladdin pantomime theme (with all the cross-dressing inherent therein), it also references the underground gay politico author Jean Genet. In 2003, Goldfrapp's excellent single, 'Strict Machine', reinvented the 'The Jean Genie' riff for the 21st Century, proving that old riffs never die.

LADY GRINNING SOUL

Sensuous and beautiful, this depiction of the preamble to love-making is intense in its honesty and quite incongruous within the Bowie canon. Again, Mike Garson's piano has the starring role. Echoes of Franz Liszt and Chopin mixed with a touch of Liberace make for a glittering ending to a fine album.

THE THIRTIETH ANNIVERSARY EDITION

Continuing EMI's Thirtieth Anniversary series, *Aladdin Sane* comes with new liner notes and timeline and is digitally remastered and expanded to include as second disc (details below). CD 2, of course, showcases Bowie's own unusual version of 'All The Young Dudes', the song he gave away to Mott The Hoople, along with the superb sax-driven version of 'John, I'm Only Dancing', and a fascinating live acoustic version of 'Drive-In Saturday'.

CD 2: 'John I'm Only Dancing' (sax version), 'The Jean Genie' (original single mix), 'Time' (single edit), 'All The Young Dudes', 'Changes,'* 'The Supermen',* 'Life On Mars?'* (previously unreleased), 'John I'm Only Dancing',* 'The Jean Genie'**, 'Drive-In Saturday'*** (previously unreleased).

* Recorded live at the Music Hall, Boston, 1/10/72
** Recorded live at the Civic Auditorium, Santa Monica, 20/10/72
*** Recorded live at the Public Hall, Cleveland, 25/11/72

THE FORTIETH ANNIVERSARY EDITION

With no new tracks, sleeve notes or anything to tempt the collector, this new version might on first-inspection seem perfunctory. However, the remaster by the original engineer, Ray Staff, brings the album truly alive. If you 'love Aladdin Sane', you have to hear it in its full decadent pomp.

PIN-UPS

(Original UK issue: RCA Victor RS 1003, released 19 October 1973; UK CD: 521 9030; US CD: Virgin 21903. UK chart: 1 [Total weeks in chart: 37]; US chart: 23 [21])

Actually Ziggy hadn't broken up the band – at least not yet. Unsure of his next move after the 'retirement' gig in early July, and under pressure from RCA for new product, Bowie took the Spiders minus drummer Woody Woodmansey to the Château d'Herouville studios in France to record *Pin-Ups* as an interim measure.

By 1973, rock's history was almost 20 years long and already there were signs of revivalist notions. British glam rock itself was full of fifties re-runs. On the one hand there was Roxy Music who often brilliantly re-invoked fifties kitsch for their seventies vignettes. Then there was glam rock's pop side with groups such as Showaddywaddy, The Rubettes and Mud all repackaging nostalgia for the pre-teenies. *Pin-Ups*, a collection of covers of Bowie's favourites from the London scene between 1964 and 1967, like Bryan Ferry's *These Foolish Things* (also released in the autumn of 1973), rode the Zeitgeist of British pop history's first real wave of retroactivity and made an effortless début at number one in the UK.

The album does sound good now in its latest 1999 remastering, and it swings along at a fine pace, with each song segueing neatly into the next. At 33 minutes and 42 seconds, it is

Bowie's shortest studio album. Produced by Bowie and Ken Scott, the band was essentially the old Spiders unit, with Woodmansey replaced by Aynsley Dunbar on drums.

However, the album is, in truth, not classic Bowie. On occasion, his vocal is unsuited to the material, particularly the rock attack of The Who's 'Anyway, Anyhow, Anywhere', and he's even less at ease with the hip R&B revivalism of The Mojos and The Pretty Things. And many of the songs sound dated compared to with the adventurous new music crafted by Bowie at the time. When he moves on to more whimsical pop, as in the cover of The Kink's 'Where Have All The Good Times Gone', or the hammy, neo-classical version of Pink Floyd's psychedelic anthem 'See Emily Play', he's on safer ground. The album's highlight is, of course, his cover of the Merseys' 'Sorrow', the only moment when he vastly improves on the original. This, the album's only single release, became one of his biggest hits, reaching number three in Britain and staying in the charts for 15 weeks well into 1974. *Pin-Ups* itself fared well on release, entering the UK Charts at number one on November 3. Bowie was now the UK's top individual star and certainly the most exciting and original, so this was to be expected. *Aladdin Sane*, *Hunky Dory*, *Ziggy Stardust* and *Space Oddity* were also still in the UK Top 40 and *Pin-Ups* would eventually chalk up an impressive five weeks at number one. Yet, despite Bowie's huge popularity, many critics remained unconvinced. Ian MacDonald at *NME*, for example, called the album, 'a shoddily-carpentered dove-tail-joint that by simply not fitting into its slot, will have the fragile edifice of its maker's credibility tottering for some time to come.' However, such predictions of Bowie's career hitting the buffers proved spectacularly ill-judged, as 1974 would confirm.

Finally, this would be the first of three albums to be credited simply to 'Bowie'. David Jones was now thinking of his musical and performing self as curiously abstracted from the real self. He was now a one-word legend of the Twentieth Century, alongside

Elvis, Garbo, Brando and Hitchcock. A little under a decade later, Prince and Madonna would aspire to greatness using the self-same tactic.

ROSALYN

(Jimmy Duncan/ Bill Farley)
Bowie is nothing if not a pop *aficionado*, as evidenced by this unearthing of a number 41 hit by The Pretty Things. It's a riffy if unremarkable pop song.

HERE COMES THE NIGHT

(Bert Berns)
Originally a number two hit in 1965 by Them, this gets the full honking Bowie sax treatment and contains one of the album's standout moments with Bowie's opening yodelling scream.

I WISH YOU WOULD

(Billy Arnold)
Originally by The Yardbirds, this is where Bowie really shows himself up as a wooden and limited R&B singer.

SEE EMILY PLAY

(Syd Barrett)
The original by Syd Barrett's Pink Floyd (and the distinction is important) reached number six in 1967. It's one of British psychedelia's signature songs and Bowie does it proud with some 'Bewlay Brothers'-styled cockney for the choruses and an overblown classical flourish at the end.

EVERYTHING'S ALRIGHT

(Crouch/Konrad/Stavely/James/Karlson)
Boring re-run of a Mojos 1964 hit.

I CAN'T EXPLAIN

(Pete Townshend)
Slowed-down sax-driven version of The Who's first hit included on the set list of some of the early *Serious Moonlight* concerts a decade later.

FRIDAY ON MY MIND

(Young/Vanda)
Bowie's in Anthony Newley mode yet again for this cover of The Easybeats' 1966 hit.

SORROW

(Feldman/Goldstein/Gottehrer)
A great Bowie single and far and away the album's highlight – lush strings, beautifully paced sax solo and a fine vocal performance, even though Bowie does sound oddly (if somewhat faintly) reminiscent of Bryan Ferry. It was originally a number four hit for The Merseys in 1966.

DON'T BRING ME DOWN

(Jonnie Dee)
Not Lennon's great late-period Beatle B-side but a superfluous cover of a 1964 Top 10 hit for The Pretty Things.

SHAPES OF THINGS

(Samwell-Smith/McCarty/Relf)
The futurism of this 1966 Top three hit for The Yardbirds obviously appealed to Bowie but it's hard not to conclude that in the intervening years his own songs had revisited similar themes with far more telling effect.

ANYWAY, ANYHOW, ANYWHERE

(Pete Townshend/Roger Daltrey)
Bowie's vocals had yet to undergo the transformation which would make him in the mid-seventies a genuinely technically great vocalist. Here he's straining and can't match Roger Daltrey for dynamic attack on this cover of The Who's second UK hit from May 1965.

WHERE HAVE ALL THE GOOD TIMES GONE

(Ray Davies)
Absolutely fine cover of a Kinks song, and the suitably fatalistic lyrics fit *Pin-Ups'* nostalgia trip perfectly. In 2014, Bowie penned the sleeve notes for the compilation, *The Essential Kinks* and wrote, 'I've never heard a Kinks song that I didn't like.' High praise indeed.

DIAMOND DOGS

(Original UK issue: RCA Victor APLI 0576, released 24 May 1974; UK CD: EMI 521 9040; Thirtieth Anniversary Edition 7 June 2004 UK CD: 577 8572. UK chart: 1 [Total weeks in chart: 34]; US chart: 5 [25])

Now bereft of the Spiders, Bowie was truly a solo artist once again, and *Diamond Dogs*, recorded late in 1973 and early 1974, shows him both at his most indulgent and at his most creative. Far from being the *folie grandeur* which many critics have suggested, the album encapsulates what truly makes him tick. It is a masterpiece of invention, cinematic in its scope, breathtakingly audacious in its execution and, finally, scary as hell. It also single-handedly brought the glam rock era to a close. After 'Diamond Dogs' there was nothing more to do, no way forward which would not result in self-parody or crass repetition.

Bowie replaced Ken Scott with Keith Harwood who had worked with Led Zeppelin and the Rolling Stones who were recording their new album, *It's Only Rock And Roll* at Olympic Studios Room A, as Bowie, with considerably more industry, worked in Studio B. Bowie took on the role of lead guitarist, with the help, on some songs, of Alan Parker, while pianist Mike Garson is once again on hand to add a touch of eccentricity. Tony Visconti, then building his own recording studio, and having freed himself from the task of producing Marc Bolan's increasingly formulaic pop, was reconciled with Bowie and was

brought in to arrange the strings for '1984' and to mix the album. A 16-year-old tape-op, Andy Morris, working under Harwood, vividly recalls Bowie's burning focus at the time: "David was like Orson Wells! He was a visionary, highly intelligent. We would layer and layer different songs. His approach was cinematic. I think David already had a vision of the tour, the show, and how he would present the music live. With '1984' I don't know how long we spent on that song. That was the song we spent the most time on because David wanted to get it perfect, and it turned out perfect, it's a masterpiece."

Bowie had originally intended to produce a musical of the classic George Orwell novel *1984*, but when Orwell's widow refused him the rights, he found himself with a collection of songs dealing with the apocalyptic totalitarian themes of the book and nowhere to put them. He therefore created his own future urban nightmare environment, Hunger City, a sort of post-nuclear, technologically primitive hell populated by tribes of proto-punks looting their way through the streets. Again, as with Ziggy, the actual narrative remains under-developed. Like all of Bowie's best work there are plenty of unanswered questions, gaps and contradictions to allow listeners to construct their own meaning of events.

The music on the album is densely packed with piano, strings, sax, synths and guitars melding together beautifully, particularly on the criminally underrated 'Sweet Thing'. *Melody Maker*'s Chris Charlesworth noted that, "For most of the tracks, he's adopted a 'wall of sound' technique borrowed not a little from Phil Spector". Bowie's songwriting had also become influenced by the cut-up technique, pioneered in literature by the American writers William Burroughs and Brion Gysin. The lyrics are now consciously more fractured and less figurative as images collide with each other in a spiralling non-sequential private universe. The spoken narrative of 'Future Legend' is particularly Burroughsian, reading like an off-cut from *Naked Lunch*. A remarkable work and probably Bowie's finest album from the seventies.

The cover art work by Guy Peellaert, which showed Bowie as half man/half dog, caused a minor rumpus when it was noticed that the dog's genitals were in full view. The albums were recalled by RCA for the offending area to be airbrushed out although a few originals slipped through the net to become collectors' items. The genitals were restored to rude health for the Ryko reissue in 1990 and are once again on full view here. The striking photographs for the cover artwork, taken by Terry O'Neil in April 1974 were the last to feature Bowie with his famous spiky red hair. A promotional shot for the album remains one of the most memorable in Bowie's long career. Bowie wearing a fedora sits impassively holding the leash of a huge dog that, during the shoot, suddenly reared up on his hind legs and starts barking: "This terrified the life out of everyone in the studio," according to O'Neill's official website, "except Bowie who didn't even flinch."

Regarded by his hardcore fans as a classic, *Diamond Dogs*, like so many Bowie albums of the time, was given a bumpy ride by many a critic. As Bowie was breaking America in the summer of '74, *Rolling Stone* said this of the album: "Unfortunately, the music exerts so little appeal that it's hard to care what it's about. And *Diamond Dogs* seems more like David Bowie's last gasp than the world's."

 ### FUTURE LEGEND
The tone is immediately set by this minute-long narrative introduction in which Bowie details the horrors of Hunger City: 'Fleas the size of rats sucked on rats the size of cats'. The opening hyena-like howl is both as chill a moment as any committed to tape by Bowie and a demonstration of the camp, kitsch-like quality of Bowie's cartoonesque imagery.

 ### DIAMOND DOGS
Musically this title track was always too long and too slowly-paced to cut it as a single (in the UK it limped, dog-tired, to number 21 in the summer of 1974). The narrative continues with the introduction of the Halloween Jack character. For Hunger City, Bowie had drawn on a story his father,

who worked for Barnado's children's homes, had told him about the visit of Lord Shaftesbury to poverty-stricken areas of London where he found children in rags living on the rooftops. Hence, Halloween Jack 'lives on top of Manhattan Chase'. Bowie also references Tod Browning, the maker of the then banned 1932 film *Freaks*. The film was populated by actors with real-life freakish deformities, and the name-check in the song reflects the circus freak-show of the album artwork and Bowie's anthropomorphic transformation. Bowie sang the song on the ensuing 1974 tour, lassoed by dancers Gui Andrisano and Warren Peace.

 ### SWEET THING/CANDIDATE/ SWEET THING (reprise)
The album's highpoint. As a piece of music this is seamless and dramatic, showcasing a new maturity in Bowie's work. 'Sweet Thing' opens with Bowie's vocal deep and growling, and builds, courtesy of Garson's finest performance yet, into a seedy ballad of prostitution and druggy Americanised low-life.

'Candidate', originally a song in its own right and included as a bonus track with the thirtieth anniversary re-issue, is here much-changed. Combining some of Bowie's most powerful writing – 'We'll buy some drugs and watch a band/And jump in a river holding hands' – it segues neatly into a reprised 'Sweet Thing'. Some critics would argue that it was on moments such as these that Bowie's reputation as one of rock music's premier acts was built. Indeed, as the music folds away to reveal a deadeningly mechanical guitar feedback solo at the end of the song suite, the effect is stunning. Mike Garson, who arguably outstrips his work on the *Aladdin Sane* track, cannot remember much about laying down his parts, other than to say, "I recall Olympic Studios. It had a very heavy vibe. The studio played me as I played it!" A strange alchemy was at work.

 ### REBEL REBEL
The last of his bona fide glam singles, 'Rebel Rebel' was a UK number five hit in early 1974. It's a superb

riff from Bowie, guitarist Alan Parker having helped him shape its contour in the studio. This is definitely another mini-manifesto for all the Bowie Boys and Bowie Girls, who were one of the most conspicuous aspects of pre-punk youth culture, and the lines 'You got your mother in a whirl/She's not sure if you're a boy or a girl' sum up early seventies gender-bending perfectly. Bowie performed a mimed version of the song for *Top Pop* in Holland in pirate chic with eye patch and neckerchief.

ROCK 'N' ROLL WITH ME
(Bowie/Peace)
There are definite hints of Bowie's 'plastic soul' phase, particularly in the infectious piano part, in this cute pop song which builds to a rousing chorus. With the lyric, Bowie addresses the star/fan nexus in a positive, upbeat manner: 'When you rock and roll with me,' he sings, 'There's nowhere else I'd rather be'. The music was written at Bowie's London home of the time, Oakely Street, with the help of his friend Geoff

McCormack (AKA Warren Peace). "He got up, and I started fiddling around with a chord sequence and stuff that I had just written," McCormack told the author in 2004. "David said, 'Hang on a minute, play that again!'"

WE ARE THE DEAD
A twisted, piece of Gothic grotesquery, this is one of Bowie's most underrated songs, courtesy of a keyboard line straight out of a horror movie score, it evolves into something even doomier than the dystopia of *1984*. Bowie here is identifying with Winston Smith, the central character in the Orwell novel, and, his inevitable re-assimilation after an illicit sexual affair, into the totalitarian state. But the song reaches beyond a simple depiction of the novel, transporting the listener into a new stratum of the freakish and the unnatural. Yet another exercise in short-changing the fan, RCA were later to release the track as the B-side of 'TVC 15' in 1976.

1984

In 1971, Isaac Hayes helped kick-start what later became known as disco music with his theme tune to the film *Shaft*. Alan Parker's guitar licks borrow heavily from that track's guitar work and, together with some on-the-button Philly strings, provides the clearest clue yet of his upcoming disco phase. The song was covered by the resurrected Tina Turner on her *Private Dancer* album of 1984, a bizarre choice of song for that most middle-of-the-road of soul-stresses, filled as it is with gloomy predictions for the future of mankind.

BIG BROTHER/CHANT OF THE EVER CIRCLING SKELETAL FAMILY

In which Bowie returns once again to the idea of the 'strong man', the 'homo superior', as a means of salvation, this time through taking on the Big Brother of the Orwell novel, whose totalitarian grip was ultimately absolute. It was this fascination with supermen of one persuasion or another, whether it be his own fictionalised rock personae, or the figures of myth, legend, philosophy (through an interest in Nietzsche) or novels, which would culminate in Bowie's own delusions of grandeur during his flirtation with Nazi-chic two years later. With hindsight, we can all see it coming. Whatever, 'Big Brother' is a daring, insistent, somehow frightening paean to the Super God, and the way in which it segues into the 'Chant Of The Ever Circling Skeletal Family' (a truly mesmeric and frightening chant in 5/4 time) is one of the greatest moments Bowie has committed to tape.

THIRTIETH ANNIVERSARY EDITION

Diamond Dogs was reissued in 2004 complete with new artwork, a timeline and a booklet, and, of course, a bonus CD. Of particular note is the original version of 'Candidate' which is an absolutely superb Bowie track. The music rolls beautifully, if nonchalantly, with piano to the fore, while Bowie delivers one of his most sexually-suggestive couplets: 'Inside every teenage girl, there's a fountain/Inside every young pair of pants, there's a mountain.' Also included are two versions of 'Dodo'. Between October18 and 20, 1973 at the London Marquee, Bowie recorded *The Midnight Special* for US TV, showcasing material from his just-released *Pin-Ups* album, featuring a duet with Marianne Faithfull, tastefully attired in a nun's habit slashed at the back to reveal her *derrière*. The show was aired on NBC, but has never been shown on British terrestrial television. 'Dodo' (then entitled 'You Didn't Hear It From Me') was performed as part of a medley with '1984'. It was the last time Bowie worked with Ken Scott. What would Scott do with a Bowie track now? It would be utterly intriguing to hear how the producer of Bowie's 'classic period' would capture the Bowie of today.

Bonus Tracks: '1984/Dodo', ' Rebel Rebel (US Single Version)', ' Dodo', 'Growin' Up', 'Alternative Candidate', 'Diamond Dogs (K-Tel Best Of... Edit)', 'Candidate (Intimacy mix)', 'Rebel Rebel (2003 mix)'.

DAVID LIVE

(Original UK Issue: RCA Victor APL 2 0771, released 29 October 1974; UK CD: EMI DBLD 1; US CD: Rykodisc RCD 1038/39; UK chart: 2 [Total weeks in chart: 12]; US chart: 8 [21])

In April 1974 Bowie left England for the States to launch what is now regarded as one of the most theatrical and elaborate tours ever attempted. In 2014, journalists would gush over the stagecraft of Kate Bush on display at her residency at the Hammersmith Apollo, as if pop music had never seen such values before. A full four decades earlier, fans of Genesis who saw *The Lamb Lies Down On Broadway* tour and those lucky young Canadians and Americans who saw Bowie in the flesh in June and July 1974 might like to point out even more daring feats of fancy, and ones which travelled from state to state, or, in Genesis' case, across continents.

As the cover shot for the *David Live* album shows, the *Diamond Dogs Revue* revealed Bowie ashen and painfully thin, the Ziggy crop discarded in favour of a peroxide-orange parting and the Kabuki trappings of yore replaced by suits and braces. With Mick Ronson gone and the Spiders a fast-fading memory, Bowie assumed the mantel of *Diamond Dogs*' central character Halloween Jack in what was, in essence, a one-man show. On stage he performed in a re-creation of the album's 'Hunger City', all decaying skyscrapers and crumbling bridgeheads. "A lot of people feel that it has never been

bettered," said Bowie in 1993. "I mean, it was such an extravaganza, and it was so weird, it just came from such a strange place. It really did look like one of those expressionist movies come to life, it was like *Metropolis* meets *Caligari*, but on stage, in colour and it had a rock'n'roll soundtrack to it. It was something else, it really was."

Most audaciously, for 'Space Oddity' he was lofted several rows out above the audience by a cherry-picker crane, to sing the song into a microphone masquerading as a telephone. "All you saw was this arm coming out over the audience, and I was about 20-foot out over the audience, over their heads, singing, and, of course, the nights when it wouldn't go back in and I was bloody stuck out there, God, I had to sing three or four songs until they got me back in. That in itself was so totally Dada because I'd be singing three or four songs into a telephone, it was so ludicrous. And one night I had to actually climb back on the pole to get back into the window because it just wouldn't come back in again. Never work with props. We had a bridge that used to go up and down and a bridge that went from one building to another, the full span of the stage, going asymmetrically from one side to the other. Occasionally that would go plunging down at the speed of light, and I would jump off it when I assumed it would hit the bottom, and I would be in the air so that I didn't come to some catastrophic end."

David Live can only give an aural, and therefore partial, idea of what must have been a fascinating rock theatre experience. Only Alan Yentob's brilliant Omnibus documentary *Cracked Actor* gives any taste of what this stunning revue must have looked like. We haven't even mentioned Bowie singing to a skull for 'Cracked Actor', let alone perhaps the strangest prop of all, a crystal cabinet in which Bowie sang 'Big Brother' and which stripped away to reveal a huge mechanical hand at the start of 'Time'.

The double live album was recorded at the Tower Philadelphia towards the start of the tour in July. However, band morale had been sorely tested and Bowie's new lead guitarist, New Yorker Earl Slick, remembers: "They didn't even tell us ahead of time that they were recording the shows. Herbie Flowers [Bowie's new bassist] put two and two together when we got to the gig. He confronted them [Bowie's management Mainman]; they made us an offer at that point which was insulting. Eventually, they negotiated a figure and we went on, but not before things had got ugly, very ugly. On top of that, we still didn't get paid. In the end, we had to sue David, and that was when we were still on the road with him."

According to Kevin Cann's *David Bowie: A Chronology*, UK promoters turned down the chance to stage the tour at the Empire Pool, Wembley in 1975, because Bowie's management Mainman were demanding around £7.00 a ticket, then deemed an unacceptably high price. The fact that the Diamond Dogs tour did not make it to Europe undoubtedly played a role in the semi-stalling of Bowie's career in the UK during 1974 and 1975. Between April 1974 and July 1975, Bowie released five singles, only one of which reached the UK Top 10.

David Live (its original title was, in fact, *Wham Bam Thank You Ma'am*) is a tense, unnerving album: his vocals seem cracked and tired. Bowie, himself, has been dismissive of the album, even going as far as to refer to it as 'David Dead'! It does, nevertheless, contain some fine performances, notably an intriguing cabaret version of 'All The Young Dudes', a brilliantly re-worked 'Width Of A Circle' and a marvellously overwrought and slowed-down version of the epic 'Rock And Roll Suicide'. 'Aladdin Sane' sashays with a cool Latino rhythm while Slick's searing guitar lines power through 'Panic In Detroit.' 'Knock On Wood', a cover of the old Steve Cropper and Eddie Floyd rhythm-and-blues Stax standard, reached number 10 in the UK.

The early nineties Ryko reissue includes 'Here Today, Gone Tomorrow', a song which appeared to have been transported on to planet Bowie completely by surprise.

The most recent version of *David Live* was released in 2005 with significantly better artwork and an improved new mix by producer Tony Visconti. Three tracks, 'Space Oddity', 'Panic In Detroit', and 'Time', hardly piffling items, are included too, making this a faithful document of a standard summer '74 set-list. By September however, new, as then unreleased songs, were being slotted in to the show. Bowie was morphing again… into soul man.

Tracks on 2005 reissue:
Disc 1: '1984', 'Rebel Rebel', Moonage Daydream', 'Sweet Thing/Candidate/Sweet Thing (Reprise)' 'Changes', 'Suffragette City', 'Aladdin Sane', 'All The Young Dudes', 'Cracked Actor', 'Rock 'N' Roll With Me', 'Watch That Man'; Disc 2: 'Knock On Wood', 'Here Today Gone Tomorrow', 'Space Oddity', 'Diamond Dogs', 'Panic In Detroit', 'Big Brother', 'Time', 'The Width Of A Circle', 'The Jean Genie', 'Rock 'N' Roll Suicide'.

YOUNG AMERICANS

(Original UK Issue: RCA Victor RS 1006, released 7 March 1975; UK CD: 521 9050; US CD: Virgin 21905; UK chart: 2 [Total weeks in chart: 13]; US chart: 9 [51]) Special Edition [CD + DVD] EMI B000LW9PY4, March 2007.)

Bowie's work from *The Man Who Sold The World* to *Diamond Dogs* form some sort of sonic and conceptual unity; full of themes of dread, alienation and apocalyptical visions, as if the world was entering some sort of 'End Time'. Today, over 40 years later, they seem frighteningly predictive, as each decade appears more unsafe than the last. His next move saw Bowie attempt to restore some sort of emotional and musical equilibrium. In one famous interview Bowie would say that he was 'glad I'm me now'. What he didn't know was that he was entering the most personally unstable period of his entire life.

During a late-summer break in the Diamond Dogs Review, Bowie decamped to Philadelphia and the Sigma Sound Studios to record the lion's share of what would go on to be one of the most influential albums of the seventies. In 1974 disco music, hitherto the preserve of gay and Latino communities, broke big with US number ones in the shape of the Hues Corporation's 'Rock The Boat' and George McCrae's 'Rock Your Baby'. Bowie's conversion to disco/soul, although perplexing at the time and certainly an audacious step, was not quite unforeseen. Both *Aladdin Sane* and *Diamond*

Dogs had displayed a rougher R&B slant, and '1984' off the latter was a clear sign of his future direction. Indeed, one song, 'Takin' It Right', reportedly demoed for *Diamond Dogs*, would later be included on the new album in a re-recorded form as 'Can You Hear Me?' Disco also had many things in common with glam rock. Both had attracted the marginalised in society; with glam it was the sexual experimenters, with disco it was women, gays and blacks. Both sets of fans were narcissistic and embraced consumerism in a way progressive rock or folk fans would have baulked at. This fitted in well with Bowie's stance.

Bowie assembled a bona fide R&B band including bassist Willy Weeks and saxophonist David Sanborn. His knack for unearthing new talent still hadn't deserted him. Playing rhythm guitar on the sessions would be Carlos Alomar, who be part of Bowie's musical lifeblood for the next 13 years. One of his friends, invited to the studio, was a then totally unknown singer, Luther Vandross. Bowie tried him out, and very soon Vandross became an integral part of Bowie's vocal ensemble along with Geoff McCormack, Ava Cherry and Alomar's wife, Robin Clarke. One of Vandross' own songs, 'Funky Music', would be reshaped by Bowie into one of the strongest cuts on the album, 'Fascination'.

The version of *Young Americans* that everyone involved in the project considered basically complete at the end of those Sigma sessions in August '74 was not that eventually released. For a start, it was entitled *The Gouster* (a Gouster was a sharp-dressed dandy-cum-gansgster-styled hipster) and the sessions included at least eight songs which would not make the final album, two (possibly three) of which have never been released although definitely exist (for more information, see the section 'Crypto Bowie' towards the end of this book).

Months after finishing the album, Bowie went back into the studio, this time with Harry Maslin as producer to record 'Fascination', 'Win', and, after a spontaneous recording session with John Lennon, a Beatles' cover, 'Across The Universe', and the collaboration between Lennon, Bowie and Carlos Alomar, 'Fame'. These additions strengthened, not weakened the album, although many fans and even those who worked on the original Sigma project were saddened to find out that songs such as 'Who Can I Be Now?' and 'It's Gonna Be Me' had been dropped.

With hindsight, *Young Americans* is a curious album; in places it sounds now like an authentic musical reconstruction of then-current black sounds; in others it sounds a most parochial oddity, as Bowie's self-conscious jiving betrays a very stylised English manner. In fact, at other times, Bowie creates (whether deliberately or not is an open question) a beguiling tension between the 'blackness' of some of the music and the Englishness of his lyrics and their intonation and delivery. *Young Americans* is ripe for psycho-analytical literary deconstruction and could easily be a required text on cultural studies courses! Dubbing the music on the album 'plastic soul', Bowie shortly after its release argued that this was a peculiarly contrived version of the real thing: "It's the phoniest R&B I've ever heard... If I ever would have got my hands on that record when I was growing up I would have cracked it over my knee."

In 1976, Bowie explained the music like this: "I was left to meddle around a bit not having a concept to work on, and I thought, 'Well, I'll be the radio'. In 1979, he referred to the album as being recorded during his 'cynical period'. Later, he would reflect more kindly on the record: 'I advanced myself – tumbling over myself with ideas.' No record in the Bowie canon up until that point divided opinion quite like *Young Americans*. It appeared that Bowie was trying to de-spirit himself of his former selves, to make an album saner and more accessible. *Sounds'* review of the album claimed 'Bowie Takes Time-Warped Weirdness to the Cleaners.' Yet others were more sceptical of the new Bowie. In sections of the rock press, soul and disco were synonymous with frivolity.

"Bowie: Destroyed by commercialisation?" ran one picture caption in the *Melody Maker* letters pages.

By crossing over into disco/soul music he helped pave the way for the greater commercial success later in the decade of the Bee Gees, although Scotland's Average White Band, now decamped to New York, had beaten Bowie to the punch by enjoying a number one hit with the dance instrumental 'Pick Up The Pieces' the previous year. The Bowie model of white, blue-eyed soul would be hugely influential for the likes of ABC, Spandau Ballet and Simply Red as the eighties unwound, and British soul boys and girls everywhere have this pioneering album to thank. Looking back at *Young Americans* from the vantage of 1985, *Face* writer Robert Elms wrote: "10 years later, it's all come true. We're a nation living in a disco... [Bowie] was the first English artist to tart up black music and sell it back to the Americans since The Beatles did it in '64..."

YOUNG AMERICANS

Bowie kicks off proceedings with a frantic reconstruction of the mundane nature of American everyday life. Bowie's lyrics sound second-hand, as if they are an imagined version of American exotica, and the band, with a groovy sax-line well to the front, swings along with an almost Latin rhythm. Released as the album's first single it reached number 18 in the UK and number 28 in the US. A performance of then then unreleased track on the *Dick Cavett Show* was used in the UK as an unofficial promo for the song on *Top Of The Pops*. Bowie hasn't played the song live since 1990.

WIN

'Win' is an outstanding track, with Bowie beginning the process of unearthing his 'true' self after years of role-playing. When he sings 'Well you've never seen me naked and white' you can hear the struggle between the distanced, contrived posturer and a newer, 'real version'. A haunting melody (Earl Slick reports that he helped worked out the song's basic chord structures on acoustic guitar in Bowie's hotel room), rippling synth refrain, and some melting backing vocals give this exercise in positivity – 'All you've got to do is win' – a haunting quality, and the resigned vocals betray an uncertainty at odds with the song's message.

FASCINATION
(Bowie/Vandross)
Based on Luther Vandross' original, 'Funky Music (Is A Part Of Me'), this is another fine song which would have made a classy single. There's a great riff too, and Bowie's singing is instantly impressive. Carlos Alomar, brought in to record with Bowie on the sessions and a mainstay of Bowie's touring and recording band for the next decade, waxed lyrical: "David Bowie is a singing fool, make no doubt about it. That means he's got chops galore. This dude can wail – that's the best compliment I can make."

RIGHT
'Right' is undoubtedly the most authentically blue-eyed cut on the album, with Bowie and backing singers bouncing off each other in true call-and-response style. The message merely reiterates the central arse-kicking theme of the previous two tracks as Bowie, now descending into the mire personally, is recognising the signs of collapse.

SOMEBODY UP THERE LIKES ME
Lyrically this is one of Bowie's finest songs, containing a typically disingenuous critique of the corrupting powers of the media, disingenuous in that here Bowie is criticising the very image of what he has purposely become: 'There was a time when we judged a man by what he'd done/Now we pick them off the screen/What they look like/Where they've been'. Some great sax too.

ACROSS THE UNIVERSE
(Lennon/McCartney)
Lennon himself commented during their impromptu recording sessions that he was puzzled by Bowie's choice of Beatles cover, regarding the 1970 original from *Let It*

Be to be unrealised. This overwrought version has actually stood the test of time well and the powerful playing and overall air of invulnerability seems to capture Bowie 1975 vintage with an unerring and unforgiving eye. A few months later, a troubled Bowie would talk cryptically of the necessity of a new Hitler figure. This cover, like many of the songs on *Young Americans*, seems to obsess about super-confidence: 'nothing's gonna change my world'. The track played out over the end-titles of episode two (fittingly called 'Stardust') of the 2011 documentary *Wonders Of The Universe* by Professor Brian Cox.

CAN YOU HEAR ME
A swooning, yearning song which teeters at times on the verge of cliché, and came as a huge shock to those space cadets still fired-up from the full-tilt pop/rock of the previous year's 'Rebel Rebel'. One of Bowie's most conventional songs, it provides further evidence of his continued fascination with the real and the imaginary, with the admission that he still might simply be 'fakin' it all'. Again, like 'Fascination', it would have made a perfect single.

FAME
(Bowie/Lennon/Alomar)
Bowie's big US breakthrough single came courtesy of this commentary on the pressures and pains of stardom. 'Fame, what

you want is in your limo/Fame, what you get is no tomorrow'. This wonderfully spiteful song now seems like a direct message to his about-to-be-ex-manager Tony Defries. The musical structure is one of rock's greatest examples of a cut up. Bowie took a riff created by guitarist Carlos Alomar for Bowie's own version of The Flare's 'Footstompin'' (1961), and then added his own brilliant guitar line, "the long Wah and the echoed Bomp! Sound", Bowie remembered in 2006. John Lennon features on acoustic guitar and, more noticeably, backing vocals, and Bowie created a sonically astonish ending, which saw Bowie and Lennon's vocals step from an impossible high down to unsingable low.

In 2006 the album was re-issued again with sleeve notes by the author, a timeline by Kevin Cann, unseen images and three bonus tracks, 'John, I'm Only Dancing (Again)', 'Who Can I Be Now?' and 'It's Gonna Be Me (With Strings)' and a bonus DVD which included the entire album again, and two songs '1984' and 'Young Americans', performed on *The Dick Cavett Show* from December 1974. The interview with Cavett, a mixture of fun banter, dread seriousness and extreme discomfort, is mesmerising viewing. Bowie obsessively plays around with his latest prop, a cane, sniffs repeatedly, and at times seems to glaze over completely. In 2013, Cavett said that at the start of the interview, he thought he would 'witness a live nervous breakdown', adding, 'performers know that nerves can hit you and stay there but usually if you're out there a while it abates and it did with him… He was very personable… [and] a shockingly good performer.'

STATIONTOSTATIONDAVIDBOWIE

STATION TO STATION

(Original UK Issue: RCA Victor APLI 1327, released 23 January 1976; UK CD: EMI 521 9060; US CD: Virgin 21906; UK chart: 5 [Total weeks in chart: 18]; US chart: 3 [32]) Special B003UTUQ3E and Deluxe Editions B00FZ0PJIS 5CD /DVD/3LP). Box set 2010.

In 1975 Bowie famously pronounced rock dead. "It's a toothless old woman," he cried. "I've rocked my last roll." During the summer, he completed work on his first, and probably still best, major film to date, *The Man Who Fell To Earth*. In this cult sci-fi classic Bowie plays the role of an alien who is forced to come to Earth in search of resources for his dying planet, falls prey to mankind's corruption and is unable to return. Bowie imbued the role with a frozen demeanour and he brought the same sense of detachment and rootlessness to his next musical project.

Originally entitled *The Return Of The Thin White Duke*, this was, for almost 20 years, the last album to feature Bowie in character and it was his least empathetic character yet. The Thin White Duke, lofty, Aryan ('making sure white stains'), was a projection of Bowie's own deluded attachment to the magical symbols of the Far Right. There's a glacial, yearning quality to the music, from the epic title track through to the breathless interpretation of Dimitri Tiomkin's 'Wild Is The Wind'. *Station To Station* is a rivetingly

sea change, and I think that was part of the excitement, something absolutely new. Nothing in pop had been absolutely new probably since Elvis Presley in the 1950s."

An immensely rich listening experience, this shows Bowie at his very best. Earl Slick once again takes the role of soloist, and the rhythm section of Alomar, Murray and Davies conjures up an intriguing mélange of 'black' and 'white' styles. Harry Maslin, who had engineered the *Young Americans* sessions, was brought in as producer. "Haunting and beautiful still, and utterly timeless, it is full of a quiet grief, and lovely tunes," is how writer and broadcaster Tony Parsons sums up an album that Bowie himself has only the very vaguest recollections of even making. An essential purchase and the greatest album of all time to play in life's desperate moments.

emotional album but it's the emotion of an individual who has become desperately and spiritually bankrupt.

Recording began in October 1975 at the Cherokee Studios in Hollywood, and again Bowie wrote most of the album in the studio. Bowie was living reversed hours, sleeping during the day and often recording through the night. In 1976, a disgruntled Earl Slick commented: "Bowie used us like a radio. He turned us on when he needed us. He ignored us when he didn't." Yet, today, Slick is more sanguine about the whole period, remembering a very troubled time in which friendships were strained: "I don't think any of us looked that great at times back then. The executives of the record companies weren't clean, the managers weren't clean. Everybody was fucked up. And I'm not just saying that to be funny, it's the goddam truth!"

Finally re-titled *Station To Station* and released early in 1976 it proved to be a bigger commercial success in America than in Europe. That said, musically it was beginning to move away from the 'plastic soul' of its predecessor towards a new, thrilling hybrid as music writer Paul Du Noyer comments: "There was something thrilling innovative about the music, the possibility of a crossover between white European electronic music and black American funk music, which in due course would be one of the most significant developments of the next twenty years. *Station To Station* was one of the first premonitions of this impending

STATION TO STATION

This is one of Bowie's best ever. It starts with a synthesized train sound rebounding from speaker to speaker and, through a hypnotic and gradually intensifying rhythmic figure, builds dramatically towards Bowie's entrance: 'The return of the Thin White Duke/Throwing darts in lovers' eyes'. The imagery is redolent with references to magical transformations, and his vocal is ominously multi-tracked. The music in the first half of the track is the perfect fusion of the new sounds coming from Germany, the music of Kraftwerk and Neu! in particular, and the hard funk of the band. In later interviews, Bowie has often admonished the lazy assumptions of journalists who have drawn a direct link between the track and Kraftwerk's 'Trans Europe Express', a track which would be released over a year after this.

At the time, Bowie was studying the esoteric works of the theosophist Madame Blavatsky and various other occultist and Cabbalistic teachings, and this influence, filtered through Bowie's own unhinged mindset, created a spell-like and quite disturbing piece of music. Bowie would later joke that the entire record was 'Black Magic – the musical!', yet sections such as the opening of the title track are as far away from jollity as one could conceive. Then, suddenly, mid-way through, the piece turns round on itself and, after the killer lines, 'It's not the side effects of the cocaine/I'm thinking that it must be love', rocks out passionately until Slick's solo closes the proceedings. An ambitious and awesomely realised piece of music, it's Bowie's own 'Sympathy For The Devil' for the seventies, a godless, desperate record written by a desperate and unbalanced young mind.

 GOLDEN YEARS
Alomar remembers that the song originated when Bowie was fooling around with a Broadway vibe: "David goes to the piano and plays 'They say the neon lights are bright on Broadway... Come de dum ma baby...'," and viola! Bowie's best dance track ever recorded is born. Earl Slick, however, remembers differently: "The riff at the beginning of 'Golden Years' is mine. And in all honesty I kind of ripped it from an old song called 'Funky Broadway'. I twisted it a bit but that's where it came from. It's not verbatim but it's the same vibe." Whatever the origin, the insistent riff is a killer, and its most obvious musical cousin is the late addition to *Young Americans*, 'Fame', a track which would sonically have fitted *Station To Station* better. Add in cool castanets and a catchy refrain, not to mention Bowie's rather good whistling, and some of his most intriguingly oblique lyrics. Bowie stumbled on the wasted side of elegant through the song on *Soul Train*, a performance which would serve as a de facto promo for the song. 'Golden Years' became a transatlantic Top 10 hit early in 1976.

 WORD ON A WING
Around the time of *Station To Station*, Bowie began wearing a cross as a form of talismanic protection, and this quite beautiful song is no less than a hymn. Roy Bittan, from Bruce Springsteen's E Street Band, is on hand with some delicious piano on what is essentially a plea for salvation from a man fully aware that his lifestyle, his obsessions, and his addictions were killing him. It's music so raw, so vulnerable, and so sad that, at times, it's almost painful to witness. This is the sound of a young man in total despair.

 TVC15
Showing Bowie in lighter vein, this is your average run-of-the-mill song about a girlfriend-eating television set! Influenced by the Thomas Newton figure in *The Man Who Fell To Earth*, who overdosed on the cathode ray in front of a bank of television screens (a trick later famously, and brilliantly, ripped off by U2 in the nineties), Bowie offers up one of his simplest, and best, hooks: 'Transmission/ Transition', and the band, complete with honky-tonk piano and doo-wop backing vocals, are in jaunty mood. The second single from the album, it stalled in the UK at number 33, despite being released to coincide with the European leg of the world tour.

 STAY
Some of the best guitar work of any Bowie album can be found on this cool cut about the uncertainties of a one-nighter: 'Cos you can never really tell/When somebody wants something you want too'. Always a live favourite of Bowie's during his touring years, this version has drama a-plenty and remains one of his strongest cuts from the seventies.

 WILD IS THE WIND
(Tiomkin/Washington)
Originally recorded in 1956 by Johnny Mathis for the film of the same name, Bowie makes this epic tale of passion his own with a remarkable, highly-mannered vocal performance. The song, driven by some almost aggressive acoustic guitar, twists and turns to full dramatic effect, before falling silent as Bowie croons: 'Don't you know you're life itself'. The song then burns out in one of the most stirring and erotic endings to any pop ballad. Bowie later commented that this track among others comes close to defining his core vocal sound. The big, deep and full delivery evident would continue over the next few albums, marking Bowie out as arguably the finest British rock singer of his day.

THE SPECIAL AND DELUXE REISSUES

In 2010, *Station To Station* was reissued again and made the UK Top 30, albeit for one week. The album came in Special and Deluxe editions, the latter, at the time of writing, is fetching well over £300 on-line and includes a 24-page booklet, the 1985 RCA master, a five-track singles version EP, an unreleased edit of the title track, and various other bits of fan memorabilia. The scaled down, but still impressive Special Edition is currently available for around £60. Both editions feature a live '76 show, the much admired (and much bootlegged), Live Nassau Coliseum, a double CD. Track listing: CD 1: 'Station To Station'/'Suffragette City', 'Fame', 'Word On A Wing', 'Stay', 'Waiting For The Man', 'Queen Bitch.' CD 2: 'Life On Mars?' 'Five Years', 'Panic In Detroit', 'Changes', 'TVC15', 'Diamond Dogs', 'Rebel Rebel', 'The Jean Genie'.

The '76 tour, official called the *Isolar* tour, was hailed by many who saw it as Bowie's finest ever. This was the show seen by Kraftwerk, Madonna and Gary Numan; all three, in their own ways, with Bowie's DNA in their makeup. However what we don't get is any live concert footage and it is indeed a terrible shame that so many of Bowie's tours do not have anything approaching an official release. On stage in the first half of 1976, Bowie was the Keaton-esque Thin White Duke, a cosmic cabaret crooner in a black three-piece suit, a packet of Gitanes in his top pocket and his red hair severely slicked back, the brash intensity of the music matched only by the blinding intensity of the stage lights. Online, one can see various snippets of fan footage, and a professionally filmed rehearsal for the tour, which intriguingly includes an early version of 'Sister Midnight' (later to become an Iggy Pop song on *The Idiot*), and which, next to 'Station To Station', is the best exemplar of the new hard rock/funk/electronics fusion. The most revealing piece of footage which does exist comes in a remarkable short documentary made by French TV, *David Bowie Ou La Rêve De Natacha* about a sexagenarian Bowie fan who set up a David Bowie fan club and her meeting with a very charming singer before his final gig of the tour in Paris, May 1976. Three clips of Bowie onstage are also shown.

Finally, the cover is returned to its original, a black and white still of Bowie in *The Man Who Fell To Earth* with the intriguing capitalised and no-word-breaks of the front and back in red and in font close to Franklin Gothic (STATIONTOSTATIONDAVIDBOWIE). A brilliantly minimalistic cover.

LOW

(Original UK Issue: RCA Victor PL 12030, released 14 January 1977; UK CD: 521 9070; US CD: Virgin 21907; UK chart No. 2 [Total weeks in chart: 27]; US chart: 11 [19])

1976 was a crisis year for Bowie. Crippled by cocaine, he haunted the stage during a five-month world tour. Off-stage he faced a concerted media backlash in the wake of his alleged Nazi salute at Victoria Station, and some perversely inappropriate (given the rise in Britain of the far-right organisations such as the British Movement and the National Front) observations about Hitler and the need for a new right-wing government to seize the reins of power. In the eyes of many, despite the excellence of his recent recordings, Bowie had flagrantly abused his position as a star.

Bowie moved to France and to the Château d'Herouville studio near Paris after the tour and began work with Iggy Pop on songs which would form *The Idiot* album. Although released after *Low*, these songs revealed Bowie road-testing his new sound. Remarkable pieces such as 'Nightclubbing' and 'Funtime' mixed droll lyrics and minimalistic beats on Iggy's most ground-breaking album. By the time Bowie himself felt ready to record, his new sound was very much forming before the sessions began in August. Showing once again an unerring knack of picking the right collaborators, Bowie brought Visconti back as producer and also asked Brian Eno, late of Roxy Music, to collaborate during the

sessions. The previous year Eno had released two of the most important albums of the seventies, *Another Green World*, a meld of art rock and electronics, and the instrumental ambient album *Discreet Music,* full of slow, quiet beauty.

Low – originally entitled *New Music, Night And Day* – can be seen as an attempt to retreat from the excesses and pressures of this very stardom. At a time when punk rock was noisily reclaiming the three-minute pop song in a show of public defiance, Bowie almost completely abandoned traditional rock instrumentation and embarked on a kind of introverted musical therapy. The sonics sound clean and pure as if Bowie was attempting to exorcise the evil of his LA self, yet *Low* is still a very troubled record and spiritually is closer to *Station To Station* than its successor, "Heroes". It was recorded during the late summer of 1976 at the Château d'Herouville studio and at the Hansa studios in Berlin.

Brian Eno remembers: "What I think he was trying to do was to duck the momentum of a successful career. The main problem with success is that it's a huge momentum. It's like you've got this big train behind you and it all wants you to carry on going the same way. Nobody wants you to step off the tracks and start looking round in the scrub around the edges because nobody can see anything promising there."

One of the most unusual features of the recording process was the use of Eno's *Oblique Strategies* cards which he had developed with Peter Schmidt in 1975. They formed a sort of musical tarot ("over one hundred musical dilemmas" according to the author) and contained directives on how to work in the studio such as "Listen to the quiet voice", "Fill every beat with something", "Emphasize the flaws", "Mute and continue" and "Use an unacceptable colour". Eno urged Bowie to experiment and to think in non-linear ways about the recording process, and he went on to develop this new approach throughout the rest of the decade.

For Bowie fans the resulting album could hardly have been more challenging. He had completely abandoned narrative structures in his songs. The 'songs' which form the first side of the album sound like mere fragments or half-reported conversations. Side two, comprising four longer pieces of music, two featuring Bowie singing in an invented language, reportedly gave RCA a collective coronary and led one executive to suggest to Bowie that he might relocate back to Los Angeles and record more *Young Americans*-style hit material. Bowie, however, had the last laugh: 'Sound And Vision', the album's first single, reached number three in the UK charts.

Low, never a big seller on release, remains an uncompromising work, but it has attained almost mythic status within the rock pantheon, and is now regarded as perhaps *the* defining work of art rock. It stands as a template for adventuresome pop music which has never been equalled since. The significance of *Low* in the general scheme of things cannot be overestimated and it stands not only as Bowie's most innovative work to date, but as a landmark in popular music history. Its prescient use of ambient musical structures and Bowie's blanked-out, expressionless vocals influenced a whole generation of British post-punk artists from Joy Division to Gary Numan. Perhaps more importantly, just as punk was helping to democratise the guitar, Bowie and Eno, along with Germany's Kraftwerk, were making the synthesizer cool and poppy after a decade of Emerson Lake & Palmer and pseudo-classical meanderings. Philip Glass resurrected three tracks ('Warszawa', 'Subterraneans' and 'Some Are') for his puzzlingly jaunty neo-Romantic Low Symphony (Point Music 438 150 2) in 1993. Revealingly, *Low* has never been given the 'deluxe reissue' treatment although the 1991 Ryko reissue did include new material (see page 154). Perhaps Bowie is happy to leave what many regard as his definitive statement untouched and unadorned.

Incidentally, the cover artwork, based on a still from *The Man Who Fell To Earth* which shows a duffle-coated Bowie in profile against an unnatural, raging-fire of a sky, was intended as a punning statement on Bowie's new solitude – his Low profile! Hardly corset-snapping humour to be sure, but not bad from someone who only a year before had been surviving on a staple diet of cocaine, red peppers and milk slugged straight from the carton.

SPEED OF LIFE

Bowie's instrumental opener immediately sets the tone for the first half of the album: treated synthesizer figures, a crashing distorted snare-drum and some highly unusual melody lines (this time faintly reminiscent of the very elderly 'Whispering' recorded in 1922 by Paul Whiteman). All in all, it is one of Bowie's most successful instrumental tracks. The wonderfully spacey descending synth line was, of course, resurrected three years later for 'Scary Monsters'. A great opener to Manic Street Preacher's greatest hits tour of 2002, it was in turn resurrected by Bowie himself on that year's *Heathen* tour.

BREAKING GLASS

(Bowie, Davis, Murray)

Clocking in at just one minute 42 this song fragment shows the direct influence of Eno. Rather than ask Bowie to flesh out the song with an extra verse, Eno again opted for the 'if it's not broken don't fix it' method and the result is a song which is perfectly half-formed. The lyrical content is minimal, as if the singer is so traumatised he can hardly speak, the music is angrily insistent and there's that clever three-note synth swoop from speaker to speaker.

WHAT IN THE WORLD

A nervy, bustling song. Lyrically it continues the themes of alienation and claustrophobic introspection which infuse the album: 'So deep in your room/You never leave your room'. The song was a live favourite of Bowie's and featured on the 1978 tour, the *Serious Moonlight* comeback tour in 1983 and on some dates on the *Outside* tour in 1995/96.

SOUND AND VISION

'Sound And Vision''s crashing metronomic instrumental opening (Bowie's vocal doesn't even appear until halfway through the song), together with Mary Visconti's (née Hopkin) backing vocals and cribbed synthesized Mantovani-style strings presumably became a favourite of the director general of the BBC as it was used throughout the early part of 1977 as background music for continuity announcements. RCA must have been glad of this exposure as Bowie himself did nothing to promote it. It's justifiably one of Bowie's greatest singles. You can dance to it, marvel at Bowie's cyborg croon and enshroud yourself in its melancholic grandeur: 'Blue, blue electric blue/that's the colour of my room/Where I will live'. Bowie's ultimate retreat song.

ALWAYS CRASHING IN THE SAME CAR

Two of the resounding successes on *Low* are Dennis Davis' drumming and Tony Visconti's treatment of the snare drum using a gadget called the 'harmonizer', which created a drop in pitch. 'Always Crashing In The Same Car' utilises this effect to the full and Bowie adds some suitably violent images to go along with the stark musical backdrop. It is reportedly based on a real-life event, either in LA or in Berlin, when having rammed his dealer's car; Bowie drove around an underground car park at a life-threatening speed of abandonment.

BE MY WIFE

The second single off the album and, despite a promo (his first since 'Life On Mars?' four years earlier) featuring a frighteningly contrived performance by a hammy Bowie in full flow, a complete flop. It's another great track, with a memorable honky-tonk piano opening, great riff courtesy of Ricky Gardener and the album's most direct lyric, 'Please be mine/Share my life/Stay with me/Be my wife'. The song was dusted down as one of Bowie's own choices for the phone-your-fave *Sound + Vision* tour of 1990, and also appeared on the *Heathen* tour in 2002 and on selected shows on the *A Reality* tour 2003-2004. It is

Bowie's greatest un-charted song and also one of his own favourites.

A NEW CAREER IN A NEW TOWN

A second short instrumental closes the vinyl side one. The track is an incongruous mix of the cool, alienating timbres of the synthesizer overlaid with Bowie's harmonica. The result is a kind of battle between the European (specifically German) tradition of calculated metronomic synth music and the wholesome authenticity of the Yankee harmonica. Intriguing.

WARSZAWA

(Bowie/Eno)

This bleak, funereally slow instrumental was an attempt by Bowie to capture the textures of the Polish countryside in general, and the city of Warsaw in particular. Midway into the instrumental Bowie booms out in what sounds like a real language (but isn't) and the result is as far away from the mainstream as he has ever got. The use of phonetically constructed 'none-sense' in popular culture wasn't new (the Dadaists had evolved something called 'Sound Poetry' in the 1910s), but Bowie pioneered its resurgence, as the career of the post-punk British indie-darlings The Cocteau Twins proved.

ART DECADE

Bowie said that here he was trying to capture the ambience of West Berlin, "cut off from the world, art and culture, dying with no hope of retribution". Another slow instrumental utilising a variety of synths, piano and cello, it still sounds stark and unnerving almost four decades on.

WEEPING WALL

Philip Glass's neo-classical accumulative work, in which the process of music-making is as important as the end result, is an obvious influence on this instrumental track, which again takes Berlin as its subject-matter. Bowie plays all instruments and sets the shiny but 'real' timbres of the xylophone and vibraphone against the synths.

SUBTERRANEANS

The sombre, four-note ascending bass line was reused from a piece recorded for the Bowie/Paul Buckmaster soundtrack to *The Man Who Fell To Earth*, recorded after the sessions for *Station To Station* but never properly completed. It completes the trilogy of instrumentals about Berlin, this time dealing with the East. Bowie later commented that it was 'about the people who got caught up in East Berlin after separation – hence the faint jazz saxophones representing the memory of what it was'. A superb ending.

"HEROES"

(Original UK Issue: RCA Victor PL 12522, released 14 October 1977; UK CD: EMI; 521 9080 US CD: Virgin 21908; UK chart: 3 [Total weeks in chart: 26]; US chart: 35 [19])

In a famous advertising legend for the *"Heroes"* album, RCA proclaimed: "There's Old Wave, there's New Wave and there's David Bowie". In the year that the angry sloganeering of punk dominated the press, Bowie and Eno offered two albums which showed another, more private, musical world which would arguably go on to have just as great an influence as any Sex Pistols record.

This would be David Bowie's twelfth studio album and all but three of the first dozen are essential pieces of modern musical history. To put this into a wider context, by the autumn of 1977, Bowie had already released the same number of albums as The Beatles and Madonna, one more than The Who (although, at the time of writing, a new album is in production), four more than Talking Heads and Radiohead (to date), and six more than the ultimate studio slackers Dire Straits would come up with. Nirvana's career, although cut short by tragedy, amounted to just *three* albums. Simply put, even by 1977, Bowie's body of work was already, in numbers and in quality, the equal of any recording artist in the history of popular music. That Bowie was not even halfway through his career in terms of records released makes this all the more exceptional.

"Heroes", like its predecessor *Low*, was recorded with largely the same personnel during the summer of 1977 at the Hansa Studio in Berlin. Recording began immediately after Bowie had finished work at the same venue on a new Iggy Pop album *Lust For Life*, co-producing and contributing music to seven of the songs, including the now world-famous title track. In a December 1977 *NME* interview, Eno revealed, "It was much harder working on *'Heroes'* than *Low*," before adding: "He [Bowie] gets into a very peculiar state when he's working. He doesn't eat. It used to strike me as very paradoxical that two comparatively well-known people would be staggering home at six in the morning, and he'd break a raw egg into his mouth and that was his food for the day, virtually."

Robert Fripp, then on sabbatical from King Crimson, was brought in by Eno as lead guitarist and his contribution made for some stirring moments. Eno knew that Fripp would respond best by being surprised into action: "We put the songs on. These were songs he'd never heard... He didn't know what the chords were going to do, what the changes were going to be... He would just launch into them at full speed and somehow navigate his way through them." Overall, *"Heroes"* has a very different sonic identity to *Low*. Whereas on *Low*, Bowie's singing is often disengaged and icy, on *"Heroes"* Bowie is emotionally over-powered. There are screams, odd shifts of tone and key and full-lunged emotive salvos. The music too has changed with densely-packed collages of avant-rock; the guitars squeal, the saxophone barks and the synths, although still integral, are now darker and more disturbing. In terms of Bowie's future development, *"Heroes"* is the album which would be the most influential. *Lodger*, Scary *Monsters*, *Outside*, *Heathen* and *The Next Day* would all draw on this extraordinary palette of sounds.

However, the key to the decadent grandeur of *"Heroes"* was location. "At that time, with the [Berlin] Wall still up, there was a feeling of terrific tension throughout the city," Bowie remembered. "It was either very young or very old people. There were no family units in Berlin. It was a city of extremes. It vacillated between the absurd – the whole drag, transvestite night-club type of thing – and real radical, Marxist political thought. And it seemed like this really was the focus of the new Europe. It was right here. For the first time, the tension was outside of me rather than within me. And it was a real interesting process, writing for me under those conditions." Bowie's workplace itself would become an iconic locale.

The studio's control room, which housed the producer's console, was overlooked by armed soldiers in an observation tower on the Wall only a matter of yards away. This, as Eno was later to comment, was an environment which forced them into some sort of greatness: blandness would have been totally inappropriate as an end result. The album was completed extremely quickly, taking only a month to write and record, and many of the takes used were first ones. Only 'Sons Of The Silent Age' was finished as piece when recording began. Whereas *Low* has attained legendary status, it was *"Heroes"* which won the plaudits at the time, becoming *NME* and *Melody Maker*'s Album of the Year.

"Heroes" might have taken a rather different turn however. Michael Rother from Neu! had spoken to Bowie about a collaboration. However, either due to a miscommunication, or the meddlesome subterfuge of a record company scenting yet another 'non-

commercial' Bowie album, the collaboration never came to pass. However, what is stamped right through the music is Bowie's continued admiration for the new German sound. In 1997, Bowie said: "When I speak about influence, I'm not just talking about the soundscapes and the musical moods. I'm talking mainly about rhythm and how these Germans back then managed to knock together such breath-taking beats out of their synthesizers."

By the time of its release, punk was blowing itself out as a musical force. The clued-up were already looking for something else, and Bowie had just provided it. "'Heroes' was fantastic, particularly the second side," says Jon Savage, then a journalist on the British music weekly *Sounds*. "Punk had become very claustrophobic, London had become very claustrophobic, at that particular point, and that's why all the synthesizer music was such a boon, really, because it offered a way out."

With *"Heroes"* he retreats even further from the role of rock icon: "I feel incredibly divorced from rock and it's a genuine striving to be that way," he told *Melody Maker* soon after the album's release. *"Heroes"* has a cinematic quality, with the instrumental section, found originally on side two of the album, bettering the equivalent instrumental second side of *Low*.

"Heroes" has also been portrayed as a more emotional and positive album than its predecessor, but there is actually very little evidence of Bowie lightening up. The mood remains sombre, often brilliantly so, and the lyrics are more confused, oblique and innerved than on *Low*. His music was also becoming truly international in its scope (a trend further emphasised on the last in the Bowie-Eno tryptich, *Lodger*) and was beginning to incorporate non-Western musical motifs. Yet again, the cover design for the album showed Bowie to be the most important visual artist working in modern music. The photo by Masayoshi Sukita was inspired by the German expressionist artist Erich Heckel and his 1917work *Roquairol*. "Tomorrow belongs to those that can hear it coming," intoned Bowie in his best cockney for the album's TV ad. By the end of 1977 Bowie had reaffirmed his position as Britain's most innovative artist.

BEAUTY AND THE BEAST

The scene-setting opening salvo – weird Eno-esque 'Sky Saw' guitars, a troubled cry from Bowie, and then Fripp's dark and visceral guitar parts set the tone for most of the album: despite leading a more stable life in Berlin, there was still a lot of troublesome debris in Bowie's emotional cache to recycle. The second single off the album and a minor hit in early 1978.

JOE THE LION

The album really kicks into gear with this tale of Berlin bar-life, partly based on performance artist Chris Burden.

Burden liked being put in a bag on a motorway, being hung over a pool of water with two electrodes in his hand, and, yes, being nailed to his car. It was this idea of ritual performance art, of the body-as-art-object, that informs much of the writing on the *Outside* album 18 years later. According to Bowie, Robert Fripp's idiosyncratic guitar playing was his attempt at the blues, and the middle section – with Bowie announcing: 'Its Monday', the strange vocal pitching, and scream – 'You will be like your dreams tonight' – is one of the album's best moments.

"HEROES"

(Bowie/Eno)

In "Heroes" Bowie gives the impression that you can be like your dreams forever. This is the only piece of narrative writing on the album and is perhaps pop's definitive statement of the potential triumph of the human spirit over adversity. It is also a classic example of how music, lyrics and context must always be brought into equivalence when assessing a song's impact, as this particular song is nothing without Fripp's guitar work and the slowly building ominously repetitive musical refrain which builds into an almost excruciating climax. Yearning, romantic and theatrical, it is regarded in poll after poll as Bowie's greatest moment on record.

Bowie would later comment that the tempo and rhythm had been inspired by the Velvet Underground's 'Waiting For The Man'. Visconti has revealed that the lovers' secret rendezvous by the Berlin Wall depicted in the song was inspired by a real-life event. Visconti and backing singer Antonia Maas were spotted by Bowie kissing on the street.

There have been a number of high-profile live renditions (notably at Live Aid) and the music was also extensively used throughout the 2012 London Olympics. Released in an unsatisfactorily edited form as a single in the autumn of 1977, in view of its acclaim it is actually quite shocking that it only reached number 24 in the UK charts.

SONS OF THE SILENT AGE

Here Bowie serves up a slice of nostalgic futurism, as if we've been transported to some time centuries hence and are listening to a re-telling of the story of a long-gone era. Again, it's the incongruity of the structure of the song which is of interest, with its doomy, leaden, sax-driven verses and almost schmaltzy choruses. Played live on 1987's *Glass Spider* tour, but not revisited since.

BLACKOUT

There was some speculation among Bowie fans at the time that this song referred to Bowie's own collapse (sensationally reported as a heart attack) in 1976, but this has been denied by the man himself. It's another lyrical and musical cut-up *à la* 'Beauty And The Beast', but this time Bowie's vocals have a breathless, haughty manner ("Me I'm Robin Hood and I puff on my cigarette") and there's some great drumming from Dennis Davies, recorded live with no overdubs.

V-2 SCHNEIDER

The album really releases its charms with the four instrumental pieces which could be found on the original vinyl side two. Here Bowie leads the band through a goose-stepping piece of music with an off-the-beat sax part (Bowie had begun his part on the wrong beat but decided to keep it like that), some military-style drumming and great guitars. The title of the song is in part a tribute to Kraftwerk's Florian Schneider.

SENSE OF DOUBT

This is a good example of how Bowie and Eno were able to build up the expressive quality of their music using what is in essence a very simple piece of musical information. As notes on a page there's very little going on with this track, but the main four-note descending refrain has such awesome resonance and the high synth line is so disturbing and funereal that the result is a minimalist masterpiece.

This track appeared as the B-side of the 'Beauty And The Beast' single and, as such, found its way on to a few pub juke-boxes. Bowie fans with a droll sense of humour liked nothing better than to observe its effects on a cheerful crowd of drinkers.

MOSS GARDEN

(Bowie/Eno)

From funereal to ethereal on this highly effective, slowly moving piece of music. It's obviously meant to carry Japanese musical connotations and Bowie's koto (a stringed instrument similar to the guitar) works well. Eno's influence is felt everywhere on this track, as the musical structures change almost imperceptibly. In the eighties and nineties Eno's video installations would visually re-create the minimalism of his seventies music with their slowly changing image collages.

NEUKÖLN

(Bowie/Eno)

'Moss Garden' segues straight into this instrumental. The Zen tranquility is disrupted by, again, some fine guitar work (again with a five-note descending riff) and Bowie's asthmatic sax. By the end of the piece the sax is alone and Bowie booms out like a ship in a fog-bound harbour. Neukölln (to give it its correct spelling), is an area in Berlin which at the time had a large population of Turkish immigrants, hence the plaintive, melismatic music.

THE SECRET LIFE OF ARABIA

(Bowie/Eno/Alomar)

This vocal track has tended to be ignored, which is a shame as, along with the title track, it's the album's best song. There's an infectious groove which builds and builds in a typically Bowiesque repetitive manner and Bowie once again returns to the camp theme of real life being merely a bit-part acting role: 'You must see the movie/The sand in my eyes/I walk through a desert song/When the heroine dies'. Another in the long line of Bowie songs that should have been singles.

STAGE

(Original UK Issue: RCA Victor PL 02913, Released 8 September 1978; UK CD: EMI EMD 1030; US CD: Rykodisc RCD 10144/45; UK chart: 5 [Total weeks in chart: 10]; US chart: 44 [13])

'All the world's a stage… And one man in his time plays many parts'…The Euro-funk of the 1976 Thin White Duke tour yielded a number of high quality bootleg recordings but this, Bowie's second live double album to be released (if not recorded), was met with dismay by many on original release. Fans were disappointed by the release delays. Some moaned that the tracks didn't in fact sound very live (Chris Brazier at *Melody Maker* went so far as to write: "…the album almost demands to be considered a studio recording"), or that the tracks appeared to have been slowed in tempo (reportedly Bowie did instruct the band to play in more deliberate manner and bootleg recordings of the tour do reveal sprightly-tempoed versions) and that the audience appeared to have been turned down (in fact this was not the case as producer Tony Visconti had recorded the band and Bowie largely through direct feeds which minimalized audience noise), while others muttered about the decision by Visconti, with Bowie's full approval, to re-order the songs chronologically. Despite the massive critical success of *"Heroes"*, there were some lukewarm reviews of both tour and album. The most scathing, if inconsequential, comments came from *NME*'s Julie Burchill calling Bowie: "That toothless old piece of

meat… proving that, just like his good friends Lou and Iggy, all he's good for is hanging out with other has-beens." Bowie and his fans would have to get used to the tide turning against them as the years went on.

The 1978 tour (officially called Isolar II) saw Bowie's fanbase, still loyal, in transition. The 'Bowie Clones' were still there, but fewer in numbers. Bowie's new look of alternately astonishingly voluminous pants, or slightly punky PVC trousers, plastic hoodie, sailor's cap, white shirts and cool jackets made the 31 year old dashing rather than alien. The staging was, once again, masterly in its minimalism, a cage of white fluorescent bars at the back and overhead provided stunning light show. Those old enough to have seen the tour would retrospectively claim this to be the end of the 'classic' Bowie stage shows before commercialism broke him in the eighties. Nobody would have guessed that it would be his last tour for a full five years.

Bowie had never been in such good voice and *Stage*, culled from four shows from the tour (two from the Spectrum, Philadelphia, and shows at Providence and Boston), draws heavily on *Low* and *"Heroes"* while also containing a large chunk of *Ziggy Stardust* (the entire album was, reportedly, rehearsed but only around half the songs were regularly played). The *Ziggy* material was given a very different, but no less good, interpretation. Whereas the Spiders were a tight, proto-punk rock act, the new band with the tried and trusted Alomar/Murray/Davis rhythm section swung (Dennis Davis drumming is brilliantly expansive and flamboyant), Sean Mayes' piano and Roger Powell's synths work a certain magic, while Adrian Belew on lead guitar (headhunted from Frank Zappa's band), Simon House on electric violin, added surprising avant-rock flourishes. 'Breaking Glass' was put out on an EP with 'Ziggy Stardust' and 'Art Decade' and reached number 54 in the UK charts.

In 2005, *Stage* was revisited by producer Tony Visconti and the track listing was returned to the original running order of the concerts. 'Be My Wife' and 'Stay' were added, along with Bowie's excellent rendition of Kurt Weill and Berthold Brecht's 'Alabama Song', originally included as a bonus track on the 1991 Ryko reissue of the album. Brecht and Bowie proved a good fit and Bowie's version knocks the Doors' version into a cocked hat. The new 2005 version is superior sonically and comes repackaged and improved. Shame that songs played during these shows, including 'Jean Genie', 'Suffragette City' and 'Rebel Rebel', originally discounted from inclusion on *Stage* because they had appeared on 1974's *David Live*, did not make the new edition.

Full track listing, Disc 1: 'Warszawa', "Heroes", 'What In The World', 'Be My Wife', 'Blackout', 'Sense Of Doubt', 'Speed Of Life', 'Breaking Glass', 'Beauty And The Beast', 'Fame': Disc 2: 'Five Years', 'Soul Love', 'Star', 'Hang On To Yourself', 'Ziggy Stardust', 'Art Decade', 'Alabama Song', 'Station To Station', 'Stay', 'TVC 15'

LODGER

(Original UK Issue: RCA BOW LP 1, Released 18 May 1979; UK CD: EMI 521 9090, US CD: Virgin 21909; UK chart: 4 [Total weeks in chart: 17]; US chart: 20 [15])

By early 1979 Bowie was being 'out-Bowied' by Gary Numan, a new-wave rocker turned robotic androgyne, with a head full of Bowie, whose band Tubeway Army hit number one in the UK with 'Are Friends Electric?', and John Foxx-era Ultravox. Another Bowiesque single, 'Cars', also reached the UK top spot. In the absence of a big UK hit for Bowie in over two years, it looked as if his natural constituency of the emotionally dispossessed had found a new, if not exactly unfamiliar, icon. Numan has justifiably gone on to become a cult artist of great repute but, at the time, the hardcore Bowie fans looked on dispirited and unaccepting at a man considered to be nothing more than a Bowie copyist.

The *Lodger* album, which hit the shops just as Numan-mania was breaking out, was a demanding affair, its working titles including *Planned Accidents* and *Despite Straight Lines*. Recorded during a gap in the 1978 world tour and completed in early 1979, it revealed the Bowie-Eno collaboration in its final throes. For *Lodger* Bowie returned to a more narrative style of writing, and one suspects that this was beginning to grate on Eno's pioneering ambient stance.

This collision of styles (the rock idol beginning to grasp for mainstream acceptance once again, the pop pioneer deepening his interest in ambient structures) makes for an uneasy, though often brilliant musical trip. The album has unjustly suffered in the eyes of posterity, not least due to Eno's constant dismissal of it in a succession of interviews. Its main flaw is that its sound is 'graced' with one of the most demanding mixes of any Bowie record. Unless it is played on superior hi-fi equipment the vinyl *Lodger* sounds unclear and soupy, the top end dulled, while the bass lacks any resonance. On CD the sound is much improved but still not great. In 2013, co-producer Tony Visconti revealed that he and Bowie may one day revisit the tapes and produce a better-quality version.

Although the album boasts the trans-sexual hit single 'Boys Keep Swinging', its eclecticism and experimentation have lessened its mainstream appeal; a pity since much of *Lodger* is really exciting and the use of ethnic musics on side one extremely prescient. *Lodger* is loosely thematic, with the first half commenting on Bowie's wanderlust and the second on Anglo-American consumer society. A vastly underrated work, it's there for anyone interested in Bowie's more daring musical legacy. And the cover, in the form of a postcard and showing Bowie on the mortuary slab with nose and legs squashed at right-angles, is one of his most innovatory.

Reviews were mixed. Although *Record Mirror* got in early with a pre-release five-star review, Jon Savage at *Sounds* was underwhelmed: "*Lodger* is a nice enough pop record, beautifully played, produced and crafted, and slightly faceless. Is Bowie that interesting? …. Projection: will the eighties really be this boring?"

There was a sense, too, that the wanderlust Bowie enunciated in the tracks on side one reflected his need to move on career-wise. Although he owed them one more album, which would turn out to be *Scary Monsters*, his record contract with RCA was drawing to a close. For too long he'd been the label's biggest star, perhaps taken for granted, and RCA was fast diminishing as a force in the record industry. Perhaps this was why the only promotion he personally undertook for *Lodger* was to appear at a luncheon in RCA's London boardroom, glad-handing executives, while their press office was left to stage a 'listen to *Lodger*' session for media types in the same office the following week. Low-key was the message.

A final point: *Low*, "*Heroes*" and *Lodger*, the so-called Berlin trilogy or triptych (even though only one of the albums was recorded there in full) were co-produced not by Brian Eno, but by Tony Visconti. Eno was at the sessions, co-writing many of the songs, and adding his own particular magic, but he was *not* there as producer.

Low, "*Heroes*", *Stage* and *Lodger* are also available as discount-price box set, *David Bowie: Zeit! 77-79* (Released 6 May 2013 EMI B00BQ8ZWO4).

 FANTASTIC VOYAGE
(Bowie, Eno)
After the jagged, ominous music of

"*Heroes*", Lodger starts off with a surprisingly delicate, mandolin-led ballad which harks back to the narrative styles of *Hunky Dory*. It also indicates the beginnings of a certain politicisation in Bowie's work, dealing as it does with the threat of the holocaust and the 'depression' of our leaders. Incidentally, the song has apparently exactly the same chord sequence as 'Boys Keep Swinging'. Occasionally played live on the *Reality* tour, it's another fine Bowie song awaiting full rehabilitation.

 AFRICAN NIGHT FLIGHT
(Bowie, Eno)
This is the most innovatory piece of music on the album. Suitably jungle-like noises abound, and the musical fabric is dense with Eno's synthesized 'cricket menace'. Bowie's vocal delivery, as he was later to comment, is a sort of white rap delivered at break-neck speed and is extremely eccentric, the whole giving the impression of great velocity. The listener feels as if she is being dragged through the undergrowth along with a babbling Bowie. Narratively, the 'song' deals with some German fighter pilots Bowie had met in the bars of Mombasa who felt so culturally alienated that they couldn't return home. More Man Who Fell To Earthisms.

 MOVE ON
Another unusually intense ballad, this time with a melody far superior to 'Fantastic Voyage'. Thematically it's the key-note song on the first half of the album. The rhythm is busy, galloping, propulsive to match the restless lyric describing a peripatetic rootless lifestyle. He is 'just a travelling man' and in a typically corny moment Bowie croons 'Cyprus is my Island/When the going's rough/I would like to find you/Somewhere in a place like that'. *Lodger*'s finest track and, to my knowledge, never performed live.

 YASSASSIN
Fine vocal phrasing is the feature of this catchy, Middle-Eastern 'Fame' re-write, which was surprisingly left as an

album cut only. Bowie sings 'We walked proud and lustful/In this resonant world' and stretches the first syllable of 'resonant' over five notes, imbuing the line with an appropriate melismatic quality. Simon House's violin is pretty good too. ('Yassassin' is Turkish for 'long life')

RED SAILS

(Bowie, Eno)
In which Bowie gambles on a piece of ambient-pop with a Motorik beat sounding good on your average hi-fi equipped with a darning needle as a stylus. I'll let Bowie try and explain what's going on here: "Here we took a German new music feel and put against it the idea of a contemporary English mercenary-cum-swashbuckling Errol Flynn, and put him in the China Sea. We have a lovely cross-reference of cultures. I honestly don't know what it's about". The ending, in particular, is one of my favourites, with Bowie yelling "The hinterland, the hinterland/ We're going to sail to the hinterland". Barmy.

D.J.

(Bowie, Eno, Alomar)
There's a marked shift in focus now, as Bowie abandons his Marco Polo, roving pop-God act. 'DJ' is a good song, but, even in an edited form, proved too tangled structurally for the singles charts, peaking at its début position of 29 in the UK. Again, the use of violin works well and Bowie's in great 'amateur operatics' form vocally, but you need to see the video too for the song to really take off.

LOOK BACK IN ANGER

(Bowie/Eno)
This song, about a rather seedy angel of death and possessor of a fabulous video, never actually became a single in the UK. A pity since it's one of the most dramatic moments on *Lodger*, fast percussive beat again indebted to the Motorik of bands such as Neu!, with a great droning quality and a super, funky-yet-ambient guitar break from Carlos Alomar. It proved a worthy opener to many of the *Serious Moonlight* concerts four years later, and was revived on the 1995 *Outside* and *Heathen* tours.

BOYS KEEP SWINGING

(Bowie/Eno)
Bowie famously instructed the band to swap instruments in order to get a raw, garage rock sound, and the closing guitar solo at the end of the track is fanatically awkward and discordant. Released as the lead-off single it reached number seven in the UK charts but deserved much better. Lyrically, Bowie has rather cheekily pastiched The Village People's 'YMCA'/'In The Navy' for this tale of hetero/homo-sexual laddishness: 'When you're a boy/You can wear a uniform/When you're a boy/Other boys check you out'. Who could forget Bowie being chased around the studio by Kenny Everett as 'Angry of Mayfair' complaining, 'You know I was in the war/But I didn't see you there/I fought for people like you/And I never got one!' on *The Kenny Everett Video Show*? Well, I certainly haven't, and as for that video...

REPETITION

In this most alarming piece of descriptive writing Bowie tells a tale of wife-beating and marital disharmony in a mundane, matter-of-fact way. The metronomic guitar riff mirrors perfectly the repeated blows dished out by husband to wife. An undervalued song and one of his best.

RED MONEY

(Bowie/Alomar)
Here Bowie takes back the music written for Iggy Pop's great 'Sister Midnight' and sets against it some observations on consumer society and the responsibility money brings. Although an absolute killer riff still, one just wished it wasn't quite so buried in the mix. 'Project cancelled,' sang Bowie, drawing a line under the Eno collaboration. Where was he heading next?

SCARY MONSTERS (AND SUPERCREEPS)

(Original UK Issue: RCA BOW LP 2, released 12 September 1980; UK CD: 521 8950; Super Audio CD 543 3182: US CD: Virgin 21895; UK chart: 1 [Total weeks in chart: 32]; US chart: 12 [27])

For many Bowie fans, the release of *Scary Monsters (And Supercreeps)* in the autumn of 1980 marked the end of a golden era. It was the last album to feature the production skills of Tony Visconti and the rhythm section of George Murray, Dennis Davis and Carlos Alomar (though the last named has worked with Bowie on subsequent projects). Although booked to produce the *Let's Dance* album late in 1982, Visconti was dropped at the last minute in favour of Chic's Nile Rodgers. In 1983, Visconti worked with Bowie on the UK leg of the Serious Moonlight tour, when he was asked to sort out the sound mix for the Edinburgh and Hammersmith shows, but there would then be a 15-year hiatus in their working relationship. Visconti claims that the rift was caused by certain comments to Bowie biographers which were perceived as disloyal by Bowie. Bowie claims Visconti talked too much to the media about his son Joe. Whatever the real reason, his absence almost certainly contributed to the drop in standard of Bowie's output in the mid-eighties.

On *Scary Monsters* Visconti and Bowie, this time without Eno, fashioned what is

unarguably one of Bowie's finest records to date. The sound is uncompromising – a huge, cavernous drum sound and some truly manic guitar work from Robert Fripp. These are guitar solos without any of the machismo and predictability which characterises most rock guitar-playing, and they teeter, screech and tear through the songs, far and away the best pieces of guitar work yet on any Bowie album. Indeed, the whole set shows Bowie at the height of his powers: musically he's adroit at pulling off both the wondrous synth swoop of 'Ashes To Ashes', the dementia of 'It's No Game' and the New York-styled funk of 'Fashion'. Lyrically, Bowie plays the role of battered and wearied narrator, in turn both cautionary (as on 'It's No Game', and 'Teenage Wildlife'), and predicatory (as on 'Scream Like A Baby'). Vocally the set runs the whole gamut from the 'Newleyesque' cockney of the title track to the burnt-out resignation of 'It's No Game Part II'.

A more dynamic and commercial work than *Lodger*, *Scary Monsters*' success was founded, however, on one of his strongest ever singles – 'Ashes To Ashes' – which became Bowie's second UK number one. With Bowie the packaging has always been as important as the music itself, and in 1980 he hit upon the perfect blend of commerciality and innovation wrapped up in the disguise of a Renaissance clown, a perfect trailblazer for the New Romantics on the horizon. At the time, the mannequin-like Pierrot-Bowie which adorned the covers of both album and single, and which featured in that unforgettable video, looked just like the latest instalment in the continuing cartoonesque trawl throughout the many untapped characters of the Bowie psyche. Little did we know that it was to be the end of an era. Greeted with almost unanimously good reviews at the time (*Record Mirror*'s Simon Ludgate famously awarded it seven out of a maximum of five stars!), *Scary Monsters* is an essential item.

Incidentally, Bowie never promoted the album live, choosing instead to play (with some distinction) the role of the crippled

John Merrick in stage productions of *The Elephant Man* in Chicago and New York. Bowie did talk of a 1981 tour and of playing a select number of shows which could be then beamed into cinemas live across the world. It was an idea he would revisit over 20 years later.

IT'S NO GAME (PART 1)

The sound of a vacuum cleaner, the Cobra-like hollow rattle of a castanet and then a lurch straight into this remarkable opening salvo. The die is cast – a huge ambient snare sound echoes through the mix, and then Bowie tries to out-scream Japanese singer Michi Hirota, who replies to Bowie's lines with a Japanese translation. Bowie said that he wanted to 'break down a particular kind of sexist attitude about women and I thought that the Japanese girl typifies it, where everybody sort of pictures a geisha girl – sweet, demure and non-thinking. So she sang the lyrics in a macho, samurai voice'.

UP THE HILL BACKWARDS

This was the album's fourth, and least successful, single (UK chart number 32). The lazy, non-committal stance in the lyrics, and the shuffling, almost Bo-Diddley-like beat, is turned around in a blazing final minute as Robert Fripp's exhilarating guitar figures give the piece a most committed ending.

SCARY MONSTERS (AND SUPERCREEPS)

Fripp's guitar again detonates to wild effect in this tale of a girl who's 'stupid in the streets and can't socialise'. Although at the time Bowie was keen to impress on his public that his drug period was over, songs such as these, redolent as they are with images of paranoia and violence, give a strong hint that drug-induced schizophrenic states were not something he had totally left behind. Indeed, in interviews in the nineties, Bowie admitted that his association with hard drugs lasted well into the eighties. The music also has a foreboding, mellismatic, Middle-Eastern quality which was later

echoed in rock by tracks such as Echo & The Bunnymen's 'The Cutter' in 1983 and the excellent PIL single 'Rise' in 1986. The third single off the album, it reached the UK Top 20 in January 1981.

ASHES TO ASHES

With the addition of some Goons-like frivolity in the instrumental break in the middle, this version is slightly more extended than the single release. A classic pop song, incantatory (what *is* he saying in the background during middle eight?) and multi-layered, this is Bowie recapturing his melodic touch in a huge wash of synthesizers and treated guitars. 'Ashes To Ashes' updates the Major Tom saga from 'Space Oddity' and remains the only sequel to reach number one in the UK Charts. And Bowie got the queasy, Edwardian, nursery rhyme-like quality just right in the sing-along dénouement: 'My mother said/To get things done/you'd better not mess with Major Tom' – a sneaky and sinister re-write of a children's nursery rhyme ('My mother said/that I never should/play with the gypsies in the wood'). Although it might be stretching it a bit to say so, it could be argued (given the synthy music, Bowie's *Scary Monsters* pierrot persona, and, of course, the video) that 'Ashes' was the first and (unless you count Adam & The Ants) only New Romantic UK number one single!

FASHION

According to Tony Visconti, Bowie had a riff based around the word 'Jamaica' which refused to take the form of a song until the very end of the recording session. That this almost-lost song fragment went on to become one of Bowie's live staples and a sizeable hit (UK number five) is testimony to Bowie's quicksilver improvisatory talents and Visconti's production skills. The result is both a jaundiced view of the very musical culture Bowie was using to such good effect, that of dance and disco ('It's loud and it's tasteless and I've heard it before'), and a sly put-down of style fascism – something Bowie could be accused of himself. There's also a great, driving rhythm section and the gloriously arrogant 'Listen to me/Don't listen to me' middle eight.

TEENAGE WILDLIFE

This sprawling, ambitious track has for too long been regarded as a just an inferior "Heroes" re-write. In fact it's a fine song which lyrically continues 'Fashion''s theme of world-wearied, patrician pessimism, with Bowie, then the 33-year-old paternal figure, pronouncing on youth culture from a marked distance. In fact, *Scary Monsters* reveals a Bowie heading towards an uncertain middle age and commenting on this uncertainty (unlike 'Let's Dance', which seems to revel in maturity and being well-adjusted). The vocal performance on this track is gargantuan and the epic quality of the music makes for an underrated, and often ignored, Bowie classic.

SCREAM LIKE A BABY

This track has a calculated New York, New Wave feel, and is based, musically, on a track Bowie wrote back in 1973 for Ava Cherry's group The Astronettes called 'I Am A Laser', which was available on the CD *People From Bad Homes* (Golden Years, GY005). 'Scream Like A Baby' continues the Bowie tradition of nostalgic science fiction. This time Bowie, as narrator, re-tells a futuristic tale of incarceration and sexual persecution in a distant past. The best moment comes towards the end of the track when Bowie, through the use of two vari-speed vocals, brilliantly captures the sense of a mind being split in two and the sort of schizophrenic horror which had troubled him in real life through much of his career as a singer.

KINGDOM COME
(Verlaine)

This Tom Verlaine song roots the album's creative spiritual home in the late-seventies American post-punk scene and as a homage works well. The highlight is of course the astonishingly contrived vocal performance in which Bowie attempts an almost psychotic Barry Gibb-like phrasing.

BECAUSE YOU'RE YOUNG

This, the weakest song in the set, would still have cruised on to the set-list of any of the subsequent Bowie recordings in the eighties. Pete Townshend lends some characteristically springy, jagged guitar, but the theme of past master commenting on the trifles of youth is now overplayed and Bowie's overblown vocal finale can't rescue it.

Bowie later commented on how surprised he was to note that, in the studio, Townshend played with the same athleticism he brought to his stage performances, jumping around and even spinning his right arm while playing.

IT'S NO GAME (PART 2)

The vinyl version ended with this re-working of the opening track. Both band and singer sound exhausted after the sonic bruising they've just administered, and the line 'Put a bullet in my brain and it makes all the papers' with hindsight proved a gruesome prediction for a famous friend.

In early December Radio 1's Andy Peebles went out to interview Bowie about his new album and recent theatre triumph in *The Elephant Man* on Broadway. Peebles unexpectedly also caught up with John Lennon and found him in optimistic mood and talking of a future tour. Two days later he was shot dead. What the full effect of the murder of a good musician friend had on Bowie is hard to tell. However, his disappearance from the music scene for two-and-a-half years and his re-launch as a pop idol without the schizoid and obsessive trappings of old might just have been a response to the ultimate example of fan-worship taken too far.

LET'S DANCE

(Original UK Issue: EMI America AML 3029, released 14 April 1983 ; UK CD: EMI 521 8960; Super Audio CD 543 3192; UK chart: 1 [Total weeks in chart: 56]; US CD: Virgin 21896; US chart: 4 [68])

1983 was the biggest year yet for David Bowie. In January he finally split from RCA and signed for EMI America in a deal reputedly worth 17 million dollars. In the spring his new single 'Let's Dance' became a transatlantic number one and the album of the same name became his biggest-selling album to date. Reviews were often gushing: "Utterly worth the wait, *Let's Dance* is irresistible. You should be ashamed to say you do not love it," wrote Charles Shaar Murray in the *NME*. There was no hint that Bowie was selling out; *Let's Dance* was seen as a flashy and classy move back into a funkier direction as *Young Americans* had been eight years earlier. Two major films starring Bowie, *The Hunger* and *Merry Christmas Mr Lawrence*, were also released in 1983. There were also two videos, shot and co-directed by David Mallet in Australia for 'Let's Dance' and 'China Girl'. Telegenic rock stars such as Bowie were perfect for the new video medium and both began heavy rotation on MTV in North America and around the world. A world tour, entitled Serious Moonlight, began in Europe in May and what was expected to be an arena tour soon saw extra dates added in open-air stadia to meet demand. This was the biggest exposure of his career; the year the world

met David Bowie. On July 16 Bowie had a staggering ten albums in the UK Top 100 album chart, as throngs of new admirers snapped up his illustrious back catalogue which had just been re-released by RCA at a special-offer price.

What was the key to this memorable comeback? Firstly, the album itself hit all the right response buttons. Although its predecessor *Scary Monsters* had been brilliant, it was still too awkward for mainstream consumption in the States. *Let's Dance* was warm, humanistic and funky and, 'Ricochet' apart, overtly commercial. Co-produced by Chic's Nile Rodgers it positively swung along, driven by a great honking sax section and some genuinely bluesy guitar from Stevie Ray Vaughan.

It was also five years since the last Bowie tour, and almost three since his last studio album. The strong showings of some unlikely interim measures such as the collaboration with Queen on 'Under Pressure' in 1981 (UK number one), and the then five-year-old and totally freaky duet with Bing Crosby on 'Little Drummer Boy/Peace On Earth' (UK number three) at Christmas 1982 proved that his commercial stock had never been higher. Since 1980 the unjustly maligned New Romantic movement headed by Visage, Culture Club and Duran Duran had peopled Planet Pop with little David Bowies. The garish narcissism of New Romanticism brought disco and club culture back on to the agenda after the largely monochrome, anti-star culture of punk. Bowie was their hero and in 1983 they welcomed him back home.

The main problem, though, was that the new normalised Bowie was a very different beast from the sex-change style guru they remembered from only a few years before. He told *NME*'s Chris Bohn: "I don't have the urge to continue as a songwriter and performer in terms of experimentation – at this moment." With hindsight, this statement is not quite true. Many British acts had attempted a fusion of rock, pop and disco/R&B and had never pulled it off. And *Let's Dance* certainly did not sound like any other record of 1983. However, Bowie became a victim of his own success. *Let's Dance*, despite its classiness and playability, appealed not perhaps directly to Bowie's existing audience, but to a new, upwardly-mobile mass audience. This would prove to be a huge hindrance to Bowie as the eighties unfolded.

MODERN LOVE

A sparkling opener, one of the best pop songs Bowie has written, and as different from Bowie's Enoesque late-seventies introspection as you can get. A great spoken opening – 'I know when to go out/I know when to stay in/Get things done' – gets the ball rolling and there's that thunderous cyclical chorus (a re-write of the 1963 hit 'Tell Him', recorded by Billie Davis among others, and echoed by Bowie ten years later in 'Miracle Goodnight'), and some fine sax. One of the album's main lyrical themes, the relationship between God and man, comes through strongly too, with Bowie putting his trust in 'God and man' against formalised religion, which merely 'gets you to the church on time'. It was the third single to be taken off the album and reached a deserved number two in the UK charts (number 14 in the States).

CHINA GIRL
(Bowie/Pop)

More famous now for its video, depicting Bowie rolling around in the surf with the actress and then love-interest Jee Ling, all bare buttocks and sandy bits, in a pastiche of Burt Lancaster and Deborah Kerr in the film *From Here To Eternity*, this is in fact another fine pop song and his best Iggy Pop cover to date (the very different original can be found on Iggy's 1977 *The Idiot* album). Nile Rodgers serves up a cheeky little oriental riff for the beginning and Bowie croons admirably through this eminently hummable ditty. Its musical accessibility has, of course, helped to draw attention from the lyric's darker themes, dealing as they do with cultural imperialism and megalomania.

Bowie screams, 'I wander into town/Just like some sacred cow/visions of swastikas in my head/Plans for everyone/It's in the white of my eyes'. A curious and incongruous lyric for the new 'normal' Bowie to resurrect, the single peaked at number two in the UK and number 10 in the States.

LET'S DANCE

Possibly Bowie's greatest-ever single (if not song) is this, the title track, in all its seven-minute and three-second glory. Musically, it's simple, direct and emotional, while the big band-style arrangement, impassioned vocal delivery, thudding bass and killer hook made it an instant dance-floor staple. It's the song on which producer Nile Rodgers' production skills are shown off to their best effect. On the surface it appears lyrically naïve, but look closer and there's a hint of an impending apocalypse. The almost whispered delivery intones, 'Let's Dance – for fear from grace should fall/Let's Dance – for fear tonight is all'. Is this the last dance before the bomb goes off? Had Bowie been listening to Prince's '1999' by any chance?

WITHOUT YOU

Essentially a filler, this is a very simple love song quite well sung. Released as a single in the USA, it reached number 73.

RICOCHET

This is the only track on the album to contain the same gravitas as his seventies work, although musically it is very different. Driven by a stark, military, indeed ricocheting drum figure it builds well with sax, horns and guitar. Lyrically again there's a religious theme as contemporary ills – 'the world is a corner waiting for jobs' – mean that we must 'turn the holy pictures so they face the wall'.

CRIMINAL WORLD
(Godwin/Browne/Lyons)
An inspired choice by Bowie, this is a cover of a 1977 song from Metro, which was fronted by Peter Godwin, and a fine version it is too with another excellent bass-line, some nice flute and one of the best couplets on the album: 'You caught me kneeling at your sister's door/That was no ordinary stick-up'! According to writer Bob Stanley, the song was banned from BBC playlist at the time due to its sexual imagery. A few years ago co-writer Sean Lyons messaged on *YouTube*: "It was lovely to hear Stevie Ray Vaughan playing my guitar parts and great to meet Mr Bowie at Milton Keynes on his Serious Moonlight tour."

 ### CAT PEOPLE (PUTTING OUT FIRE)
(Moroder/Bowie)
Bowie had written the lyrics to the theme for the 1982 film *Cat People* and the song had been a minor hit in April of that year, reaching number 26 in the UK charts. This version replaces the Moroder sound with a dose of hard rock but fails to improve on what was already a pretty good original. Stevie Ray Vaughan's searing guitar lines dominate. It acted as a taster for the album being the 'B-side' of the single, 'Let's Dance'.

 ### SHAKE IT
The album ends with the most dance-oriented track of the set. A cool, funky groove is the perfect backdrop to Bowie's fond-of-himself lyrics which directly echo the album's lunar and pugilistic leitmotif: "I duck and I sway/ I shoot at a full moon/So what's my line?"

ZIGGY STARDUST: THE MOTION PICTURE

(Original UK Issue: RCA PL 84862, released October 1983; UK CD 30th Anniversary 2CD Special Edition: released 24 March 2003, EMI 541 9792; UK chart: 17 [Total weeks in chart: 6]; US chart: 89)

On July 3, 1973 the 'leper Messiah' finally bit the dust and so ended Bowie's first experiment in genetic pop engineering. At the time it was thought that Bowie had simply retired from the stage and his real reason for this temporary secession of live activities has become peculiarly entangled with his own myth. Bowie has gone on to say that he was merely retiring from playing Ziggy and that, since he had lived out his fictional character in real life, then it would only be fitting that he bury him in actuality too. In fact what happened was that he needed a break, both from the non-stop schedule of touring, and from his band. Bowie had grown bored with the restraints the Spiders placed on him musically, and, with less rock-oriented projects probably already in mind, needed to free himself from the Jeff Beck-isms of Ronson and co.

Again, it might be overly-pedantic, but we should point out that this was the final show, not of the *Ziggy Stardust* but the *Aladdin Sane* tour, complete with beautiful piano from Mike Garson. Although Bowie himself, as we have noted, would later conflate the two personae, at the time, a sharp

distinction was made as evidenced by the section in Alan Yentob's *Cracked Actor* when Bowie is pulling out Kabuki-designed costumes for the tour.

The resulting live album is probably only of interest to *aficionados*. That said, there's some fine moments, notably a medley of three of his best songs 'The Wild Eyed Boy From Freecloud'/'All The Young Dudes'/'Oh! You Pretty Things', a chilling version of Jacques Brel's 'My Death' with its iconic ending, a moment frozen in time as the fans complete the final line of the song, a version of 'Hang To Yourself', which is to all intents and purposes a punk rock song, and the final Ziggy version of 'Rock And Roll Suicide' complete with last words: "Bye bye we love you" and appropriate audience screams. Little did they know that this was only the beginning of Bowie's musical odyssey.

'White Light/White Heat', a cover of The Velvet Underground song, complete with Ronson's rather off-key guitar work in one section, was released as a taster for the album and just missed the UK Top 40 at the end of 1983.

EMI's award-winning new edition of the double live album, featuring a vibrant mix by Tony Visconti and Richard Tozzoli using the original 16-track tapes, restores Bowie's between song pronouncements and band introduction, and includes a full-length 15-minute version of 'A Width Of A Circle' which may prove tortuous for all but the most hardcore of the hardcore. The only fly in the ointment is that Jeff Beck, who guested on three cuts that night ('The Jean Genie', 'Love Me Do' and 'Round And Round') still won't let Bowie use them.

Full track listing: Part 1: 'Intro' (incorporating: *Beethoven's Ninth Symphony* – arranged and performed by Wendy Carlos), 'Hang On To Yourself', 'Ziggy Stardust', 'Watch That Man', 'Wild Eyed Boy From Freecloud'/'All The Young Dudes'/Oh! You Pretty Things', 'Moonage Daydream', 'Changes' 'Space Oddity', 'My Death' (Jacques Brel), Part 2: Intro (Incorporating: *The William Tell Overture* by Rossini, performed by Wendy Carlos) , 'Cracked Actor', 'Time', 'The Width Of A Circle', 'Let's Spend The Night Together' (Mick Jagger/Keith Richards), 'Suffragette City', 'White Light/White Heat' (Lou Reed), 'Farewell Speech' (spoken word), 'Rock'n'Roll Suicide', 'Finale: *Pomp And Circumstance*' (Edward Elgar).

TONIGHT

*(Original UK Issue: EMI America DB 1,
released 24 September 1984; UK CD:
EMI 521 8970; UK chart: 1 [Total weeks
in chart: 19]; US chart: 11 [24])*

If *Let's Dance* and the subsequent *Serious
Moonlight* tour had made Bowie more
popular than ever in 1983, the following year
saw the beginning of a commercial and
artistic free-fall that lasted for almost a
decade. The global success of the new
'normal' Bowie, and the less-than-radical
musical soundtrack that accompanied this
new model, proved to be his undoing. *Let's
Dance* had brought Bowie a sizeable
mainstream following which he felt he
needed to appease. In so doing, he lost sight
of those very qualities, the sense of drama
and adventure, which had won him support
and respect in the first place, and he began
consciously to distance himself from the
cutting edge. It turned out to be a no-win
strategy. His new audience balked at his
theatricality on stage and his half-baked
attempts at becoming mainstream on record
fell between two stools, failing to engage the
new and less critical audience while at the
same time alienating the more discerning
fans who had appreciated his visionary zeal.
With hindsight, it would have been wiser to
have taken 1984 off, to have worked on new
material, maybe to have put out a live album
as a holding operation. But Bowie had a
hungry new record label to feed and,
perhaps with that in mind, booked sessions
for a new album a mere five months after
finishing off the exhausting world tour.

For *Tonight*, recorded at Le Studio, Morin
Heights in Canada, Bowie was woefully short
of new material and the album should never
really have been released in this form,
comprising as it did just two new songs of
any note ('Loving The Alien' and 'Blue Jean').
For some inexplicable reason, Nile Rodgers,
who had provided such a wonderfully
distinctive production for *Let's Dance*, was
not asked to work on its follow-up. Even
Bowie himself, in a moment of almost
painful self-realisation during an interview
with Charles Shaar Murray to promote the
album, recognised that he had lost the plot:
"I feel on the whole fairly happy about my
state of mind and my physical well-being and
I guess I wanted to put my musical being in
a similar staid and healthy area, but I'm not
sure that that was a very wise thing to do."

Tonight just isn't up to the standard expected
of Bowie: the production (courtesy of the
three-man team of Bowie, Derek Bramble
and Hugh Padgham) is both confused and
uneven, the performances below par, the
music generally insipid and the
arrangements wholly conventional. Padgham
was shocked by just how far below par some
of the material was, and did as good a job as
possible on finishing off the album after
Bramble's departure from the sessions. Even
the promotional photographs for the album
are truly awful, with the master of seventies
chic pictured wearing the kind of gaudy,
tasteless suits and shirts that make your jaw
drop in disbelief.

The EMI 1999 reissue, however, almost
manages to rehabilitate the album. The
booklet, featuring stills of the deliciously
over-the-top de Chirico-inspired promo for
'Loving The Alien', and the overall punchier
sound manage to regain our interest once
again. Over half of this is listenable and
likeable, although when *Tonight* hits the self-
destruct button, it really is Bowie at his most
forgettable.

This did not stop *Tonight* becoming a UK and
Dutch number one, Top 10 in 13 other
countries, selling a million copies in the US,

or for its lead-off single, 'Blue Jean', becoming a transatlantic Top 10 hit. And, once again, the critical reception of the album at the time was at direct odds with the critical consensus today. Richard Cook's review in *NME* on September 29, 1984 refers to 'Loving The Alien's' "extraordinary lyric… as a brilliantly supple, epic music flexes around the picture", the "blowsily exaggerated and vicariously enjoyable" 'God Only Knows', and concludes: "If this is an introverted muddle it's also an intensely playable one." Over 30 years on time has been kinder to *Tonight* than many might think. One to play in life's calmer, more settled periods, while it has none of the angsty invention of *"Heroes"* or *Scary Monsters*, it's intriguingly like Bowie wishing himself a more normal life, a pretence of fitting in. Yet it's not quite working… how could it, if you have been David Bowie?

LOVING THE ALIEN

The only track on the album with the gravitas of much of his earlier work, this is a truly astonish piece of writing, dealing, as it does, with the confusion brought about by religious identity and referencing directly passed conflicts between Christianity and Islam. The sci-fi conceit of our creator actually coming from another world is the secondary narrative of the song, and less original. Released as a single in May 1985 it peaked at number 19 in the UK with a much-criticised, though actually beautifully over-the-top video. Richard Skinner introduced it on *Top Of The Pops,* shaking his head in disgust at its supposed lavishness. Such was the anti-Bowie feeling at this point that even cloth-eared *TOTP* presenters felt moved to show their disapproval on screen! Bowie would perform an acoustic version of the song live on his *Reality* tour. A demo of the song, said by Bowie to be superior to the recorded version, remains in the Bowie vaults.

DON'T LOOK DOWN

(Pop/Williamson)
Bowie had sometimes commented in the press that reggae was a style with which he never felt comfortable. However, emboldened by his 22-year-old producer and bassist Derek Bramble's mastery of the style, Bowie pulls off a successful re-interpretation of the Iggy Pop original. The music shines, Bowie sings well, and, in the context of the time with the recent success of the Police (one of Padgham's production chargers) and UB40, the only criticism which could be made is that Bowie had attempted the experiment a few years too late to present it as an innovation. One can only wonder what sort of album *Tonight* might have been if it had been a coherent white/reggae/world music fusion instead of the style-hopping twitch it is.

GOD ONLY KNOWS

(Brian Wilson/Tony Asher)
The impulse to cover extremely well-made and well-known classic songs should be resisted at all times. This lifelessly bathetic version of the Beach Boys classic is an artistic failure on every level. Apparently, Bowie recorded a very similar version back in 1973 which remains unreleased

TONIGHT

(Bowie/Pop)
Only four songs into the album, and the third cover version so far has Bowie reconstructing Iggy Pop's tortured 1977 druggy epic into an extremely conventional, reggae-calypso love song. Never has Bowie had such a flimsy song as a title track. Tina Turner is drafted in for a spot of duetting, but she remains totally buried in the mix. This was the album's second single, and surprisingly a complete flop, despite its pandering to the mainstream in such an obvious and rather galling way.

NEIGHBORHOOD THREAT

(Bowie/Pop)
Yet another cover version, but this time a successful one: Bowie remakes the Iggy original into a fierce rock track which swings along at a fine pace, along with brutal

drum figures, and strident guitars. Bowie's vocal is one of the best on the album

BLUE JEAN

The only real contender for a hit single was this 'sexist piece of rock'n'roll' (Bowie's own words) and it made a respectable number six in the UK. Musically it harks back to Ziggy-era Bowie and the accompanying video showed Bowie dripping in make-up for the first time since the great 'Ashes To Ashes'.

TUMBLE AND TWIRL

(Bowie/Pop)

On Iggy Pop's *Blah Blah Blah* album of 1986, the Bowie/Pop co-creative juices were in full flow, with such classics as 'Shades' and 'Isolation', tracks which sounded more like Bowie than Bowie's own material did. With its vaguely Latin rhythms and half-baked lyrics, this is, however, a totally uninteresting foray into world music.

I KEEP FORGETTIN'

(Leiber/ Stoller)

This is a completely redundant cover version of a beefy, powerful original recorded by the American R&B artist Chuck Jackson in 1962. Bowie's version is merit-less. By this stage in the album, the heart of most Bowie fans had sunk very low indeed. A Bowie album with just two really good songs on it? Can he redeem it with a classic ending...?

DANCING WITH THE BIG BOYS

(Bowie/Pop/Alomar)

Erm, no...Throughout the mid-eighties Bowie was searching for a particular horn sound and this fractured piece of dance-pop is probably the closest he ever got to finding it. A far superior Arthur Baker re-mix can be found on the B-side of Jellybean's equally interesting 12-inch re-mix of 'Blue Jean' (EMI America 12 EA 181).

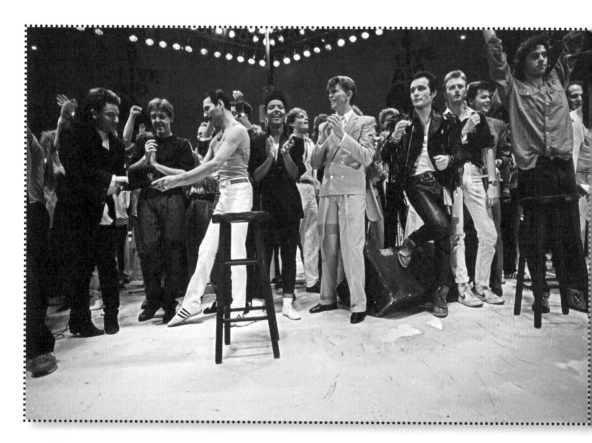

LABYRINTH

(Original UK Issue: EMI AML3104, released 23 June 1986; UK CD EMI AML 3104 UK chart: 38 [Total weeks in chart: 2]; US chart: 68)

Featuring five David Bowie songs, and an instrumental score by Trevor Jones, *Labyrinth* is not a 'proper' Bowie album per se. That said, one could argue that at least three of the Bowie songs are as strong as the majority of Bowie's mid-eighties output. Bowie's record label seemed once again to have the knack of unwitting sabotage. 'As The World Falls Down', a pretty ballad and hugely commercial, was all ready to go as a single, complete with glossy video, just in time for Christmas and to coincide with the UK release of the film (the USA release was six months earlier). Then, inexplicably, the song was pulled from the schedules and an almost certain Top 10 hit deftly avoided.

On release *Labyrinth* the film was given lukewarm reviews and fared poorly at the box office. Today, its rehabilitation is complete. Telling the tale of Jareth the Goblin King (played in a Kabuki wig and *those* trousers by Bowie) who kidnaps the baby brother of teenager Sarah (played by Jennifer Connolly), and with an assortment of loveable if completely un-frightening monsters, *Labyrinth* became a video, TV and now DVD/Blu-Ray hit. In fact, many born in the eighties and nineties remember David Bowie not as Ziggy, or the Man Who Fell To Earth, but as Jareth, in his Escher-styled maze waiting for Sarah.

The highpoint of the film is Bowie's 'Magic Dance', and the film sequence is, in effect, a pop video. The eagle-eyed will notice that at two minutes six seconds Bowie very naughtily mimes putting cocaine up his nose. Taken together with the revealing nature of his manhood-hugging joggers, it is a wonder a whole new generation of under-twelves were not completely corrupted. With its frankly great tune and bouncy music, 'Magic Dance' has gone on to become one of Bowie's most popular songs. At the time of writing both it, and 'As The World Falls Down', are in the UK Top 30 best-selling Bowie downloads on i-Tunes, and the parent album is Bowie's third-best selling download album! Despite this, neither song appeared on the 2002 *Best Of Bowie** or the 2014 compilation, *Nothing Has Changed.** Only 'Underground', the first single release, and a modest UK number 21 hit, has appeared on greatest hits compilations. A riotous gospel song with guitar from Albert Collins and backing vocals from Cissy Houston and Chaka Khan, its mood prefigured that of Madonna's 'Like A Prayer' by three years. Two other songs, the cheeky 'Chilly Down' (with a piano part a close kin to the melody of 'Absolute Beginners') and the hammy 'Within You' complete Bowie's contribution. Trevor Jones went on to a successful career as a composer, mainly for film (*Richard III*, *In The Name Of The Father*, *Notting Hill*) while the singer who, in the eighties, was as visible on the big screen as he was in the music world, would return to the studio, firstly to work again with Iggy Pop, then on his own material. But it had been a fun and ultimately successful immersion into the mainstream. *Labyrinth* isn't classic Bowie but it's worthy of much more than a footnote.

Tracklisting: 'Opening Titles Including Underground' (Music by Jones, Lyrics by Bowie), 'Into The Labyrinth' (Jones), 'Magic Dance' (Bowie), 'Sarah' (Jones), 'Chilly Down' (Bowie), 'Hallucination' (Jones), 'As the World Falls Down' (Bowie), 'The Goblin Battle' (Jones), 'Within You' (Bowie), 'Thirteen O'Clock' (Jones), 'Home At Last' (Jones), 'Underground' (Bowie).

NEVER LET ME DOWN

(Original UK Issue: EMI America AMLS 3117, released 27 April 1987; UK CD: EMI 521 8940; US Virgin 21894; UK chart: 6 [Total weeks in chart: 16]: US chart: 34 [26])

Like many artists who at times struggle to remain relevant, David Bowie is unlistenable when they try too hard to be listenable (R.E.M., Genesis, Bryan Ferry, Elton John, Manic Street Preachers all hang your heads in shame now). A new breed of music writers and magazines emerged in the mid-eighties, and in 1987 they sharpened their claws and pointed them in the direction of David Bowie. At the inkies (*Sounds*, *NME*, *Melody Maker*), there was a rump of Bowie-lovers (championed by Chris Roberts and Steve Sutherland) while a new monthly, *Q*, the UK's answer to the 'serious' American publications, injected a tone of cynicism and weariness to music writing that still exists to some extent to this day. Almost all of the early *Q* reads as if it is written by the same person (a thirty-something, white middle-class male who doesn't even suffer his friends gladly), so strong are the 'house rules'. It was time to give Bowie a good kicking, and, boy, did they.

At Live Aid in 1985, Bowie was supreme; confident, relaxed and in full control of his skills, better than almost everyone else on the bill in fact, but this was a false dawn for less than two years later *Never Let Me Down* was the nadir that gave Bowie's literary

assassins a juicy target. It wouldn't have mattered much what Bowie released in 1987; the climate had changed and, with it, the view of Bowie too. Prince ruled the hearts of the tastemakers, while dance and Indie was trusted as the new *Ur* music. John Peel, an early Bowie supporter, had long-since abandoned Bowie as a tired, corporate face and was now filling his shows with the Smiths, the Cure (both great to be sure) but a lot of lo-fi shit. The new pop aesthetic, which would find its crowning glory five years later with Nirvana, hated anything that might look dressed-up, colourful and articulate. If Bowie felt out of place then his fans, many of them still in their early twenties, felt like there was nowhere to go.

It didn't help that almost all of Bowie's contemporaries were releasing music of a frankly dire quality. Eno, cleverer than everyone else, turned his skills to production, Bryan Ferry was stuck in the departure lounge, the Rolling Stones were infighting and already frail, the Who had stopped (for the time being at least), Elton went sickly sweet, Pink Floyd had decapitated itself and Stevie Wonder was writing mawkish drivel. The new kings and queens of the CD era – Dire Straits, Sade, Queen, Fleetwood Mac, Genesis – played music that was a perfect fit for the aspirant Thatcherite thirty-something with big hair, a big phone and a crap-sounding CD player. Some of the music was still excellent, but much made one envy the deaf.

One of the criticisms later levelled at Bowie is that after *Scary Monsters*, his albums still contained great songs, songs to match his finest work, but they inhabited maybe half the playing time of the whole. Never is this criticism so powerful than with *Never Let Me Down*. The man who gave us some of the best album titles (and album covers) followed the inexplicably dully-named *Tonight* with the hostage-to-fortune-shot-in-the-foot title of *Never Let Me Down*. And unlike *Tonight*, whose artwork had some merit, *Never Let Me Down*'s cover was a complete omnishambles. It resonated with no one and, one suspects, not even with Bowie himself, the singer as

Barnumesque tramp circus star in a clutter of visual signifiers, signifying nothing.

It was not as if Bowie was suffering writer's block. Earlier in 1986, he had worked again with Iggy Pop, for his *Blah Blah Blah* album. Two songs - 'Shades' and 'Isolation'- were easily better than almost everything on *Never Let Me Down*.

For the first time in his career Bowie was genuinely divorced from the cutting edge of popular music. An interview with Dave Thomas of *Today* in 1986 makes depressing reading: on music ("The music is so awful here... I've dropped out of radio, I play my old record collection"); on Live Aid ("I think the potential in Paul Young is extraordinary"); on his music ("Music starts to mellow... I don't have the riveting desire now to persuade people that what I have to say is right"); and finally on his audience ("What's the point of me trying to write for teenagers? The only way I could do that would be as some kind of father figure"). In short, Bowie had abdicated his position as Britain's most innovatory pop icon since The Beatles.

Never Let Me Down, recorded at the Mountain Studios, Switzerland and co-produced by David Richards, was written and recorded with the road in mind, as Bowie was committed to a large-scale stadium tour the following year. Long-standing side-kick Carlos Alomar and old school-chum and guitar virtuoso Peter Frampton are the band's central points, while the astonishingly versatile Erdal Kizilcay is nothing if not a hell of an impressive one-man band. But the resulting album now has a fair claim to being Bowie's all-time recording low spot. Critics and fans have a tendency to be overly critical of Bowie's more unadventurous moments; he has set himself such high standards that when he falls short, the sense of disappointment turns into something akin to a feeling of personal affront. Yet, a poor David Bowie album is still pretty good by most other people's lower standards. But on *Never Let Me Down* there is only one great song, 'Time Will Crawl', and one good one,

the title track itself. On the rest of the album, with its noisy and dull soloing, horrid synth figures, bombastic singing and cluttered production, Bowie is as uninterested as he could ever be. He appears sonically distanced from the events; nowhere does the music actually sound like he has been involved with it. In later interviews, he admitted to being less than committed to the recording and arrangement of the album. The music, all grand gestures which don't come off, and busy, fussy arrangements, is almost like someone else's idea of what David Bowie should sound like. Sonically constipated, the enema of *Tin Machine* was just two short years away.

The *Glass Spider* tour of 1987, which showcased a large selection of current material, was almost universally panned. Hammy, uninteresting and, frankly, at times unwatchable, it attempted to be avant-garde, yet to many ended up looking like a bad rock musical. Bowie put way too much effort into fiddly detail, a miscalculation which left many of those who had come to see him perform totally adrift, as the mini-vignettes which unfolded on stage were not visible to anyone behind the first 20 rows. True, there were genuine moments of fun and danger, and for those who journeyed up and down the country to watch the spectacle, it was a pleasing gathering of the Bowie faithful, yet the big audience founded on the success of *Let's Dance* looked at *Glass Spider* with troubled incomprehension.

Finally, the song 'Too Dizzy', included on the original issue of the CD, was taken off subsequent reissues at Bowie's behest, for the simple reason that he now seems to dislike it. In the original version of this book, the entry went, 'This is the album's low point, a shameless AOR rocker which should have no place in the Bowie canon but, unfortunately, does.' Well, it has now officially joined the ranks of the missing: recorded, released, but now expunged from the Bowie chronicle forever, which is a shame for its co-creator, Erdal Kizilcay who, presumably, has taken a financial knock as a result.

DAY-IN DAY-OUT

This oddly jumbled, horn-driven rock/pop hybrid was the first single off the album, reaching number 17 in the UK charts. Although by no means a classic Bowie single, the opening line, 'She was born in a handbag', surely a crib from *The Importance Of Being Earnest*, is still a joy. The accompanying video, complete with a long-haired, roller-skating Bowie, caused a rumpus with its attempted rape and succession of sordid scenes from lowlife America, which purportedly mirrored the song's anti-Americanism. The video was re-edited for a number of television shows.

TIME WILL CRAWL

The strongest song on the album by a country mile was a surprisingly unsuccessful single peaking at a meek number 33 in the UK. It harks back to Bowie's seventies work in that the lyrics are able to fire the imagination without possessing any literal meaning in themselves. Good tune too. Bowie even performed the song on *Top Of The Pops*, ten years after his last visit to croon through "Heroes", but the performance was not aired at the time as the single dropped down the charts the week of its scheduled slot.

BEAT OF YOUR DRUM

There's a classic Bowie pop/rock song *à la* 'Jean Genie' somewhere in there, but it's buried in over-elaboration. There is a genuinely fine (and rather sexy) chorus, though: 'I'd like to beat on your drum/I'd like to blow on your horn'. Indeed, Mr Bowie! And there's yet another 'Speed Of Life' synth rip-off in the musical mix.

NEVER LET ME DOWN

(Bowie/Alomar)
This song, a tribute to Bowie's personal aide Corrine 'Coco' Schwab, musically and lyrically pastiches John Lennon, particularly 'Jealous Guy'. It's actually a fine, if clichéd, pop song with the best vocal performance on the album. The third single off the album, it hung around the UK Top 40 for a month but peaked at

number 34. It fared slightly better in the States, reaching number 27.

ZEROES

The Beatles *leitmotif* is continued on this slick but rather lifeless pop song all about 'letting love in' and complete with mid-sixties mantra at the end. The most interesting moment comes with the line 'And me, my little red corvette has driven by', in which Bowie name-checks a famous Prince song and simultaneously hands over the baton of experimentation to the Minneapolis midget. Touching in a way.

GLASS SPIDER

Although the howls of derision from critics are still echoing ten years on, this is one of the best tracks from Bowie's eighties output. The song, telling a Freudian tale of a mother/child relationship in fantasy form, begins with a narration about a Glass Spider in the 'Zi Duang' Province of an Eastern country and comes across, as most narrations do within pop, as incredibly pompous and embarrassing (who can fail to remember Phil Oakey on the Human League's 1986 American number one 'Human' or Telly Savalas's 'If'?), which should appal only those without a sense of humour. The song then stirs itself with a splendid riff and a great 'Gone, gone, the water's all gone' refrain.

SHINING STAR (MAKIN' MY LOVE)

This is a white, and rather polite, rap, featuring none other than actor Mickey Rourke, and would have been all the better if the awful, tinny-sounding arrangement had been beefed up a bit. Still, some signs of the old Bowie magic here – 'Life is like a broken arrow, memory a swinging door'.

NEW YORK'S IN LOVE

This is another nod to glories past (this time the ambient funk of *Lodger*'s 'Red Sails'), but the production is flat and the song uninspired. However, the return of the Motorik beat at least signals Bowie's creative intelligence wasn't completely on standby-mode.

'87 AND CRY

This rocker, more than anything else on the album, indicated the direction his music would take with Tin Machine, although the lyrics, which desperately try and summon up some sort of anger and passion, are contrived and meaningless.

BANG BANG

(Pop/Kraal)

'A couple of pence for a cup of tea for me old, starving, impecunious mate Iggy anyone?' Yet another in the long line of 'Bowie plays Pop' – but surely there were better tracks to cover than this.

A flat and uninspired ending to what is possibly Bowie's weakest collection of songs, and certainly his most inelegantly produced record.

TIN MACHINE

(Original UK Issue: EMI-USA MTLS 1044, released 22 May 1989; UK CD: EMI 521 9100; US CD Virgin 21910; UK chart: 3 [Total weeks in chart: 9]) US Chart: 28 [Total weeks in chart: 5]

By the late eighties Bowie, or 'the Dame' as he was by then often referred to by *Q* magazine, had become a figure of ridicule in the music press, and had been largely abandoned by his early-eighties mainstream following. Bowie himself would later claim that in the period he came close to calling it a day and returning to painting full-time. Obviously desperate measures were needed, and the Tin Machine project was a radical response to a dire situation.

In fact, Bowie's creative rebirth began not with the *Tin Machine* album but a year before at a charity gig for the Institute For Contemporary Arts at the Dominion Theatre, London. Here he performed a nine-minute version of the *Lodger* oldie 'Look Back In Anger' along with, among others, American guitarist Reeves Gabrels and Canadian Dance Troupe La La La Human Steps. The result was mesmeric, possibly Bowie's greatest performance since the seventies in terms of sheer theatricality. Musically, it was stripped down and at times veered towards heavy metal. It was this sound that Bowie developed with the Tin Machine project. On that day drum machine figures lent the music a contemporary edge, but for the new album Bowie opted for Hunt Sales on drums and Tony Sales on bass. Both had worked

with Bowie on the Iggy Pop album *Lust For Life*. Gabrels was to be become Bowie's new right-hand man and the 'brains' (along with Bowie) to set against the 'balls' of the Sales brothers. Indeed, Gabrels played a crucial role in resurrecting Bowie's foundering career, encouraging him to make the sort of music he wanted to make rather than pander to the whims of his record label and the less adventurous tastes of some of his fan base.

Bowie had met Gabrels when Gabrels' then wife Sara was working on the PR for the *Glass Spider* tour. They became good friends and during summer 1988, Gabrels was invited to spend time with Bowie at his home in Switzerland. They would write, record, drink wine and watch *Monty Python* on video. For the first time, probably since Mick Ronson, Bowie had a foil. Gabrels, almost ten-years younger than Bowie, learnt from the Master, while Bowie picked up and ran with many of Gabrels' ideas and obsessions too.

However, what turned out to be Tin Machine might have had a very different makeup, sound, even name. The first name considered for the band was White Noise. Perhaps still smarting from the adverse publicity that accompanied his Nazi flirtation in the *Station To Station* era, Bowie thought the term could be construed as racist and dropped the idea; a shame since, for most, the connotations would have been of the aural, rather than racial type. Gabrels suggested Terry Bozzio (drummer with Missing Persons and Frank Zappa) and Percy Jones (bass guitarist with Soft Machine, Brand X) as a rhythm section that was distinctive and which utilised non-session musicians. Reeves Gabrels: "And then David ran into Tony Sales on the street in LA and I got home to a message on my answerphone ('I've found our rhythm section. Go and listen to *Lust For Life*'). I had never been in a garage band. Everything I had done up until then had sounded like a cross between King Crimson and *Scary Monsters*!"

With the addition of the Sales Brothers, the foursome became a band. Bowie claimed to be simply one-quarter of a democratic whole, a move that was bound to founder sooner or later, much like Paul McCartney's intention of simply being a 'member' of Wings. Since these times, established musicians have swapped bands regularly, as Damon Albarn, Dave Grohl, Peter Buck, Gruff Rhys and many others have proven. The only difference is that none of these had been the biggest superstar, in artistic terms, of his day. It was a shift many of his idolaters found a step too far.

Produced by Tim Palmer, who, after this, was offered both Pearl Jam and Nirvana to work with (he passed on the latter) and featuring Kevin Armstrong (who had worked with Bowie at Live Aid) on rhythm guitar, the album has gone down in rock history as a ghastly blunder. However, the reviews at the time were by no means poor, and the resulting record, fierce, spontaneous and uncompromising, is certainly a vast improvement on then recent solo outings. Forced to write quickly, often ad-libbing on mike, Bowie's lyrics have a tumbling stream-of-consciousness air, and the songs themselves often crash to a closure as if beheaded mid-verse. Bowie paraded a hectoring didacticism quite different to his other work, as tracks such as 'Crack City' and 'Under The God' deal with the evils of intoxicants and fascism respectively. It was hard not to read these songs as an exercise in catharthism after his mid-seventies flirtation with Nazi chic.

Tin Machine, released at the height of interest in new metal groups like Guns'n'Roses and Pearl Jam, in part reflected the musical Zeitgeist. But more than that, at times Tin Machine, along with Sonic Youth and the Pixies, extended the sonic vocabulary and were precursors of grunge. Ultimately though, as an album, it's an experiment that almost works. The sound pioneers the sort of music that would soon become known as 'alternative rock', yet often it sounds too sloppy, garagey and too retro; an artier, more sentient approach might have worked much better. Tin Machine simply confirmed the redundancy of looking back to Cream,

Hendrix and Led Zeppelin for inspiration. The sight of Bowie, now bearded, in a band with his mates, was a sight that the androgynous outsider that was Bowie in the seventies might have jeered at. Bowie's detractors wrote the whole concept off as yet another pose, another mask, while a good part of his fan base (like that, at various times, of R.E.M., Neil Young and U2) didn't enjoy it when their hero went too noisy. Still, *Tin Machine* will repay those potential Bowie fans willing to be taken on a brutal journey far away from the polished musical surfaces of *Let's Dance*. And make no mistake: without Tin Machine, Bowie might well have remained lost in the mainstream wilderness forever.

HEAVEN'S IN HERE

An infectious bluesy riff, right out of the old school, drives this unashamed tale of heterosexual lust: 'Heaven lies between your marbled thighs'. Get the idea? Actually a good song and an incredible rootsy shock after the general tameness of *Never Let Me Down*.

TIN MACHINE
(Bowie/Tony Sales/Hunt Sales/Reeves Gabrels)

Another fine riff from Reeves Gabrels, and Bowie delivers his best vocal performance of the set in this song of self-disgust: 'Raging raging raging/ Burning in my room/Come on and get a good idea/Come on and get it soon'. Released as a double-A sided single with Dylan's 'Maggie's Farm', it reached number 48 in the UK singles chart.

PRISONER OF LOVE
(Bowie/Tony Sales/Hunt Sales/Reeves Gabrels)

Yes, another fine song, this time a rock ballad with hints of T. Rex's often-aped 'Children Of The Revolution' in the backing vocals. The first hint of didacticism creeps in with Bowie's exhortation to his addressee to 'Just stay square' in the face of life's excesses. The third single off the album, it failed to break the UK Top 75.

CRACK CITY

This is undoubtedly the most direct song Bowie has ever written on social issues, and its message is delivered with an unrestrained anger. Bowie graphically depicts the horrors of addiction, rounding on the drug-pusher at the song's dénouement – 'May the ho-ho hounds of paranoia/Dance upon your stinking bed'. Musically, the song borrows from 'Wild Thing', originally by The Troggs, although famously covered by Hendrix. The purpose of this particular musical borrowing is to simplistically bring into the listener's mind one of the most resonant paradigms of rock'n'roll death through intoxicant abuse (regardless of the actual circumstances of the great man's death).

I CAN'T READ
(Bowie/Reeves Gabrels)

Possibly the best song on the album, this arty, discordant number is a distillation of one of Bowie's obsessions: an inability to feel. After the monosyllabic delivery of most of the song, Bowie screams: 'I can't read shit any more'. His vocal delivery renders the line highly ambiguous, in that it actually sounds like 'I can't reach it any more', thus becoming a comment on his recent musical paralysis.

UNDER THE GOD

Musically, this slab of hard rock re-works The Mojo's 'I Wish You Would' (a song Bowie had covered on *Pin-Ups*). It is a further view of the new, politicised Bowie, dealing as it does with the rise of neo-Nazism. A poor choice as a lead-off single, it reached a paltry number 51 in the UK.

AMAZING
(Bowie/Reeves Gabrels)

This, the simplest song on the album, is also one of the best. The basic structure of the music was recorded by Gabrels into a Dictaphone in a 20-minute burst of inspiration while waiting for Bowie to get ready for a night out at the movies. The lyric was Bowie's imagined take on the relationship between Gabrels and his then wife. The obvious choice as a single, it remains an album cut only.

WORKING CLASS HERO
(John Lennon)
Tin Machine owed a debt to Lennon's earlier politicking, and this is obviously intended as a homage to that cause. However, this cover replaces the acoustic spite of the original with an overbearing posturing.

 ### BUS STOP
(Bowie/Reeves Gabrels)
This short and beautifully silly song about a man who finds God at the bus stop, displays a Bowie in fine full-cockney regalia. It was an attempt to write a fast, sharp, shock of a song, with the Mekon's 1978 single, 'Where Were You', the template. Great tune too.

 ### PRETTY THING
This is the weakest song in the set, the band power on remorselessly and Bowie sings as if in search of a decent tune. And the 'Tie me down, pretend you're Madonna' line is crass.

 ### VIDEO CRIMES
(Bowie/Tony Sales/Hunt Sales)
As on 'I Can't Read', Bowie ransacks his late-seventies period for more blanked-out numbness. Interesting, but it doesn't quite work. Cracking drums by Hunt Sales though.

 ### RUN
(Kevin Armstrong/Bowie)
This track has very little of Bowie's personality stamped on it but it's pleasant enough with some pretty guitar work.

 ### SACRIFICE YOURSELF
(Bowie/Tony Sales/Hunt Sales)
Another dose of heavy metal bluster but by now it's all wearing very thin: more guitars, more advice for the potentially misguided. The musical is monotone and the message old.

 ### BABY CAN DANCE
This song could have been a classic Bowie rocker had it not been subjected to a rather-overdone guitar freak-out from Gabrels at the end. Here is the best chorus on the album, and the Stones-inspired rhythm-and-blues shuffling beat ought to have secured a better result.

TIN MACHINE II

(UK CD: London 8282721; released 2 September 1991; UK chart: No. 23 [Total weeks in chart: 3] US Chart: 126)

Although, with the first Tin Machine album, Bowie had succeeded in transfusing some purpose into his music after his mid-eighties coma, the follow-up was a decidedly mixed bag. The radical metal approach was finessed. Gabrels states that he wanted to add a greater harmonic sophistication to the second Tin Machine album. However, the material is generally weaker than on the first album and the whole sounds much more like a traditional Bowie album but without much of the magic of his best work. If the first Tin Machine album stamped its feet and raged, the second sat in the corner and sulked; a period of introspection after an almighty temper tantrum. Perhaps, the limitations of the four-piece were showing themselves up and the tension between the four was cancelling out each other's strengths. By 1991, it was also a complicated dynamic within the band as Hunt Sales was battling substance addiction.

Unlike the first Tin Machine album which was written and recorded quite quickly, the weakness of this sophomore effort may lie in

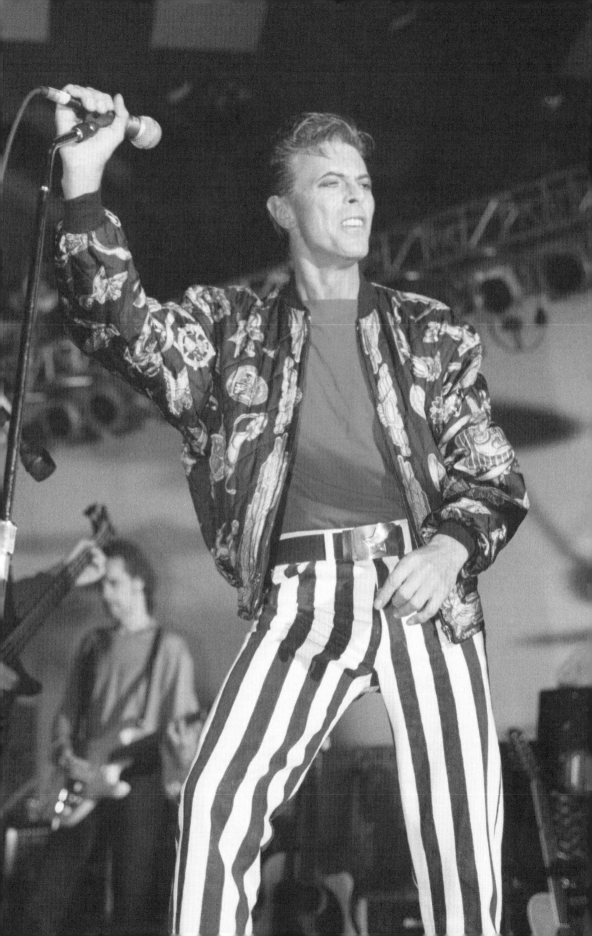

its protracted birth. The record was started in Sydney, Australia in autumn 1989, with Tim Palmer co-producing, and with some song ideas being worked up from the sessions for the first album. Then there was a gap of several months, with Bowie already committed to a major tour.

In 1988, Bowie had agreed to the buy-me-again *Sound + Vision* tour, in which he tackled his big hits for what he promised would be the last time. A small North American company, Ryko, were working on an audacious re-issue programme and Bowie felt obliged to promote his catalogue. To keep himself honest, the touring band would reflect the 'old is the new, new' aesthetic of Tin Machine: that music was best when played by a classic configuration of drums, bass, guitar and vocal. Only a synthesiser/keyboard player would be added to this and instead of Gabrels (who was offered the chance to play on the tour), Adrian Belew was brought back as Bowie's guitarist and main foil. Live, the dare sometimes worked, sometimes not ('Young Americans' without a saxophone, anybody?). Bowie himself cut a frustrated figure, wishing himself into a new future before he had quite buried the past. Visually, however, the shows were stunning, being the first to use interactive video techniques in stadia. These shows served as a stark contrast to the chain-smoking, bearded rocker, power-chording his way through the previous year's Tin Machine tour. Secondly, sometime during 1990, Bowie and EMI fell out. Rumour has it that, presented with the tapes to *Tin Machine II*, EMI decided to pull the plug. Apart from *Let's Dance*, Bowie's EMI material had veered from the good to the atrocious (by Bowie's standards) and it now seemed likely that the company had simply had enough.

Gabrels would bring tapes of the new recordings on tour for Bowie to work on in May 1990. Further sessions followed the end of the tour (although Bowie's filming commitments for the flop film *The Linguini Incident* caused further delays), with recording continuing into 1991 with sessions

in LA in March. By the time *Tin Machine II* came out, almost two years since the sessions began; momentum (and interest) had waned. From 1988 to 1991, it seemed as if Bowie was being tugged in two opposite directions at once. The musical salivary amylase was dribbling down his chin at the sight of the new, raw meat of Tin Machine and a future making music for himself, not his bosses. Yet his advisors (and perhaps his wicked, more venal, superstar self) kept getting in the way with the temptation of big bucks on the road, and film stardom.

When *Tin Machine II* came out in *September* 1991 on the London label, Bowie's recording career seemed not simply to have stalled, but to have gone into reverse. It garnered what are politely called 'mixed reviews' (*NME* actually liked it!) before slipping out of the charts after a paltry three weeks, despite extensive media promotion (including two *Top Of The Pops* appearances, a Radio 1 session and a seven-month world tour). Most Bowie fans simply hated seeing their idol in a lime-green suit in a rock band with the lads. During its weakest moments, *Tin Machine II* sounded compromised and diluted, with Hunt and Tony Sales pulling the more sentient Bowie and Gabrels into more traditional American rock areas, and Bowie and Gabrels bringing in elements of ambient, acoustic rock and experimental music which suggested a very different direction. It was obvious from that moment on that Bowie was unhappy with Tin Machine's 'democracy' and would be forced to resume his solo career again.

Tin Machine II has not been included in any of Bowie's reissue campaigns of recent years and, as such, is increasingly difficult to track down. Largely a set for die-hard Bowie fans only, and rock fans at that, the album did have a few worthwhile moments in among the stodge, not least the stomping opener...

 BABY UNIVERSAL
(Lyrics Bowie: music Bowie/Gabrels)
This frantic three-minute rocker was the second single off the album, scraping to Number 49 in the UK charts. Reminiscent of

something from *Scary Monsters*, though without that album's studied weirdness, it's a fine, under-valued song. In 1996 and 1997, it would be performed live by Bowie as a solo artist with an improved, electronic rock, arrangement.

 ### ONE SHOT

(Lyrics Bowie: music Bowie/Gabrels/H. Sales/T. Sales)
'One thing led to a dead end/One shot put her away hey-hey'. Is this really a Bowie lyric? Whereas 'Running Gun Blues', had dealt with killings in such a twisted, ironic way, we didn't quite believe it, on 'One Shot', Bowie seems to be parroting the language of the latest American TV cop drama, or perhaps, more obliquely (and therefore much more interestingly) the mantra of a section of the US Army: '"One shot, one kill," the military snipers creed.' If one can get past the lyric, the music is some of the best Tin Machine ever made, a return to a classic verse/chorus/middle eight format, a sparkling co-production by Hugh Padgham. Gabrels: "There was this feeling that pervaded from David – 'I've written songs, I've done songs to death, the conventional song form. I don't need to worry about that.' And my attitude was, well, if the way we present our instruments is challenging, then we should cling to something like the Motown song form because that's what people are used to hearing. 'One Shot' was an example of that." The last of seven Tin Machine singles, it was a single in Europe and Australia only.

 ### YOU BELONG IN ROCK'N'ROLL

(Lyrics Bowie: music Bowie/Gabrels)
Two decades earlier, in *Changes*, Bowie the poseur had urged, 'Look out all you rock'n'rollers'. Now, some said, Bowie himself was beginning to resemble that which he had set out to replace. Many of Bowie's songs can be termed 'growers', songs which need several plays in order to hit home. With 'You Belong In Rock'n'Roll' that period has taken over two decades [in this fan's case at least]. On first few hearings there's hardly a melody apparent at all, no

form, just a trundling beat, some hammy Elvis-like vocals, and some odd hand-claps. Yet with the passage of time, it reveals itself as an ambient rock semi-classic, unlike anything else recorded in 1991. The clipped acoustic interruptions, the curtailed ambient guitar moans, the insistent drum pulse, the little chiming guitar riff, and Bowie's deeper-than-deep sax: all in all, a rather great and overlooked song. In that long-established tradition of releasing your least commercial song as lead-off single, it reached number 33 in the UK charts.

 ### IF THERE IS SOMETHING

(Ferry)
Originally to be found on Roxy Music's epoch-making first album, here the song is totally de-ironised and rather blandly presented in accordance with Tin Machine's sometimes crash-bang-wallop approach. Bowie, an ardent fan and supporter of early Roxy Music, does not appear to have much love thrown the other way, in the same manner that Bowie declined Peter Gabriel's offer to record a Gabriel song (for the project, *And I'll Scratch Yours*), Peter having recorded a version of "Heroes" (for the album, *Scratch My Back*).

 ### AMLAPURA

(Lyrics Bowie: music Bowie/Gabrels)
This stately, acoustic piece works well, although hardly breaks new ground. 'Amlapura', a district in Bowie's beloved Bali in Indonesia, was the site of a massive volcanic eruption in 1963 – hence, presumably, 'all the dead children buried standing'. Incidentally, an alternative version, with Bowie singing in Indonesian, can be found on the 'You Belong In Rock And Roll' CD single.

 ### BETTY WRONG

(Lyrics Bowie: music Bowie/Gabrels)
This is pretty dull. Introspective, reflective, and evidence of the heat cooling from the rhythm section maybe, but Bowie and Gabrels' understated attempt to be wistful and ambient needed a better melody.

YOU CAN'T TALK

*(Lyrics Bowie, music
Bowie/Gabrels/H. Sales/T. Sales)*
Musically this track re-treads *Never Let Me
Down*'s 'New York's In Love' (not the richest
musical vein for cannibalisation, one would
have thought) and the whole thing is easily
forgettable.

 STATESIDE

*(Lyrics H.Sales/Bowie: music
H.Sales/Bowie)*
This geriatric blues number must be the
nadir of Bowie's recording career to date.
Hunt Sales takes the lead vocal and bawls
out 'I'm going Stateside with my convictions',
while Bowie's attempt to rescue the situation
in the chorus with some rather unconvincing
irony makes it all worse. The most alarming
thing is that this crass homage to American
authenticity makes a mockery of everything
Bowie had stood for. Dreadful.

 SHOPPING FOR GIRLS

*(Lyrics Bowie: music
Bowie/Gabrels)*
Just when the whole set appears to have
ground to a halt, Bowie goes some way
toward rescuing it with this quite excellent
piece of reportage. Whereas on the first Tin
Machine album his 'protest' songs came
across as sermonizing, now, without playing
the heavy-handed father figure, Bowie
blankly recites a liturgy of atrocities (based
on a news report from Reeves Gabrels' then
wife, Sara) against a neat guitar riff.

 A BIG HURT

This was probably the only occasion
where Tin Machine got the dumb
hard rock pose right (and significantly it's on
a track Bowie composed alone). There's a
fabulous chorus and although it's still just a
piece of sexist rock'n'roll, Bowie's almost
comedic vocal performance carries the whole
thing off.

 SORRY

(Lyrics and music: H. Sales)
Sloshy, repetitive, ballad sung by
Hunt Sales. The template is the sort of

schmaltz Dennis Wilson used to sing as an
encore when the rest of the Beach Boys
went off for a 'comfort break', but at least
'You Are So Beautiful' had a decent tune.
Another bummer from the drummer, and yes,
you weren't the only one who was sorry,
Hunt. Undoubtedly, a great drummer;
unquestionably, don't give up the day job.
Together with 'Stateside', this was the surest
indication that the band were dividing into
two camps, and targeting two different
audiences.

 GOODBYE MR ED

*(Lyrics Bowie: music
Bowie/H.Sales/T.Sales)*
One of the finest Bowie track never to be
released as a single? This is quite simply a
great pop song. Bowie's resigned vocals relay
a series of observations about the built-in
nostalgia of contemporary American culture
over a beautiful melody, reminiscent of, of all
things, Acker Bilk's 1961 mega instrumental
hit 'Stranger On The Shore'. This fine song,
concluding an album that few pop fans will
ever get round to listening to, is destined to
remain an undiscovered gem.

Tin Machine II actually ends with an
uncredited minute-long instrumental with
Bowie's saxophone to the fore. It's an edit of
a track called 'Hammerhead', to be found on
the 'You Belong In Rock And Roll' CD single
(London CD 305), but it's not essential
Bowie material.

TIN MACHINE LIVE: OY VEY, BABY

(Original UK Issue: Victory Music 828 328 1, released 27 July 1992; UK CD: Victory 828 328 2.)

Tin Machine Live was the first Bowie-related album to completely miss the US and UK Top 100. It is a record with very few admirers. In fact, while it was refreshing to see Bowie close-up in small auditoria after a decade of stadium gigging, the band often made Bowie sound hoarse and ordinary as a singer. Listening to Gabrels' live mix Bowie is reported to have commented that the album sounded like 'deconstructionist R&B'. However, most found it noisy and difficult – smatterings of great playing and fine songwriting, but overall a testing listening experience. The track listing is predictable (Tin Machine had quite successfully covered The Pixies' 'Debaser' on tour, which would have made an interesting curio if included) and, 'Goodbye Mr Ed' and an extended re-work of 'You Belong In Rock And Roll' aside, this is, sadly, almost completely superfluous. And we are not even spared the dreaded 'Stateside'. Incidentally, the title is a 'side-splitting' pun on U2's towering *Achtung Baby*, reportedly coined by Hunt Sales.

The last rites of Tin Machine came at the Budakan Hall in Tokyo. "After the last show at Budokan, David realised that that was it and that he didn't have to put up with four personalities and that he could go back to being David Bowie," is how Reeves Gabrels

puts it. *Oy Vey, Baby* was released when Bowie's commercial and critical stock was at its lowest ebb. It was almost a decade since his last major commercial success with *Let's Dance*. Almost all of the projects Bowie had undertaken subsequently, not just albums but tours and film appearances, had been given a mixed reception. Whereas everything up to *Let's Dance* had seemed like the scared un-rolling of some ineffably great plan, there seemed neither rhyme nor reason to the schedule thereafter. A cameo in a film here, a one-off collaboration there, and then, during Tin Machine, Bowie was still off and about doing solo work. Was Tin Machine, as Max Bell wrote in 1991 for *Vox*, just "an expensive hobby"? Bowie was bordering on becoming a figure of fun, dismissed as an irrelevance by hosts of music critics. Take Paul Mathur's review of *Oy Vey, Baby* in *Melody Maker* which, even by the journalistic standards of the time, was cruel: "This is the moment where finally, categorically and, let's face it, lumpily, he ceases to exist as an artist of any worth whatsoever", before the final Matador kill of, "It's not just dying, it's ensuring that posterity will never know he existed."

However, despite the band's mixed legacy, many Bowie fans look back on the Tin Machine period with a degree of fondness, as a time when Bowie seemed re-engaged with music and his audience. Many who would slate Tin Machine simply followed the pack mentality, accepting received wisdom that the period was musically bankrupt without having even listened to the music. We may not have heard the last from the band either. Hinting at a potential box set release, according to Gabrels, there are around eight Tin Machine tracks that have never been released, including an alternate version of 'Heaven's In Here'. Let's hope that *Oy Vey, Baby* is not the band's epitaph.

Full track listing: 'If There Is Something', 'Amazing', 'I Can't Read', 'Stateside', 'Under The God', 'Goodbye Mr Ed', 'Heaven's In Here', 'You Belong In Rock & Roll'.

BLACK TIE WHITE NOISE

(Original UK issue UK CD: Arista 74321136972, US CD: Savage 74785/50212/2; released April 5 1993; Reissued August 8 2003 EMI CD 584 8140; UK chart: 1 [Total weeks in chart: 11]) US CD: Virgin; US Chart: 39 [8]

It is often hard to make the love-struck sound as convincing as the lovelorn as many a saccharine pop ballad has told us. Yet in 1992, this was exactly Bowie's mien. He was in love and, in April that year, married for the second time to Iman Mohamed Abdulmajid, known to the world as model and actress Iman.

According to Bowie in interviews to promote *Black Tie White Noise* during the first half of 1993, the impetus for his first solo record in six years was his marriage. Although the desire to write his own wedding music might have kick-started the creative process, a solo album had been planned for several years. Tracks had been laid down around late 1990 with members of Bryan Adams' band, but never released, except for a cover of Dylan's 'Like A Rolling Stone', to be found on Mick Ronson's solo album *Heaven And Hull* (Sony, 474742 2) released in 1994.

Also, outside the Tin Machine project, Bowie had guested on Adrian Belew's 1990 album *Young Lions* (Atlantic, 7 82099 2), on two tracks, the infectious and sadly overlooked 'Pretty Pink Rose' (a demo of which had been recorded with Reeves Gabrels in 1988, although Gabrels is not credited as co-writer)

and the less essential 'Gunman'. The commercial failure of *Tin Machine II*, and, perhaps more importantly, the restriction the band must have placed on Bowie in terms of control of the final product, led directly to him once again stepping into the limelight as a solo artist. In 1995 Bowie told *Interview* magazine that he saw the Tin Machine phase as a necessary period of self-evaluation: "Once I had done Tin Machine, nobody could see me any more. They didn't know who the hell I was, which was the best thing that ever happened, because I was back using all the artistic pieces that I needed to survive and I was imbuing myself with the passion that I had in the late seventies."

The slate wiped clean, he resumed his solo career with an overtly commercial offering. Bowie has mythologised his career in order to give the impression that he has always been a cult artist, has never sold many records, and has never wanted mainstream popularity, but at various stages he has always back-pedalled and gone for the mainstream by the jugular.

Nile Rodgers was once again brought in as producer, but *Black Tie White Noise* is no re-run of *Let's Dance*. Whereas on the latter Bowie seemed to be willing to give Rodgers full reign creatively in helping to shape the overall sonic terrain, on the sequel it is Bowie who is calling the shots, with Rodgers helping to put the action onto tape with a commercial sheen.

And there is action a-plenty. For a start Bowie sings wonderfully well, giving perhaps his best vocal performance yet. On the more recent tours his vocals had shown signs of strain and he had lost some of his upper range – hardly surprising after years of almost constant gigging and nicotine abuse. On *Black Tie White Noise* the songs fit the voice perfectly, however, and Bowie's lower, richer, rounded vocal is just the ticket. Lester Bowie's excellent trumpet playing, taking over the role of soloist from the lead guitar, provides a novel twist, however, and Bowie's asthmatic sax-playing is prominent for the first time in 15 years. With bass-heavy dance structures well to the fore in most songs, the overall sound is very much state of the art for

1993. It is also, *Young Americans* aside, Bowie's 'blackest' album to date. In fact it was conceived as a musical re-creation of, and comment on, not only the racial mix in his marriage but also the active creative process which had long infused his work: taking 'black' styles and overlaying a European melodic sensibility.

While the album still falls short of his best seventies work (the sense of desperation infused with megalomania which made his earlier work often spine-chilling is simply not there), three tracks at the heart of the set – 'Jump They Say', 'Nite Flights' and 'Pallas Athena' – provide a musical trio worthy of comparison with anything from his seventies work.

Early 1993 should have been an extremely propitious time for a new Bowie album. Seattle-grunge denim-clad anonymity was giving way in the UK to arty, camp, laddish 'Britpop' and some excellent new groups such as Blur, Elastica, Suede, The Auteurs and Pulp all carried echoes of Bowie somewhere in their music, their packaging or their approach to music-making. Suede in particular, fronted by Brett 'a bisexual man who has never had a homosexual experience' Anderson, borrowed heavily from the Ziggy era's glam-slam, and it must have given Bowie some satisfaction to see *Black Tie White Noise* depose the début Suede album from the top of the UK charts on its first week of release. However, from that moment on, it was all downhill for the Bowie comeback. In America he had signed with the small Savage label, which promptly went bust at the time of the album's release, seriously affecting promotion and distribution. Bowie's decision not to tour the album must have significantly affected sales too. Also the Bowie camp, long renowned for their inability to pick a single, blundered badly by relegating the outrageously catchy 'Miracle Goodnight' to third-choice single release. Had that led off the campaign, the album *might* have become one of Bowie's biggest sellers.

Reissued by EMI in 2003 ten years after its original release, and containing a bonus CD

and DVD, it might not be essential Bowie, but it has some of his catchiest melodies and funkiest beats, and is certainly one of his most instantly likeable and good-humoured efforts. For perhaps the first time in his career, Bowie actually sounds happy. But it wasn't to last, and his subsequent releases in the nineties just kept getting darker and darker.

THE WEDDING

The opener, an instrumental update of one of the pieces composed for that wedding, is one of three quite excellent instrumentals to be found on the album. Since Bowie's family were Church of England and Iman's Muslim, Bowie wanted to create a piece of music which mixed the two elements. Church bells open the track, giving way to an infectious bass-line, with some great melismatic sax work by Bowie giving that 'eastern' touch.

YOU'VE BEEN AROUND
(Bowie/Gabrels)

This song had been played live, in a radically different form, by Tin Machine, but never released. It's another strong song – the 'real' Bowie vocal only cuts in after the first verse's treated vocal. Bowie's self-mocking, self-referential 'Ch-ch-ch-ch-changed' line, some great trumpet by Lester Bowie, and a glorious bassline add up to a delight. Reeves Gabrels does solo at the end of the track but, rather naughtily, is mixed so far down by Bowie (in what might have been a deliberate gesture of defiance against the democracy of Tin Machine) that he is barely audible above the rhythm track!

I FEEL FREE
(Bruce/Brown)

A cover version to send purists running for that CD remote control fast forward button but which actually works rather well. Bowie completely reconstructs the song into a rocky techno freak-out and Mick Ronson makes his last performance on a Bowie album with a fine guitar solo. Bowie's vocal is hilariously deep at one stage too, causing severe aural distress, one might imagine, to dogs, cats, budgies and the like.

BLACK TIE WHITE NOISE

Inspired by the LA riots, this is Bowie back on 'I told you so' mode and duetting with soul singer Al B Sure! It's a good enough song but, call me an old cynic, my idea of what Bowie is about just doesn't fit with the moralizing man presented on this track, even if we all agree with the general sentiments of striving for racial harmony and strength through recognising (and respecting) cultural difference. A minor hit single in the summer of 1993, it reached number 36 in the UK charts.

JUMP THEY SAY

This is simply a fine pop song, undoubtedly a classic Bowie single, and a welcome UK Top 10 hit after a seven-year gap. Thematically it draws on the life (and death) of Bowie's step-brother Terry, who committed suicide in 1985. Musically the song has the same repetitive drive which characterises so much of his best work, a backwards sax line again adds an 'Eastern' wailing quality, and Bowie's cautionary/predictive vocals ('They say jump', 'Watch out!') give the song a chilling cinematic quality. The video is superb too. Of course, on another level, 'Jump They Say' was a metaphor for Bowie's entire career – the artistic leap into the unknown that made him but almost destroyed him. The song's intensely personal nature was confirmed by Bowie in a 1993 interview. He was, he said, still looking for some sort of emotional support in a life he found mystifying. "It's also connected to my feeling that sometimes I've jumped metaphysically into the unknown and wondering whether I really believed there was something out there to support me, whatever you wanna call it; a God or a life-force?"

NITE FLIGHTS

(Engels)

The disquiet of 'Jump They Say' is continued in this excellent cover of The Walker Brothers' 'Nite Flights' (originally from the 1978 album of the same name). It's a hard-edged dance track with Bowie's brooding vocals and a soaring speaker-to-speaker synth line among its many charms.

Undoubtedly one of Bowie's best-ever cover versions along with 'Sorrow', 'Wild Is The Wind' and 'Criminal World'.

PALLAS ATHENA

The second instrumental on the album is probably the best of a very good three. A sombre violin line gives way to the sort of experimental dance music Bowie should have done more of, with both Bowies soloing to good effect. For all you budding Bowiephiles, Pallas Athene (or Minerva) was, according to Brewer's book of *Myth And Legend*, fabled to have sprung, with a tremendous battle-cry, fully armed from the brain of Jupiter. Ouch!

MIRACLE GOODNIGHT

The catchiest track on the album, based around an ever-circling riff which, as Bowie commented, "just keeps coming and coming". There's a great synthesized orchestral break in the middle and even some hi-life guitar. I have it on good authority from someone who lived in Bali that the five-note riff which runs through the track sounds exactly like the Balinese frog chorus at night. Having heard a tape of the aforementioned frogs, I have to agree!

DON'T LET ME DOWN AND DOWN

(Tarha/Valmont)

The tone of the album, which was lightened by 'Miracle Goodnight', continues in much the same vein for the rest of the set. It's a good slowie, nothing outstanding, apart from Bowie's strangely accented vocals.

LOOKING FOR LESTER

In which Nile and Dame David bring jazz to the pop masses. Although not a jazz fan myself, I became more interested in the genre (which goes to show how impressionable I am) after listening to this groovy track, which sets three solos (from Lester Bowie, Bowie and the re-called Mike Garson) against a slab of thudding techno. An incongruous success.

I KNOW IT'S GONNA HAPPEN SOMEDAY
(Morrissey/Nevin)

The original Morrissey track (to be found on the Mick Ronson-produced 'Your Arsenal' album of 1992) ended with a re-run of the dénouement of Bowie's own classic, 'Rock'n'Suicide'. Bowie's version is thus a homage to a homage (making it a postmodernist's dream text) but, rather inexplicably, leaves out the slice of 'Rock'n'Roll Suicide' Mozza had originally sampled. It's a not altogether successful cover. Bowie is a little too studiously melodramatic in his attempt to produce a *Young Americans*-era vocal and piano mix, and the whole serves to remind all Bowie fans of just what a great lyricist Morrissey has become (better, it has to be said, than Bowie himself at the time). Would have made an acceptable single, though. On hearing the cover, Morrissey was reported in the press as saying, 'Ooh it's grand.'

THE WEDDING SONG

Here Bowie admits to having deliberately written a clichéd, gushing, saccharine-sweet love song for his bride. This is basically the opening track with words on, and it's fine in itself, though inferior to the instrumental version. Still, an effective way to end the 'official' set.

THE 2003 EDITION

The 2003 edition of the record contains a limited-edition bonus CD and DVD. I've often thought that the trend towards endless remixing of material is one of the least agreeable developments in modern music, and the old cynic in me says that it's just a device to keep remixers and musicians in a job. However, for those who like that sort of thing, CD 2 has a rich bounty of extended versions. Also featured is the catchy if lightweight 'Real Cool World' a single from 1992, and 'Lucy Can't Dance', a song which should beyond doubt have found a place on the album proper, CD 3 is a DVD version of the promotional video made at the time of the CD's original release and contains interview footage and some slightly cheap-looking mimed versions of several of the songs. Not vintage Bowie.

Limited Edition CD

'Real Cool World', 'Lucy Can't Dance', 'Jump They Say (Rock Mix)', 'Black Tie White Noise (3rd Floor US Radio Mix)', 'Miracle Goodnight (Make Believe Mix)', 'Don't Let Me Down & Down [Indonesian Vocal Version]', 'You've Been Around [Dangers 12" Remix]', 'Black Tie White Noise [Here Come Da Jazz]', 'Pallas Athena [Don't Stop Praying Remix No 2]', 'Nite Flights [Moodswings Back To Basics Remix]', 'Jump They Say [Dub Oddity].'

Limited Edition DVD

'Introduction', 'with Lester Bowie', 'On Reeves Gabrels', 'You've Been Around', 'Expanding and Experimenting', 'Nite Flights', 'Otherness', 'Miracle Goodnight', 'on marriage', 'Black Tie White Noise', 'with Mick Ronson', 'I Feel Free', 'with Nile Rodgers', 'I Know It's Gonna Happen Someday', 'Miracle Goodnight', 'Jump They Say', 'Black Tie White Noise', 'Credits'.

THE BUDDHA OF SUBURBIA

(Original UK Issue: UK CD: Arista 74321 170042, released 8 November 1993; released 31 October 1995; US: Virgin America; UK chart: 87)

When the BBC planned to turn Hanif Kureishi's 1990 novel and Whitbread Prize winner *The Buddha Of Suburbia* into a television play, it was particularly fitting that Bowie was asked to provide the music. The novel deals with issues of race, sexuality and stardom in the seventies, and Bowie as a cultural icon was drawn upon for the construction of one of the characters, Charlie, who rifles through a succession of personae – from hippy to glam rocker to punk before relocating, Billy Idol-style, to the States.

The most important point to make is that this is not a soundtrack album, despite the legend on the album's original front cover. The music here completely reconstructs the incidental music used in the BBC adaptation – this is a bona fide solo offering. Its extremely poor chart showing is probably attributable to four factors: firstly the album was released at the same time as EMI put out *Bowie: The Singles Collection* and thus got lost in the pre-Christmas retro-rush. Secondly, the mis-marketing of the album as a soundtrack obviously confused potential buyers perhaps expecting a vocal-less flow of background music. Thirdly, Bowie did very little in the way of interviews to promote the the work. And lastly, it might just be that Bowie fans don't like jazz very much. Of course, there had been moments of Garsonic madness before on

Bowie albums, notably *Aladdin Sane*. However, the music never gave itself up totally to improvisational jazz and stayed broadly within a rock/pop format. This could not be said for several tracks on *Buddha*. Bowie's much-trumpeted single 'Sue (Or In A Season Of Crime)' in 2014, a full-scale modern jazz wonk-out was likewise greeted by some Bowie fans with indifference, and by a few with a degree of distress.

Recorded in a mere six days, and co-produced with David Richards, on it Bowie shares instrumental duties with multi-instrumentalist Erdal Kizilcay, who had played on the previous two Bowie tours. Mike Garson provides piano parts for 'South Horizon' and 'Bleed Like A Craze, Dad'. While we might wish for a more nuanced and expansive sound, the fact that Bowie was writing and recording quickly, and with the minimal number of interlocutors, is significant.

As a result, what gives the album its identity is Bowie's apparent sense of liberation. In Tin Machine he was always one-quarter of the whole; on *Black Tie White Noise*, the contribution of Nile Rodgers, while not as evident as on *Let's Dance*, is there, and Bowie's use of session musicians and soloists, gives the work a certain tone. On *The Buddha Of Suburbia*, it seems, for the first time since *Scary Monsters*, that Bowie is calling the shots, and is in control of the sound and the repertoire.

What also gives the album a real sense of purpose is that Bowie has an overriding theme; to create a dialogue between the nineties and the seventies. So we have an updated Motorik beat for 'Dead Against It', a mimicked Bromley Dave delivery for the title track, and a pumped up kick of late-seventies Roxy Music for 'Strangers When We Meet'.

The CD booklet contains an essay by Bowie on the project, his influences and working procedures, and an assessment of the state of pop in the nineties. The best bit is the list, "the stockpile of residue from the 1970s used to oil the creative juices" … Pink Floyd, Harry Partch, Bromley, Die Mauer, The O'Jays and Drugs all feature. The essay ends with a piece of flag-waving which re-establishes Bowie's Englishness in the wake of 'Britpop'. Here is a taste of the polemic: "We have so much un-nurtured talent in this country it borders on the criminal", while "In America popular music has never been more divisive, both racially and socially".

The album was given its first release outside of the UK in October 1995, together with new art work (the new cover was based on an idea by Mark Adams, soon to be Bowie's webmaster). One of Bowie's own personal favourites, it's ripe for rediscovery.

BUDDHA OF SUBURBIA

'Sometimes I fear/that the whole world is queer,' sings Bowie in this, the big hit that never was. Peaking at a disappointing number 35 in the UK chart, this is a fine, stirring 'Bewlay Brothers' meets 'Absolute Beginners' title track. The music quotes 'Space Oddity' and the lyrics 'All The Madmen'. It is also a Bowie-esque theme – the boredom and the stifling condition of suburban life with its uniformity and conformity. Arcade Fire were obviously listening.

SEX AND THE CHURCH

After the opening title track which mores the album in more-or-less conventional rock/pop discourse, the album reveals its true experimental colours with 'Sex And The Church', a track which, more than anything else on the album, points the way to the next album, Outside. Based on a slow, almost Prince-like funky groove, Bowie's vocals come in and out of focus, incantatory, and so heavily treated, that Bowie appears to be speaking in tongues before the ending, which sounds like the ominously futuristic sound of a robot orgasm. Bowie mentions the word 'sex' a total of 50 times by the way.

SOUTH HORIZON

Bowie's favourite track on the album showcases some beautiful piano work from Garson on a fractured jazz instrumental which splits in two halfway through; a musical cut up of New York jazz and electronic beats.

THE MYSTERIES

This instrumental is the closest Bowie has come to a solo ambient instrumental à la Eno and particularly some of his work with Harold Budd. It is also in the same lineage of some of Bowie's own recordings such as 'Moss Garden' and 'Crystal Japan.' It has a backwards slowed-down keyboard drifting lightly in and out of phase. This is immersive music at its best, and the third track in a row which demonstrated that Bowie was making a clean break from his eighties self.

BLEED LIKE A CRAZE, DAD

In some of his work in the previous decade, Bowie's lyrics had lacked meaning, but also lacked any force of emotive power. They just sounded nonsensical and empty. On 'Bleed Like A Craze, Dad', Bowie dives into the fug and mystery of the incomprehensible, but comes out the other end appearing seer-like and wise. Musically, the song is one-long riff, and a great one it is too, while the tumble of half-heard *Sprechgesang* make us look back fondly at the Burroughsian Bowie of the seventies. Selfdom was Bowie as weird and as cryptic as this. The title, apparently, is a punning reference to the then jailed London crime duo, Ron and Reggie Kray.

STRANGERS WHEN WE MEET

Bowie moves back musically into pop with this, a fantastic track reminiscent of Manifesto *and Flesh and Blood* -era Roxy Music, particularly the Garry Tibbs-like bass line. It is the more bouncy and arguably superior version of a song that would be re-recorded for Bowie's next studio album.

DEAD AGAINST IT

We're back in the club in 1979 for this one, with the shades of Talking Heads, Blondie and Neu! lurking. It is the sort of artful pop song Bowie crafted at the time too, tweaking the received expectations of how a pop song should behave with an instrumental opening of over a minute, and a cyclical synthesised coda of a minute and a half. The chirping and chipper 'Cricket Menace' from *Lodger*'s 'African Night Flight' makes a fitting return too on this, the best track on the album, apart from…

UNTITLED No. 1

…this, the strongest cut on the album. It sounds like nothing Bowie has ever made, before or since, almost a one-song sui generis genre. There's dashing contemporary beats, a beautiful vocal top-line, and a confounding mix of Raga and what sounds at one stage like Mrs Mills'-styled knees-up piano. The emotional connection to the seventies is made with a more-than-passable impersonation of Marc Bolan towards the end, something which, of course, neatly sources Bowie's own 'Black Country Rock' from 1970. Stunning, and should have been a single.

IAN FISH, U.K. HEIR

This instrumental was certain to send *Let's Dance*-era Bowie fans fleeing in panic or for the remote. Bowie, playing around with form and content in traditional ambient style, loads a funereally slow re-tread of the musical motifs of the title track with copious dollops of surface static. The result is a Lo-fi Hades, all the darkness and ambiguity of the seventies rendered almost listenable by the sonic recreation of a knackered stylus and worn-out vinyl.

BUDDHA OF SUBURBIA

Why the album has not already ended is a puzzle. The tenth track is track 1 again, but this is no *Scary Monsters* 'It's No Game'- Part Two reinterpretation but essentially the same song with a Lenny Kravitz guitar solo. While there's no doubting Kravitz's musical tekkers and production savvy, his repertoire hardly seemed compatible with that of Bowie's, particularly not on this, one of his most daring albums. Pointless and perfunctory, it perhaps indicated that even Bowie needed a 'big name presence', if the album was going to get any headspace. A loss of nerve at a time of a great leap forward, it showed Bowie (or, we can guess, perhaps more accurately, his advisors) still wanted some sort of mainstream acceptance. Or maybe Bowie is a big Lenny Kravitz fan?

1. OUTSIDE

(Original UK Issue: RCA 74321 31066 2, released September 25 1995; UK chart: 8 [Weeks in chart: 4]; US CD: Sony US: chart: 21 [6])

For years it seemed a good bet that Bowie and Eno would never work together again. During the late eighties, while Eno was making his fortune as U2's producer and being rehabilitated as the ambient godfather and Bowie was dabbling in hard rock, it looked as if the two ex-collaborators were light years apart musically. Bowie was going for a live, band sound, while Eno had never been interested in using the recording process as a means of capturing 'real' performances.

The first hint of a team-up came in October 1992 when this writer managed to quiz Eno in Munich during one of his (always very good) lectures. If memory serves me right, he told me that Bowie had been asked to write a piece of music to commemorate the 1,200[th]

anniversary of the institution of the city of Kyoto, Japan, in November 1994, and that Bowie had asked him, Eno, to collaborate. Nought came of this, but it was obvious that Eno was finding Bowie's increasingly textural music more to his liking. Around the beginning of 1994 they started work on what would eventually become *Outside*.

Outside is littered with references to Bowie's musical past, particularly the underrated *Lodger* and the still towering *Diamond Dogs*. The really astonishing thing about it is the way in which Bowie has been able to re-summon all the paranoia, pomposity and eclecticism of his seventies work so utterly convincingly, once again proving adept at ransacking images from high art and playfully bastardising them through his music. On *Outside* the preoccupation is with ritual art and neo-paganism. In the nineties Bowie's own dabbling in art became less a hobby and more a vocation. He became a member of the editorial board of the magazine *Modern Painters*, began befriending figures such as the British artist Damien Hirst (infamous at the time for exhibiting a dead sheep in a tank of formaldehyde), and in 1995 exhibited his own paintings and sculptures for the first time. The video for the first single 'Hearts Filthy Lesson' says it all. Directed by Sam Bayer, who made Nirvana's famous video for 'Smells Like Teen Spirit', it shows a Bowie surrounded by almost holocaust-like images of deprivation: hangings, decapitations, his own body of flesh and blood covered in powder paint as if bodily fluids, skin and paint have somehow been mixed to form one primeval medium.

Outside is probably Bowie's bleakest album yet (and that's saying a lot). It deals with the murder of Baby Grace Blue, a 14-year-old victim of an 'art crime' (her innards having been exhibited as art) and the investigation into the death by Professor Nathan Adler, art detective. After years of avoiding overt characterisation on stage and on record, Bowie went wild on *Outside*, creating and impersonating other figures too, such as the 22-year-old prime suspect Leon Blank, a 78-year-old art-drug and DNA print dealer

Algeria Touchshriek, the omnipotent leading lady Ramona A Stone, and the Minotaur! In typical Bowie fashion this is a concept album with the concept left out. There is a narrative of sorts, but its direction and the extent to which the William Burroughs-styled cut-ups are actually meant to convey any literal meaning, is open to debate. And in truth, it's hard to get that involved in the story in the first place. Whereas Ziggy's cartoon-like imagery instantly struck a chord and *Diamond Dogs* proffered a re-write of a familiar novel, *Outside*'s obsessions are likely to remain mainly those of their creator.

All this chicanery left Bowie open, as always, to accusations of wild pretentiousness from many in the British media. In the end, though, *Outside* was, on balance, well-received by the press. Long-time Bowie-watcher Charles Shaar Murray called it "a mad, bad, dangerous album, by turns, chilling, pretty, ugly, scary, gripping and vastly intriguing" and even the British inkies,

Melody Maker and *NME*, who had been on Bowie's back for over a decade, gave grudgingly good notices too.

Outside, first mooted to be the first of a five-CD cycle taking us into the new millennium, is a mud-pie of styles from jungle and techno to avant-garde jazz. There are a couple of lame moments (and the narrative sections sometimes hit a seven out of ten on the Bowie Cringeometer), but whereas, for example, *The Buddha Of Suburbia* had four genuinely great tracks, *Outside* has more than twice as many. There's some fine drumming from Soul Asylum's Sterling Campbell, some funky and instantly recognisable rhythm guitar from Carlos Alomar, and Reeves Gabrels, ex-Tin Machine, puts in some excellent work too. The lead instrumentalist, however, is Mike Garson, although his piano contributions are at times overdone and lose their cranky emotive power. And of course, there's Eno everywhere in the mix with some of the most wonky, nutty and dangerous sounds you'll ever hear on CD. *Outside*, which comes complete with a booklet containing an excerpt from the 'Nathan Adler Diaries' (a largely and deliberately impenetrable Bowie narrative) and a succession of computer images which show Bowie morphed into the album's characters, is another essential Bowie purchase.

Twenty years since its release, *Outside* has become a firm favourite with Bowie's hard-core fans. It shows Bowie at his most daring and uncompromising. And by deleting the segues, the trimmed down album is undoubtedly one of his best. *Outside* took many months to record. After an initial session in Switzerland which produced many tracks through improvisation such as 'Hearts Filthy Lesson', Bowie wrote more songs later, according to Reeves Gabrels, he was under commercial pressure to make the album more appetising to a major record label: "The business people got involved and they took it around and could only get half of what David usually got because it was so improvisational and they didn't know what to make of it. David thought that to get some record company

behind it he needed to write some singles or some more commercial tracks. That's when 'Strangers When We Meet' got redone."

Outside or *1.Outside* to give it its pedantically correct title, was meant to be the first part of a succession of albums with *2. Contamination* the reported follow up. The plan was abandoned for reasons which have never been fully explained. Perhaps the dynamic within the band was too complicated? Perhaps, the relatively poor sales were also a factor? Or, had Bowie, as usual, got tired and wanted to move on? Since its release, the album has appeared in various formats, in an excerpted version, as part of box sets, or as reissues. This is about the only Bowie album where I would discourage any vinyl junkie to look for a CD or download purchase given that editing out the segues gives one a total running length of a manageable 65 minutes and also, a better album.

Finally, we may not have heard the last of this, one of Bowie's most creative periods. Leaked from the sessions and doing the Bootleg rounds is an astonishing piece of music. *1. Outside Outtakes* containing over an hour of previously unreleased music, dates from 1994. See Cryptobowie section for more information.

LEON TAKES US OUTSIDE
(Music: Bowie/Eno/Gabrels/Garson/ Kizilcay/Campbell: Lyrics: Bowie)
Outside begins with this almost incantatory jumble of sound and monologue as the scene is set temporally sometime between 1977 and 1999. It's all very reminiscent of the opening of U2's *Zooropa* album, which is no bad thing at all.

OUTSIDE
(Music: Armstrong/Bowie: Lyrics: Bowie)
Those of you brave enough to have attended the first Tin Machine tour in 1989 might have heard an underrated track called 'Now', which was featured on two of the UK dates. It forms the basis for 'Outside', which builds anthemically, courtesy of some rousing

drumming from Sterling Campbell which crashes from speaker to speaker, into one of the album's best songs. Vocally, Bowie is understated and the lyric helps to herald in the new, fully-fledged post-modern Bowie, aching to blur past and present into a perpetual 'Now'. Theoretically he may be ten years out of date, but in pop and rock, late is always better than never.

THE HEARTS FILTHY LESSON
(Music: Bowie/Eno/Gabrels/Garson/ Kizilcay/Campbell: Lyrics: Bowie)
By this, the albums third piece, it is obvious that the listener is locked inside the same emotional terrain that Bowie had worked within on the albums from *Station To Station* to *Scary Monsters*. This is not music, such as that found on *Hunky Dory* or *Ziggy Stardust*, which reveals its charms instantly. 'Hearts Filthy Lesson' is a track which simply gets better with each listen and with every passing year. On first few listens, its dense structure and lack of instant melodic appeal was unpalatable. On repeated exposure, the song's stunning production values hit home along with the demonic groove, Garson and Gabrels' neat riffy interventions and Bowie's Edgar Allan Poe-like voice from the interned: 'I'm already five years older, I'm already in my grave', although in this case the feeling is that Bowie is speaking from the afterlife not still alive in the casket.

Like the best Bowie songs, it is also a maze of interconnections and red herrings. Why does the title have no apostrophe? Is it in any way or important or simply the result of some very poor text editing? The main piano line sounds very much like a sample from Iggy & The Stooge's 1973 song 'Raw Power'. While the video, directed by Sam Bayer, has some of the same weight in grotesquery as that made a year earlier for Nine Inch Nails' classic 'Closer', a video made by Bowie collaborator Mark Romanek based on a song whose deadly pulse is a lift from Bowie's own beat created for Iggy Pop's 'Nightclubbing'. 'Hearts Filthy Lesson' is a jumble of sounds, associations and liaisons, particularly when one considers that Bowie and Nine Inch Nails would tour the US together in the autumn of 1995.

A SMALL PLOT OF LAND
(Music: Bowie/Eno/Gabrels/Garson/Kizilcay/ Campbell: Lyrics: Bowie)
Who's been listening to Scott Walker's *Tilt* then? Well, Bowie's almost operatic vocal on this track is a direct borrowing from the AWOL American and is set against some of Garson's most bonkers piano playing. A difficult listening experience, but at least it's better than almost anything on *Tonight*.

SEGUE – BABY GRACE (A HORRID CASSETTE)
(Music: Bowie/Eno/Gabrels/Garson/Kizilcay/ Campbell: Lyrics: Bowie)
A short narrative with Bowie's vocal delivered in the guise of fourteen-year-old murder victim Baby Grace.

HALLO SPACEBOY
(Music: Bowie/Eno: Lyrics: Bowie)
In terms of plot development this doesn't fit at all, but no matter. Although thematically it revisits the 'hi, I'm bi' Seventies persona, with its distorted thrash, catchy guitar riff which spins from speaker to speaker, and kitsch sci-fi synth refrain, it is another indication that Bowie really has moved musically into dangerous territory once again. The origin of the music is actually a Reeves Gabrels' demo with Bowie done in Switzerland although Gabrels is not credited.

THE MOTEL
(Music & Lyrics: Bowie)
This track shows Bowie's minimalistic sensibilities interwoven to great effect with a wearied vocal performance set against Garson's languorous piano refrain. "'The Motel' on *Outside* is my 25-years-later version of 'Lady Grinning Soul'!" says Garson. It proved an effective, if low-key, opener to many of the early *Outside* tour dates, with Bowie taking the stage in an electrical storm of lighting and thunder effects.

I HAVE NOT BEEN TO OXFORD TOWN
(Music: Bowie/Eno: Lyrics: Bowie)
With the rather better working title of 'Toll The Bell', this is the most catchy track on the album. Bowie is at his very best in the persona of prime suspect Leon Blank, and the chorus and middle eight are top notch. And, as if you needed more, there's Alomar's clipped rhythm guitar to steal the show at the end. An obvious choice for a single, but passed over, it did find its way on to the movie *Starship Troopers* in a re-recorded form under the title, 'I Have Not Been To Paradise'.

NO CONTROL
(Music: Bowie/Eno: Lyrics: Bowie)
This dark, sombre stab at Pet Shop Boys-styled techno works really well (they're a good group to borrow from), particularly since Bowie's on top form vocally, steering a delicate path between understatement and excess, as opposed to Neil Tennant's careful path between understatement and understatement.

SEGUE – ALGERIA TOUCHSHRIEK
(Music: Bowie/Eno/Gabrels/Garson/Kizilcay/ Campbell: Lyrics: Bowie)
This is the silliest, and best, segue: Bowie is pushing eighty and yearning for another 'broken man' to rent his spare apartment.

THE VOYEUR OF UTTER DESTRUCTION (AS BEAUTY)
(Music: Bowie/Eno/Gabrels: Lyrics: Bowie)
This time big, bad Dame David is none other than the Minotaur in another slice of *Lodger*-era Bowie. The pace of the music is insistent, breathless, and the track comes alive on stage with an impassioned vocal performance and crazy Gabrels lead solo. As an aside, it was reported in the British press during 1995 that an anonymous man had offered Bowie and Damien Hirst his body (after death) for the sake of art, so that Hirst could graft on a bull's head and Bowie could reconstruct the Minotaur!

SEGUE – RAMONA A. STONE/I AM WITH NAME
(Music: Bowie/Eno/Gabrels/Garson/Kizilcay/ Campbell: Lyrics: Bowie)
Even if, for some, this may prove unlikeable, this segue is undoubtedly chilling and powerful in its execution. Which leads us on to...

WISHFUL BEGINNINGS
(Music: Bowie/Eno: Lyrics: Bowie)
One of his most disturbing songs, with Bowie's vocal lilting like a blissful torturer about to pull the wings off a ladybird one by one. A Gothic half-croak, half-cackle forms the musical bed for this, one of Bowie's creepiest efforts since 1974's 'We Are The Dead.'

WE PRICK YOU
(Music: Bowie/Eno: Lyrics: Bowie)
Bowie described this dance track, with its infectious riff and screamed chorus, as 'dotty'. With the working title 'We Fuck You', this track shows Bowie tentatively exploring proto drum 'n' bass in the fun rhythms.

SEGUE – NATHAN ADLER
(Music: Bowie/Eno/Gabrels/Garson/Kizilcay/ Campbell: Lyrics: Bowie)
After another spoken segue (Bowie now sounds like Frank Zappa's Central Scrutinizer from the Joe's Garage albums) we get...

I'M DERANGED
(Music: Bowie/Eno: Lyrics: Bowie)
A fine dance track with echoes of late Kraftwerk in the backing track and distinct reminders of another, lesser, Bowie song, the Nile Rodgers-produced 'Real Cool World' (Warner WO127CD, 1992) in the melody.

THRU' THESE ARCHITECTS EYES
(Music: Bowie/Gabrels: Lyrics: Bowie)
A storming, nay blistering cut, sung by Bowie as Leon Blank with one of those swooping melodies which he has been so adept at since the mid-Seventies. One of the rarest of

beasts too in that it is a song about the majesty of Modernist/Post-Modern architecture (American architect Philip Johnson and Britain's Richard Rodgers are name-checked). Musically one of the most conventional tracks on the album it prepares us neatly for...

SEGUE – NATHAN ADLER

(Music: Bowie/Eno: Lyrics: Bowie)
A very short spoken section and then...

STRANGERS WHEN WE MEET

(Music & Lyrics: Bowie)
A fine Bowie pop song, this time a re-working of a track from the criminally underexposed *Buddha Of Suburbia*. Bowie and Eno really try to make this a 'son-of-"Heroes"' complete with a one-note sustained lead-guitar, instantly hooky bass guitar line (with clear echoes of Spencer Davis Group's 1967 hit, 'Gimme Some Lovin') and a beautiful melody which builds perfectly. So, an incongruously poppy ending to an otherwise uncompromising album, and just a hint of a loss of nerve. The second single off the album and a minor UK Top 40 hit.

1. OUTSIDE UK REISSUE (27 September, 2004)

Sony reissued *1. Outside*, *Earthling* and *hours...* with bonus CDs, packaged in digibook style with booklets. The separate versions of the albums are available for just one pressing, while a limited edition slipcase edition containing all three CDs is to be limited to 2,000 copies. Earlier in 2004, the three albums were also reissued by Sony America, again with bonus tracks included, as single disc editions.

1. Outside Bonus Disc:

'The Hearts Filthy Lesson' (Trent Reznor Alternative Mix) (UK CD Single); 'The Hearts Filthy Lesson' (Rubber Mix) (Out2 promo 12" or Argentinean BMG CD sampler BMG PCD 150); 'The Hearts Filthy Lesson' (Simple Text Mix) (Out2 promo 12" or Argentinean BMG CD sampler BMG PCD 150); 'The Hearts Filthy Lesson' (Filthy Mix) (Out2 promo 12" or Argentinean BMG CD sampler BMG PCD 150); 'The Hearts Filthy Lesson' (Good Karma Mix by Tim Simenon) (US CD Single or Limited UK 'Dead Man Walking' CD Single); 'A Small Plot Of Land' (*Basquiat OST* version) (*Basquiat OST* CD); 'Hallo Spaceboy' (12" Remix) (BMG HALLO 2 promo 12"); 'Hallo Spaceboy' (Double Click Mix) (BMG SPACE 3 promo 12"); 'Hallo Spaceboy' (Instrumental) (BMG SPACE 3 promo 12"); 'Hallo Spaceboy' (Lost In Space Mix) (BMG SPACE 3 promo 12"); 'I Am With Name (Album Version)' ('The Hearts Filthy Lesson' UK CD Single); 'I'm Deranged (Jungle Mix)' (Limited UK 'Dead Man Walking' CD Single); 'Get Real' ('Strangers When We Meet' UK CD Single); 'Nothing To Be Desired' ('The Hearts Filthy Lesson' US CD Single).

All bonus track produced by David Bowie and Brian Eno.

Since 2004 there have been several other reissues of the album. The latest, from 2014, and called *Outside Version 2*, adds a remix of 'Hallo Spaceboy' to the original CD 1 and six tracks on a bonus CD 2: 'Hallo Spaceboy' (Pet Shop Boy Remix), 'Under Pressure' (Live Version), 'Moorage Daydream' (Live Version), 'The Man Who Sold The World' (Live Version), 'Strangers When We Meet' (Radio Edit), 'The Hearts Filthy Lesson' (Bowie Mix).

EARTHLING

(Original UK Issue: RCA 74321449442, released 3 February 1997; UK chart: 6 [Total weeks in chart: 4]; US CD: Sony US chart: 39 [6]

One of the most common adjectives in rock journalism is 'experimental', a word rendered almost meaningless thorough overuse. All music is an act of creation and therefore experimental by its very nature. However, experimental is less likely to be shorthand for a great leap into the unknown, a new way of seeing the world through music, or an exciting combination of sound, than to signal a situation where a major rock artist has made a poor record, with no big idea and almost always no good tunes.

Earthling is the last David Bowie album to break new ground. It is not, as we will see, the last great David Bowie album (there are two other candidates for this honour) but it is certainly the last album which leaves the listener with a sense of wonder at the shock of the new.

Unlike the *Sound + Vision* tour, during which he appeared, at times, to be performing under duress, or the Glass Spider outing which saw the ceremonial burning of the spider at the end of the tour, Bowie couldn't get enough of being on the road. Between September 14, 1995 and November 7, 1997, Bowie played 178 concerts in a variety of settings from arenas and open-air festivals to relatively intimate club gigs. Of

course, there was media coverage, yet this visibility was taken rather for granted.

By early 1996, Bowie's muse was fizzing along with ideas at a rate not seen since the late seventies. The origin of the *Earthling* album dates from this period, when the decision was made to cut down the touring band from eight to five. For the summer festivals of 1996, it would be Bowie on stage (with occasional sax) with drummer Zach Alford, guitarist and effects-wizard Reeves Gabrels, bassist and vocalist Gail Ann Dorsey and keyboard player Mike Garson. Unrecorded songs such as 'Telling Lies', 'Seven Years In Tibet' and 'Little Wonder' began making their debuts. "The design for the *Earthling* touring band in my mind was *Who's Next*," says Gabrels. "'Baba O'Riley' was the first use of electronica with a rock band. That's my favourite era of everything I did with David." Another inspiration for the new sound was Mick Jones' post-Clash band Big Audio Dynamite whose work Bowie referenced in interviews. Indeed, their use of synths, guitars, samples and big beats on tracks such as 'The Bottom Line' and their only major hit, 'E+MC2', was a daring musical cocktail with which Bowie had a natural affinity.

There was a feeling of challenge and outreach in mid-to-late nineties music that *Earthling* shares the debate with. The music of relatively new acts like Nine Inch Nails, Underworld, Prodigy, Tricky, PJ Harvey, Flaming Lips, Smashing Pumpkins, Björk, Blur, Massive Attack, Radiohead, The Chemical Brothers, and, increasingly that of already established major pop/rock acts such as Madonna, R.E.M., U2, and a rejuvenated Gary Numan, seemed to be consciously wanting to break away from how music had been made for maybe the previous 30 years. Loops and beats replaced or at least vied in importance with verses and choruses, and popular music, as it headed into the new Millennium appeared to be at its most diverse and challenging for many years.

On release, *Earthling* was often described as Bowie's 'drum and bass' album, yet this is misleading. Only four songs out of nine have a drum & bass bed, and of these only 'Telling Lies' is a fully-fledged jungle track. *Earthling* was an often thrilling fusion (not dissimilar to *Young Americans* in intent, if not sound) of European and North American contemporary music. The sound on *Earthling* is hard to easily compartmentalise fusing, as it does, not just drum and bass but Industrial, pop, rock, electronica, classical and techno. What makes the album so much more powerful than a collision of musical styles is, of course, Bowie himself and his ability to write memorable melodies. 'Little Wonder', 'Looking For Satellites', 'Battle For Britain' and 'Dead Man Walking' are nothing if not classic Bowie tunes.

Bowie had, of course, made his first forays into this sort of music on the previous album, *1. Outside*, with the brutal 'Hello Spaceboy', the techno-inspired 'No Control' and the jungle-tinged 'I'm Deranged'. However, whereas *Outside* is almost prog-rocky in its conceptualising and weird detours, its sound-layered, chattering, sometime half-heard, *Earthling* is savage, toned and extremely direct. Unlike many Bowie albums, it appears to have been mastered at a high volume and is designed for the club rather than the living room.

Therein lay a 'problem'. By now, Bowie's fan base really was approaching cult proportions. Supporters in the media were actually few and far between. Fifty-year-old rock legends were not supposed to be making records for clubs and certainly shouldn't be citing Underworld and the Prodigy as inspirations. Bowie was the first of his generation to make music which was dismissed because of ageism. By now, if they were making music at all, his seventies contemporaries were making music which spoke quite directly to their core support. The Rolling Stones had been making essentially the same record for two decades and toured an unashamedly populist set list. Bowie, however, wasn't interested in becoming a heritage act. Not just yet in any case.

Gabrels is on hot form on lead guitar, Garson plays some stupendous keyboard runs,

Zachary Alford's drumming is superb and Bowie's vocal is playful and fun. Important to the overall sound of the album was Mark Plati, responsible for programming loops, samples and keyboards, who had previously worked on a single by Big Audio Dynamite II ('additional production and mix; keys and programming') called 'Rush' which sampled 'Baba O'Riley'. "My work in the early nineties, with Big Audio Dynamite, etc, pretty much prepared me for what we were going to do on *Earthling*, though of course I didn't know it at the time," Plati told the author in 2003. "I'd been doing many records or mixes where I'd be fusing rock and dance elements, trying to get it right. *Earthling* was the culmination of that for me. After that record, I didn't program for years. I felt like I'd achieved what I'd wanted, so I went back to playing guitar in the park."

Plati added that six years down the line he was still fond of *Earthling*. "I hadn't listened to it in ages, and when I did recently it still sounded fresh, probably because it was done so fast. It was a very 'first instinct' kind of record; we really didn't think too much about it, and it felt like it just came about on its own. As such, it really captures a moment, which is part of why it is still such a high point for me. Of course, I have my favourites: the album version of 'Dead Man Walking' is a trip. And 'Seven Years in Tibet,' well, that's just huge! After that record, I didn't program for years. I felt like I'd achieved what I'd wanted, so I went back to playing guitar in the park."

During recording, which took place at Looking Glass Studios in New York in the autumn of 1996, Bowie harnessed the live power of his band at the time. Almost inevitably, of course, the jungle elements date the record. It may lack the depth, quiet menace and sheer spookiness of *1. Outside*, but parts of *Earthling* are the equal of Bowie's trail-blazing work in the Seventies. Released in February 1997, just after Bowie had celebrated his fiftieth birthday with a huge celebrity bash at Madison Square Gardens, the album has hardly ever been given the respect it is due.

Earthling was not a commercial success. Indeed, most of the media attention at the time of its release centred on the 'Bowie Bonds' scheme, the brainchild of David Pullman, which raised a whopping $55 million against future royalties. Sadly, at the time, Bowie appeared more corporate and distanced from his fans than ever before. Yet the significance of Bowie being the first major artist to release a single exclusively as a download ('Telling Lies') is an astonishing gamble and showed that, more than any other major artist at the time, he understood the way the winds of change were about to blow through the music industry.

LITTLE WONDER
(Music: Bowie/Gabrels/Plati: Lyrics: Bowie)

'Little Wonder' was originally conceived as a nine-minute jungle-electronic epic, with the middle section slammed full of effects and ideas, atmospheres and breaks. However, only the train idea after the second verse survived, in the shortened version which made the album. Released as the lead-off single, it made Number 14 in the UK charts. The vocal we hear on this track is in fact Bowie's run-through guide vocal.

LOOKING FOR SATELLITES
(Music: Bowie, Gabrels/Plati: Lyrics: Bowie)

With its gorgeous melody and rebounding rhythm, and Reeves Gabrels' astonishing one-string guitar solo, this is arguably Bowie on full creative power. "David thought that Reeves should try to play the entire solo on one string as it would shape his playing and note choices accordingly," said Mark Plati for *Strange Fascination*. "All of the attempts were recorded and we made one coherent, fantastic solo out of a few different choices. We took little pieces, moved sections around a bit. We began to see what was possible with hard -disk recording." The lyric, as Bowie so cryptically told us, was "as near to a spiritual song as I've written: it's measuring the distance between the crucifixion and flying saucers."

BATTLE FOR BRITAIN (THE LETTER)
(Music: Bowie/Gabrels/Plati: Lyrics: Bowie)

The third quality song in a row, this is an astonishing musical cocktail of programmed and live percussion units, featuring Garson's piano (for the instrumental break Bowie told Garson to play in the style of a Stravinsky octet!) and Bowie's brilliantly, vaguely Beatlesque vocal, all lightly caressed by a sensibly understated use of jungle. The song made a comeback on some dates on Bowie's *Reality* tour in 2003 and 2004.

SEVEN YEARS IN TIBET
(Music: Bowie/ Gabrels: Lyrics: Bowie)

On the face of it, this is a more traditional song, but still a great one. Bowie's opening – "Are you ok?/you've been shot in the head/and I'm holding your brains/The old woman said", is the lyrical highpoint, while the wall upon wall of Reevesian guitar, is so powerful it almost knocks you backwards in your seat. The slinky, sexy sax, Garson's farsifa organ (Gabrels' idea), and the menacing block of sound at the end lent support to Bowie's claim that he had fully regained his Midas touch. Gabrels' haunting guitar part is based, so he revealed, on Fleetwood Mac's 'Albatross'. And if all that isn't enough to captivate you, the working title for the song was, apparently, 'Muffin Lady'.

DEAD MAN WALKING
(Music: Bowie/Gabrels: Lyrics: Bowie)

Lyrically, the song deals with a theme which would increasingly preoccupy Bowie: ageing, and the sense of dignity and yet self-doubt that accompanies it. Musically, the starting point was Bowie's intention to make a techno track in the sprit of 'Underworld', then enjoying success with the single 'Born Slippy', featured in the film *Trainspotting*. For this song, Bowie dug up an old chord progression given to him by Jimmy Page which he used for the 1970 track 'The Supermen'. Exuberant, high-octane and, like almost everything on *Earthling*, superbly crafted, it inexplicable failed as the follow-up single to 'Little Wonder'.

TELLING LIES
(Music & Lyrics: Bowie)
Bowie started this authentic drum 'n' bass track in Switzerland, finishing it off at the Looking Glass Studio in New York prior to some live dates which preceded the main body of recording for the album. Released as a download-only single, it reportedly garnered a quarter of a million downloads. To be filed under 'interesting, but not essential'.

THE LAST THING YOU SHOULD DO
(Music: Bowie, Gabrels/Plati: Lyrics: Bowie)
"Reeves and I did the entire track in a day: drums, guitars, bass, programming, etc.," says Plati. "David heard it, added a synth part in the middle (the descending piano part in the break) then did a lyric and vocal in something like 20 minutes." Only a last-minute re-think secured the inclusion of this track, originally recorded as 'B'-side material. Originally, *Earthling* was feature a re-recording of Tin Machine's 'I Can't Read' (part of the soundtrack to the movie *The Ice Storm*, and eventually released as a single (Velvet ZYX 87578) in February 1998, becoming a minor UK hit, and another Tin Machine song, 'Baby Universal' which was played live during 1996. However, it's a fine track and a good musical fit, with huge washes of ferocious guitar, primal grunts from Bowie, and the reappearance of the descending synth pattern (albeit in a reworked form) lovingly handed down from 'The Laughing Gnome', via 'Speed Of Life' to 'Beat Of Your Drum'.

I'M AFRAID OF AMERICANS
(Music: Bowie/Eno: Lyrics: Bowie)
In which Bowie informs us that God is indeed an American. Originally recorded with Brian Eno for the soundtrack to the film *Showgirls* (Interscope Records, 6544 92661 2), and improved upon here, the song was eventually reduced by Trent Reznor of Nine Inch Nails to its bare bones in a remix which restored Bowie to the American charts and alternative rock programming. A staple of live shows for subsequent tours, despite its relatively meagre hook, it's obviously a Bowie favourite.

LAW (EARTHLINGS ON FIRE)
(Music: Bowie/Gabrels: Lyrics: Bowie)
"I don't want knowledge – I want certainty," intones Bowie spookily through a ring-modulator, quoting from Bertrand Russell. This techno song has a filmic, grandiose air and a mood reminiscent of *Diamond Dogs* or even *The Man Who Sold The World*, and the line "with this sound, with this sound, with this sound, mark the ground" is wonderfully evocative.

Earthling Bonus Disc (Sony 2004 re-issue)
'Little Wonder' (Censored Video Edit) (US promo only CD); 'Little Wonder' (Junior Vasquez Club Mix) (AKA Junior's Club Mix on UK CD single); 'Little Wonder' (Danny Sabre Dance Mix) (US CD single or The Saint OST soundtrack); 'Seven Years In Tibet' (Mandarin Version) (UK CD single); 'Dead Man Walking' (Moby Mix 1) (UK CD single); 'Dead Man Walking' (Moby Mix 2) (US promo 12" only); 'Telling Lies' (Feelgood Mix) (UK CD single); 'Telling Lies' (Paradox Mix) (UK CD single); 'I'm Afraid Of Americans' (*Show Girls OST* version) (*Show Girls OST* CD); 'I'm Afraid Of Americans' (Nine Inch Nails V1 Mix) (US CD single); 'I'm Afraid Of Americans' (Nine Inch Nails V1 Clean Edit) (US promo only CD); 'V-2 Schneider' (Tao Jones Index) (12" vinyl only release); 'Pallas Athena' (Tao Jones Index)

Bonus tracks – Mixed and mastered by Mark Plati. Tracks 12 and 13 recorded live in Amsterdam, 1997.

Like *Outside*, *Earthling* has been subjected to any number of re-packages, reissues and re-promotions, without anything genuinely unheard, such as the solo, studio version of 'Baby Universal', which undoubtedly exists, ever being included.

hours...

(Original UK Issue: Virgin CDV 2900, released 4 October 1999; UK chart: 5 [Total weeks in chart: 6]; US CD: Sony US chart: 47 [4])

After the febrile excesses of *1. Outside* and *Earthling*, *hours...* was seen very much as a return to melody and form and, for some, a welcome one. The advance noise before release mentioned the illustrious *Hunk Dory* in the same breath as the new music and Bowie himself wrote in his Blog that he was allowing himself to become as melodic as he had been for a good while. Yet, in the scheme of things, *hours...* (the reason for the lower case and ellipsis is unclear) is only a minor work in the Bowie canon. All of Bowie's subsequent albums, however, would contain something of the spirit of *hours...* It was as if *Earthling* had been the end of Bowie's postmodernist phase and, after the revolution, order needed to be restored. So begins the 'Neoclassical Bowie', as is in the order of things.

Sometime in 1998 when Bowie began, in earnest, writing for a new album, something of a sea-change appears to have occurred in how he wanted to relate to his music and to his audience. Gone was any intention of building on *Earthling* and its adventures; in came nostalgia and a different set of priorities. Bowie told Reeves Gabrels that he wanted to write music for his own generation, music that was 'ours' (the punning title of the album is intentional). Gabrels countered along the lines of, that

this would have to be without him, because he was ten years younger. It is certainly the case that Bowie's new music could easily have found its way onto the Radio 2 playlist.

The impulse for the album had in fact been provided by a quite unrelated project, a commission by the company Eidos to produce songs for a new computer game entitled *Omikron: The Nomad Soul.* Bowie asked Gabrels to work with him on the project. Gabrels was a natural choice, having already produced many television and film soundtracks (including David Lynch's *American Chronicles*). "The music on *hours...* was influenced by a couple of things," says Gabrels. "Firstly, we sat down and wrote songs with just guitar and keyboard before going into the studio. Secondly, the characters we appear as in the game are street/protest singers, so we needed a more singer-songwriter approach. The intention was to create a body of work which was quite different from the usual cheesy industrial metal music one would normally get."

hours... is an album full of regret for uncorrected mistakes, missed turnings and failed affairs. It looks back at a life in which apparently solid relationships somehow failed and youthful aspirations turned into the unfulfilled dreams of middle-age. It was, however, an album that confused a section of his audience. For by reaching out to his contemporaries, Bowie found out that they had just about all gone, and those that did remain had long since stopped thinking of popular music as an important part of their lives. Bowie's loyal fan base was, on average, at least ten, if not 20 years his junior. They were not 'Beatle Boys, all snowy white', but thirty-somethings.

hours... might have been a rather different album, as Reeves Gabrels reveals: "There is an earlier version that had more to do with *Diamond Dogs*. It had a different mix and Jason Cooper from the Cure played drums. It's darker, it's a little sloppier and less polished, the vocals are for the most part the same but it's a completely different mix.

'Thursday's Child' wasn't on it; it was just a shorter record. David took it back and listened to it and said, 'No, it needs to be more polished and I want different drums on it and I want fretless bass.'"

Of course, it would be fascinating to hear the original, rejected album, particularly since the actual album we have now sounds strangely unrealised. There are some cheesy and tinny synth beats, and some of the arrangements are doleful, lacking the snap of *Earthling*, the out-of-control jumble of *Tin Machine*, or the sheer finesse of *Let's Dance*. Bowie's final choice of songs for the album was a conservative one. Edgier and crankier material, such as the excellent instrumental '1917' (a perfect opener to the album surely?), 'We Shall Go To Town' and 'No One Calls', were left off the album, along with the chipper, Brit-popesque, 'We All Go Through'. However, all four tracks are available as bonus tracks in the subsequent reissues of the album.

Reservations aside, there is still something intriguing about *hours....* On many of the tracks, Bowie appears moody, spiteful and bitter. Although he professes that they were in no way autobiographical, they still carry an autobiographical or at least biographical weight. It's an album of middle-aged angst and alienation for his imaginary middle-aged audience. More so than the two albums that followed, (*Heathen* and *Reality*), *hours...* reveals a man railing against the passing of time rather than ruefully reflected on and accepting his lot. As such, many of these songs have a spice and a sense of bitterness lacking in his later work.

After the recording and release of *hours...* an exhausted Reeves Gabrels left the Bowie camp to concentrate on his solo career. His 11-year stint with Bowie split opinion. To some he was more of the Eric Morecambe school of guitar playing ('I am playing all the right notes but not necessarily, in the right order') while to others he brought a spirit of rule-breaking which made for some thrilling experiments. On balance, not all of the work they did together was completely successful,

but what is certain is that Bowie had been rescued from the mire of crowd-pleasing expectation and had regained a sense of adventure.

hours... was the first release by a major artists to be made available as a download. His subscription-based official website, Bowienet, was state-of-the-art and fun; Bowie himself appearing in web chats and in his Blog. Although the music on *hours...* was not especially adventurous, Bowie the icon was the first to realise the powerful nature of the Internet, and how it would revolutionise music. At the time, he would be criticised for diversifying and diluting his brand with unproven technology in an unseemly bid to make money. Today, with the complete revolution of the music industry and how music is listened to and acquired, Bowie seems, once again, to be so far ahead of the curve as to be seer-like.

With a new sound, came a new look: Bowie had long hair for the first time in almost 30 years, the spiky, piercing orange of the previous two years replaced by a shaggy mane of hair which, by the time of his Glastonbury performance of 2000, had grown out into almost *Man Who Sold The World*-era-proportions.

The triumph of his Glastonbury appearance, only the second of his career, was followed by the birth of his daughter Alexandria on August 15, 2000. At the age of 52, Bowie was a dad again and despite the gloom of the new album he seemed to be as happy and as settled as he had ever been at any time in his life. The feeling among many of his fans was that his career was now in a slow, but graceful downward curve. His last five studio albums had averaged around a million sales worldwide, respectable enough but the days of big sales and massive critical acceptance seemed long gone. But with Bowie, take nothing for granted.

THURSDAY'S CHILD
(Bowie/Gabrels)
'Throw me tomorrow, now that I've really got a chance,' quivers Bowie, the boy

who cried wolf, the arch dissembler, now all humanized and, well, just a bit sad? The first single, 'Thursday's Child', immediately sets the tone for most of the album – the spirit, if not weak, is in need of a lift. The contrast with the supercharged opener to the previous album, 'Little Wonder, couldn't be starker. Yet the melody is gorgeous, the slow beat sexy, and the hook: 'Monday, Tuesday, Wednesday born, I was' one of Bowie's best earworms. At one stage the song was penciled in as a cross-over vehicle for Bowie with R and B superstars TLC. Bowie cribbed the song's title from Ertha Kitt's autobiography.

SOMETHING IN THE AIR
(Bowie/Gabrels)
Undoubtedly one of the strongest songs on the CD, this is the confession of a man who has fallen out of love with the world, with himself, and with his partner. There's nothing left but empty despair, resignation and uncontrollable, angry sadness. 'Lived with the best times/Let with the worst. I've danced with you too long,' sings Bowie, before building up to a brilliant crescendo of showboating singing, his voice sweeping upwards to end this anguished song like a wounded animal. Another excellent Bowie song, albeit one destined for relative obscurity. A different, darker version of the track, remixed and remade by Mark Plati, and now including Mike Garson's piano, can be found on the *American Psycho Soundtrack* (Koch Records, 2000).

SURVIVE
(Bowie/Gabrels)
hours... continues with the third excellent song in a row. 'Survive' has a lovely melody; Reeves Gabrels, nothing if not a musician with astonishingly eclectic tastes, reins in all his outré instincts to pick out a poetic melody on lead and 12-string guitar for this tale of memory and regret: 'Beatle Boys/All Snowy White/Razzle dazzle every night/Wish I'd sent a valentine/I love you.' The second single off the album, it reached number 28 in the UK Charts.

IF I'M DREAMING MY LIFE
(Bowie/Gabrels)
The main problems with *hours...* only really reveal themselves about a third of the way into the album: the subject matter is repetitive and the pacing (mid-tempo and slightly foot-dragging) makes for a listless listening experience. It's now that Bowie's attempt to empathise with fellow mid-life crises-sufferers begin to ring slightly hollow. The music, which harks back to some of the less interesting Tin Machine forays into sixties pastiche, also fails to impress.

SEVEN
(Bowie/Gabrels)
The doleful pace continues with this pretty, acoustic song, which was re-recorded at a late stage in the production of the album to replace a much more up-tempo and commercial version. Building from a busker-like opening and a George-Harrisonesque guitar line from Gabrels, Bowie's sings, 'The Gods forgot they made me/So I forgot them too.' A minor UK hit in the summer of 2000, reaching number 32.

WHAT'S REALLY HAPPENING?
(Bowie/Gabrels/Grant)
In late 1998, Bowie's official website, Bowienet, ran a competition challenging fans to write a set of lyrics to a Bowie/Gabrels composition. The original song was posted with Bowie la-la-la-ing through the melody. While it would be rather cruel to suggest that la-las might have been a better choice than the lyric penned by the eventual winner (fan Alex Grant), it is nevertheless puzzling why these rather self-consciously Bowiesque lyrics won the day. 'Abstract' and 'non-linear' (to quote some of Bowie's favourite mid-eighties' phrases) they might be, but they do ultimately read like the sort of slightly contrived words Bowie penned circa *Never Let Me Down*. Perhaps the real issue for Alex (and the hundreds of other would-be Bowie lyricists, reportedly including members of the Cure!) is that the melody itself sounded like a rehash of ten different Bowie songs. A great idea badly executed.

THE PRETTY THINGS ARE GOING TO HELL
(Bowie/Gabrels)

There are some riffs that are so big and frightening they should only be let out after dark. For this song, Gabrels deliberately pared down his playing, aiming for what he called 'bonehead', which, according to Mark Plati, is 'the simplest Neanderthal part possible'. For the drum part, Plati records that, "Mike Levesque had been reading a biography of Keith Moon (*Dear Boy* by Tony Fletcher, available from this very publisher!)… so I think he saw an opening to rise to the occasion. I think he's the instrumental star of the track." The one genuinely rocking track on the CD, it never made it as a UK single, even though a video was put into production, though never completed featuring Bowie haunted by his past personae. Bowie re-used this idea twice. In 2003 Bowie starred in an advert for Vittel using the *Reality* track 'Never Get Old', the dad in a house full of former characters at breakfast time, and in 2013 when the original mannequins were used in the video for 'Love Is Lost'. The title, of course, references Iggy & The Stooges' 'Your Pretty Face Is Going To Hell' and Bowie's own 'Oh! You Pretty Things'. There seems to be no hope now for glam's original glitter kids: 'The pretty things are going to hell/They wore it out, but they wore it well.' The fourth and final class song on the album.

NEW ANGELS OF PROMISE
(Bowie/Gabrels)

With its vaguely Gabriel-esque melody (parts of 'New Angel' sound close to Peter Gabriel's 1982 song, 'San Jacinto'), this is Bowie breaking free from the singer-songwriter style of much of *hours…* to reach for some sort of dark theatricality. He doesn't quite pull it off, but the drumming by Sterling Campbell is worth the price of admission and, for the first time, Bowie lets his voice cut free and soar. On many of the other songs on the album, Bowie appears to 'under'-sing, and it's not often that charge can be made.

BRILLIANT ADVENTURE
(Bowie/Gabrels)

I'll let Bowie himself describe this one for you: "Brill is a luverly instrumental, again with Koto, that Reeves and I did in the front room in Bermuda."

THE DREAMERS
(Bowie/Gabrels)

By the end, *hours…* is well and truly running out of steam. Featuring some stentorian emoting, 'The Dreamers' sets out to make the sort of grand theatrical gesture only Bowie knows how to pull off, but it all gets lost in the translation and the music is underdeveloped, comprising as it does what sounds like a slowed-down version of the riff from T.Rex's 'Jeepster'. 'The Dreamers' appears to encapsulate all the failings of the album in general, sounding unfinished and in need of more production, and a sprinkle of fairy dust to make it come alive. A rather flat end to the album.

hours… Bonus Disc (Sony 2004 re-issue)

'Thursday's Child' (Rock Mix) (UK CD single); 'Thursday's Child' (*Omikron: The Nomad Soul* slower version) (Game only version); 'Something In The Air' (*American Psycho* Remix) (*American Psycho* Soundtrack); 'Survive' (Marius De Vries Mix) (UK CD single); 'Seven' (Demo Version) (UK CD single); 'Seven' (Marius De Vries Mix) (UK CD single); 'Seven' (Beck Mix #1) (UK CD single); 'Seven' (Beck Mix #2) (Virgin In House Promo CD); 'The Pretty Things Are Going To Hell' (Edit) (US Promo CD); 'The Pretty Things Are Going To Hell' (*Stigmata* Film Version) (*Stigmata* Soundtrack); 'The Pretty Things Are Going To Hell' (*Stigmata* faster actual film Version) (Film only version); 'New Angels Of Promise' (*Omikron: The Nomad Soul* different version) (Game only version); 'The Dreamers' (*Omikron: The Nomad Soul* longer version) (Game only version); '1917' ('Thursday's Child' UK CD Single); 'We Shall Go To Town' ('Thursday's Child' UK CD Single); 'We All Go Through' ('Thursday's Child' UK CD Single); 'No-one Calls' ('Thursday's Child' UK CD Single)

Bonus tracks – Produced by David Bowie and Reeves Gabrels.

Again, like *Outside*, and *Earthling*, *hours…* has been reissued and repackaged several times since the original release including a value-for-money 6-CD Sony box set of all three studio albums and their attendant outtakes and remixes. The Marius De Vries mix of 'Survive', which was used in single release and video, is particularly impressive as is the *Omikron* version of 'New Angels Of Promise'.

BOWIE AT THE BEEB – THE BEST OF THE BBC RADIO SESSIONS 1968-1972

*(Original UK Issue: EMI 5289582,
released 25 September 2000;
UK chart: 7 [Total weeks in chart: 4];
US chart: 181 [1])*

Bowie collectors waited many years for an official and complete release of the sessions recorded at the BBC and EMI didn't disappoint. The meaty bits are all on CD2, which captures the Spiders From Mars in their primal prime playing looser and more strident versions of the recorded classics. 'Starman' is perfect, and versions of 'Hang On To Yourself' and 'Moonage Daydream' pack a mighty punch. There's something instantly likeable about Mick Ronson's guitar licks, as friendly as the man himself. On 'Space Oddity', 'I'm just a rocket man' is a rather cheeky little swipe at Elton, then in the charts with a song not wholly unconnected thematically with Bowie's 1969 hit!

CD1 captures the developing talent as opposed to the fully-fledged rock God, and as a result is rather less essential. However, 'Karma Man', featuring the Tony Visconti Orchestra and 'Let Me Sleep Beside You' are clear pointers to future glories. Also included is a very early version of 'The Width Of A Circle' with the early lyric 'And I looked and frowned and looked again at me', subsequently rewritten for the actual studio recording.

A limited edition third disc captures an intimate Bowie performance from 2000 at the BBC Radio Theatre. Played in front of a select gathering of the Bowienet Brethren, plus sundry celeb Bowie fans, most of whom, you can bet your bottom dollar, didn't queue for Tin Machine tickets all night back in 1989, or dial for three solid days on the credit card hotline when the *Sound + Vision* tour was announced, or buy three different versions of *Reality* for that matter, it's a disappointing affair, the weaknesses of the contemporary Bowie all too apparent. Of course, it must have been thrilling to see him in such an intimate environment, and the fact that Bowie treated his hardcore fans to exclusive concerts is to be applauded. But, although the career-spanning repertoire from the gig is obviously stronger than on either CDs 1 or 2, the performances lack the elemental power of the earlier Bowie. It's all much too polished and perfectly played, and the arrangements on the likes of 'Ashes To Ashes' and 'Always Crashing In The Same Car' are bereft of the strategically elemental weirdness of the originals.

CD 1: 'In The Heat Of The Morning', 'London Bye Ta Ta', 'Karma Man', 'Silly Boy Blue', ''Let Me Sleep Beside You', 'Janine', 'Amsterdam', 'God Know's I'm Good', 'The Width Of A Circle', 'Unwashed And Somewhat Slightly Dazed', 'Cygnet Committee', 'Memory Of A Free festival', 'Wild Eyed Boy From Freecloud', 'Bombers', 'Looking For A Friend', 'Almost Grown', 'Kooks', 'It Ain't Easy'.
CD 2: 'The Supermen', 'Eight Line Poem', 'Hang On To Yourself', 'Ziggy Stardust', 'Queen Bitch', 'Waiting For The Man', 'Five Years', 'White Light/White Heat', 'Moonage

Daydream', 'Hang On To Yourself',
'Suffragette City', 'Ziggy Stardust', 'Starman',
'Space Oddity', 'Changes', 'Oh! You Pretty
Things', 'Andy Warhol', 'Lady Stardust',
'Rock'n'Roll Suicide'.
Extra Disc: BBC
CD 3: 'Wild Is The Wind', 'Ashes To Ashes',
'Seven', 'This Is Not America', 'Absolute
Beginners', 'Always Crashing In The Same
Car', 'Survive', 'Little Wonder', 'Man Who
Sold The World', 'Fame', 'Stay', 'Hallo
Spaceboy', 'Cracked Actor', 'I'm Afraid Of
Americans', 'Let's Dance'.

TOY

*(Recorded 2000. Original UK Issue:
None. Internet leak, 20 March 2011)*

Toy, originally recorded in 2000, was leaked
online 11 years later, and came as an
unexpected treat at a time many
commentators predicted no more music from
Bowie ever again. It may not be the final
version of the album, or the correct track list
and running order, but it sounds mixed and
ready to go. Quizzed about the album's
sudden appearance, Bowie's office refused
to comment.

Mark Plati who worked on the album as co-
producer and bandleader, told me in 2003:
"*Toy* was recorded in New York. We
rehearsed most of the tunes that would
make up the album at the same time we
were rehearsing for the Glastonbury gigs, in
May 2000. The concept was to make a
record like they used to back in the day –
we'd rehearse the songs really well, then go

into a studio and track them as a full band,
capturing for the most part the energy of the
a live performance – as opposed to the
piecemeal process that most people now
associate with record making. The idea was
to keep it loose, fast, and not clean things
up too much or dwell on perfection, and so
we ended up tracking thirteen songs in
around nine days."

'Uncle Floyd' later reworked as 'Slip Away' for
2002's *Heathen* album, opens the album.
This version is just as strong as the later
version and, in fact, is even quirkier with
Bowie's stylophone more to the fore. Next up
is 'Afraid', again, later reworked for *Heathen*.
This power-pop version is arguably superior
and would have made good singles material.
"At the time, David was reading a book by
Andrew Loog Oldham called *Stoned* where he
described locking up Jagger and Richards
until they came up with a decent tune." says
Plati. "So… I sent David off to the lounge in
the Looking Glass Studios, and told him to
stay there until he was done! Of course, we
were just kidding… sort of (he did stay there
until he was done). The third Bowie newie is
the title track 'Toy (Your Turn To Drive)'.

The rest of the album comprises re-workings
of pre-fame Bowie songs, relatively unknown
outside Bowie's hard-core fans. A few have
seen the light of day as Bowie B-sides to
later singles such as the lovely 'Conversation
Piece' but there are some complete scoops,
such as 'Hole In The Ground' originally
demoed in 1970. Best of the lot is 'Let Me
Sleep Beside You', possibly his first classic
pop song, originally recorded way back in
1967, now given an extra frisson as the then
53- year-old singer revisits this coming of
age love song.

Toy is a perfectly fine Bowie album, which
begs the question, why wasn't it officially
released in the first place? At the time Bowie
spoke of 'scheduling conflicts' which can, of
course, cover a multitude of sins, but there's
no reason to doubt Bowie's statement at the
time. Also, with Bowie and Visconti back as
friends and as collaborators (Visconti
arranged the strings on this album), it is, of

course, highly reasonable that Bowie wanted a full-bloodied collaboration with Visconti and simply went off the idea. It wouldn't be the first time that Bowie had abandoned projects after all. Another possibility is that his then record label, Virgin, had a listen and didn't consider an album with 11 remakes of obscure tracks to be the right sort of new product at a time when Bowie was still having hit singles. Bowie moved to Columbia just a year after *Toy* was scheduled. And of course, one might suspect, there may have been logistical problems in securing the publishing on such a disparate range of early music. But it's certainly no secret that *Toy* was intended as a bona fide Bowie release, and it marked a significant change of attitude from Bowie towards his very earliest recordings. In the reissue campaigns since the eighties, none of his pre-*Space Oddity* material has ever been deemed worthy of inclusion as part of the official Bowie oeuvre. *Toy* seems to indicate a willingness by Bowie to look back, find merit in, and attempt to improve upon the originals, in the same way that Brian Wilson did with *Smile*, and Kate Bush with two of her albums, *The Sensual World* and *The Red Shoes*. The hope is that one day, Bowie will green-light an official and final version of album.

Possible tracklisting: 'Uncle Floyd', 'Afraid', 'Baby Loves That Way', I Dig Everything', 'Conversation Piece', 'Let Me Sleep Beside You', 'Toy (Your Turn To Drive)', 'Hole In The Ground', 'Shadow Man', 'In The Heat Of The Morning', 'You've Got A Habit Of Leaving', 'Silly Boy Blue', 'Lisa Jane', 'London Boys'.

ALL SAINTS: COLLECTED INSTRUMENTALS 1977-1999

(Original UK Issue: EMI 533 0452, released 23 July 2001)

Being a David Bowie fan isn't quite the same as being a member of a secret cult or new religious movement, but those who really do have 'The Bowies' bad often possess something akin to the blind devotion and unrelenting zeal of the newly converted. Bowie fans feel the need to proselytise, and are mightily aggrieved when they met with stout resistance. Having got past the defence with 'Let's Dance' or 'Ziggy Stardust', and then having played them a few of the album tracks, one of the ways to really confuse any potential convert would be to play them *All Saints*. Sixteen instrumentals by who? Who apart from those in the know would even associate these weirdly brilliant instrumentals with the man who duetted with Mick Jagger? Yet these instrumentals reveal a versatility which confirms Bowie's greatness.

Although there's nothing on *All Saints* that we haven't heard before (and the absence of *Low*'s opener, 'Speed Of Life', is a major quibble), this collection, which runs from the dark menace of 'Warszawa' (not technically an instrumental, featuring as it does Bowie's invented language) through to the Zen-like beauty of 'Brilliant Adventure', is compelling listening. An essential purchase, and proof that Bowie is not just another rock'n'roll star....

In 2014 the noted drummer Dylan Howe, son of Yes guitarist Steve Howe, released an album of jazz interpretations of Bowie instrumentals called *Subterranean: New Designs On Bowie's Berlin*, a thought-provoking record, meandering, atmospheric and technically adroit, though most fans would be hard pressed to recognise them, even after listening to this album and *All Saints* back to back.

Track Listing: 'A New Career In A New Town', 'V-2 Schneider', 'Abdulmajid', 'Weeping Wall', 'All Saints', 'Art Decade', 'Crystal Japan', 'Brilliant Adventure', 'Sense Of Doubt', 'Moss Garden', 'Neuköln', 'The Mysteries', 'Ian Fish UK Heir', 'Subterraneans', 'Warszawa', 'Some Are' (Philip Glass).

The following instrumentals are new to this guide:

ABDULMAJID

The exact date of this instrumental has never been revealed, but to these ears it seems to have originated during the *"Heroes"* sessions rather than the *Low* era. It was originally included in the now deleted reissue of *"Heroes"* by Ryko. Named in honour of Bowie's then fiance Iman Muhammid Abdulmajid.

ALL SAINTS

(Bowie/Eno)

Another short instrumental and well worth inclusion as a bonus track. Bowie and Eno construct an aboriginal sci-fi apocalypse with synthesizers! Sounds impossible, but it works wonderfully with the synth aping a didgeridoo.

CRYSTAL JAPAN

All is order and tranquil in this ambient instrumental track originally recorded in 1979, then used in a Japanese Saki advert which featured The Thin White Duke himself. It was released as a single in Japan in 1980 and as the B-side of the 'Up The Hill Backwards' single in 1981.

SOME ARE

(Philip Glass)

From Glass' puzzlingly jaunty, neo-Romantic orchestral version of *Low*, the original Bowie track was included on Ryko's now deleted reissue of the *Low* album in 1991. Incidentally, both *Low* and *"Heroes"* symphonies were reissued as a double CD by Decca in 2003 and are well worth investigating.

HEATHEN

*(**Original UK Issue: Columbia 5082222 Released 10 June 2002; UK chart: 5 [Total weeks in chart: 18]; US CD: Song 86630 US chart: 14 [10]**)*

Although writing and recording for *Heathen* was underway before the attack on the Twin Towers on September 11, 2001, there is no doubt that the epoch-defining events of that sunny early-autumn morning resonates strongly throughout many of the songs. To all intents and purposes, Bowie was now a New Yorker, and most of the musicians he worked with were also based in and around the neighbourhood. This was a tragedy witnessed at first-hand, and inflicted on *his* people. "I think of David as a New Yorker and I don't think you can help but be affected on many levels by such a thing happening in your town," says Mark Plati. "After all, even when you switched off CNN you'd still see the diverted traffic, hear the sirens of the emergency vehicles and the rumble of huge trucks carting away debris, the fighter jets patrolling overhead… and, you could smell the

fires burning for months afterward, day and night, wondering what exactly you were taking in with each breath. There were constant reminders of death just walking down the street. I don't think David would set out to write a '9/11 Album' or anything like that, but I think in *Heathen* you can feel the overall mood of where we all were during those times."

Bowie was back working with his old friend and producer Tony Visconti. Significantly, it was the first record to be recorded after the birth of his daughter, Alexandria, in 2000. And, as ever, Bowie responded directly to his new environment and his status as a fifty-something parent. The album's site of production also influenced the tone of Bowie's writing in a crucial way. Much of

Heathen was written at Allaire Studios, Shokan, situated in the mountains in New York State. Paul Verna wrote, "It's hard to imagine a recording environment more physically beautiful and more conducive to meditation and creativity than Allaire." Bowie would go on to buy land in the studio's vicinity. "He would go somewhere in the mornings when he was writing these songs," Visconti told writer David Simpson in 2003. "You could see he was really struggling with questions. After a few weeks I said: 'It seems like you're addressing God himself.'"

The reinstatement of Visconti ratcheted up expectations. Without wishing to belittle Visconti's achievements as producer, it seems that his role on a Bowie record is less to do with getting the most faithful or most technically perfect possible sound, and more with getting the best out of Bowie creatively. Visconti is not just a rock producer, in the same way that Bowie is not just a rock singer. Both are able to bring all sorts of outré musical styles and techniques into the recording process from outside of rock, and Visconti seems to be the perfect producer in terms of creating an ideal environment within which Bowie can flourish. Visconti also seems to be able to get the best sounding Bowie vocal of all his producers. His masterpiece is probably the astonishing vocal on "Heroes" but, on *Heathen*, he comes close, capturing that big, full, booming voice perfectly.

Although dissimilar in musical style and overall tone, the album that *Heathen* most resembles is *Station To Station*. Both works seek to make sense out of disorder. In *Station To Station*, the disorder is in Bowie's mind; in *Heathen*, it's all around him. *Heathen*, like Bowie's best work, seems to pick up on the just-breaking, the secretly articulated, the new. On some albums, Bowie's astonishing music does this, predicting trends or weaving the unusual or the disparate. On *Heathen*, Bowie seems to be predicting a more brutal, more inflexible, more dangerous and more ideological world, a world in which dogma replaces discussion.

Heathen also had one of the strongest cover designs of his career courtesy of Jonathan Barnbrook. Bowie is re-imagined as the alien-about-town, dapper, yet totally otherworldly, eyes burning into our souls like one of Wyndham's *Midwich Cuckoos*. A series of defaced works of art and literature occur throughout the booklet, obliquely alluding to themes of censorship and 'un-art', and to cultural ignorance between East and West. In many of these images, religious icons are depicted as sightless, eyes scratched out, in the same way that the lyrics of the album are annulled too, struck through, deleted.

The album reached number five in the British charts and was the first Bowie album to be nominated for the Mercury Music Prize. It was also critically well-received; despite the tiresome comparisons to an album it scarcely resembled (*Scary Monsters*). The only thing stopping *Heathen* being a classic Bowie album was that it wandered, unnecessarily from the main theme, mainly through the inclusion of three cover versions which made the album overlong and diluted its power. That said, *Heathen* is an album that should be in every Bowie fan's collection.

SUNDAY

A brave, uncompromising opener (as if *1.Outside* had begun with 'The Motel', a song which 'Sunday' resembles in tone and pacing), and a masterstroke. A disquieting refrain picked out by guitar establishes the reflective, edgy tone of the album, accompanied by a wash of unparticularised vocal, almost Gregorian chant-like, and Bowie's startling imagery: "Nothing remains, we could run when the rain slows /Look for the cars or signs of life." Bowie told us that all the lyrics to *Heathen* were written pre-9/11. If so, they and the music eerily predict the mood of fear that followed that epic event. The moment at three minutes 45 seconds when Bowie's vocal soars free for the final line of the song, 'Everything has changed', and the band explodes into life is one of the best moments on any Bowie album to date.

CACTUS
(Black Francis)
The inclusion of three non-Bowie originals could have been taken as an indication that Bowie was short of new ideas. Not so; although only this, a cover of an album track on the Pixies' *Surfer Rosa* album, 'Cactus', is of undoubted quality. It is a superb alternative rock song, excellently framed and Bowieised for *Heathen*, and is the only track on the album that actually sounds a little like *Scary Monsters*. Bowie was known as long-time fan of the band, covered the song 'Debaser' during his *Tin Machine* years, and even brought Frank Black on to duet with him on 'Fashion' for his 50th Birthday bash at Madison Square Garden in 1997.

SLIP AWAY

A genuine Bowie classic, this possesses the album's most beautiful melody. Tony Levin's fretless bass provides just the right note of retro-activity as Bowie's song of nostalgia unfolds, building to the winning interpolation of 'Twinkle Twinkle Little Star' in the choruses, and Bowie's stylophone solo at the end. 'Slip Away' is that sort of epically-wrought melody we perhaps hadn't heard since *Station To Station*. Lurking in the sonics are spacey keys and weird refrains: think Blur's Bowiesque 'Strange News From Another Star'. In the long tradition of not releasing his best songs as singles, an album track only.

SLOW BURN

There is just something too clone-like for this to be totally successful. Although undeniably a fine song, the bass line and Pete Townshend's guitar parts are so close in style to *"Heroes"*, that they betray a lack of confidence, as if Bowie wanted to press all the correct response buttons in his recidivist brethren and say, "Look, I'm back, and I sound like the old Bowie, everything's all right". The fact that this song wasn't even a staple of the *Heathen* tour perhaps indicates that even Bowie himself doesn't rate the song too highly. Released as a promo-only single in the UK, in Germany an official CD single release saw the inclusion of four interesting curios: 'Wood Jackson' and 'When The Boys Come Marching Home', both *Heathen* outtakes, re-make of 'You've Got A Habit Of Leaving', and a version of 'Shadow Man', a hitherto unreleased song from the early seventies.

AFRAID

In his early seventies glam pomp, riffs were a commodity hardly in short supply: 'Rebel Rebel', 'Panic In Detroit', 'The Jean Genie' – some of the finest air guitar in history. In more recent years, Bowie had appeared increasingly uninterested in the concept of the rock riff, preferring more esoteric areas of the musical landscape. 'Afraid', however, sees him back at his riff-rocking best. Quite why this was overlooked for single release is mystifying. Bowie's vocal delivery is deliberately pitched to be uncertain, modulated to be, well, afraid.

I'VE BEEN WAITING FOR YOU

(Neil Young)

One of the few slightly flat moments on *Heathen* comes with this ballsy cover of a track originally recorded for Young's eponymous album of 1969. According to Johnny Rogan, the original is a "fantasy vision of a perfect woman, blessed with life-enhancing qualities". Bowie's hard-hitting version denudes the song of its original subtlety, and, although it's a perfectly fine enough track (with the Foo Fighters' Dave Grohl guesting) it should have been left as a bonus track or download-only tempter.

I WOULD BE YOUR SLAVE

With Bowie, attempts to read any autobiographical import into his lyrics are always deeply dangerous. It's also quite uncommon for Bowie to sound genuinely emotional, the point is that we are meant to admire the artifice and the distance rather than empathise with any fellow feeling. But on 'I Would Be Your Slave', Bowie appears genuinely and uncomfortably naked and bare. The music too is unique – a drum'n'bass ballad and the lovely orchestral arrangement make this one of *Heathen*'s best songs.

I TOOK A TRIP ON A GEMINI SPACESHIP

(Legendary Stardust Cowboy)

Visitors to http://www.stardustcowboy.com/, an unofficial fan site for the artist who goes by the nickname of 'The Ledge', can see a picture taken in 2002 of the original Mr Stardust with David Bowie beaming to camera. It's a little piece of rock history, since Bowie very loosely based his alter ego, Ziggy Stardust, on the career of one of the dottiest men in pop history. Bowie's remake of 'Gemini Spaceship' gives it the full techno workout, and if that isn't the sound of Bowie's saxophone making a comeback! Weirdly successful, although, again, at odds with the central theme of the album.

5:15 THE ANGELS HAVE GONE

One of the features of *Heathen* is the variety of different musical styles Bowie tackles. Here there's a very subtle reggae feel to what is arguably the record's centrepiece. 5:15 was the time the first train left central London in the morning to take the all-night revellers home. It was also, of course, the title of a Who song from1973's *Quadrophenia*. Bowie dedicated this song to the recently departed John Entwistle at the 2002's Summer Meltdown Festival, which he curated. The line, 'We never talk anymore' is sung with such passion, such conviction, and such sadness – as if a million broken relationships have been encoded in four simple words.

EVERYONE SAYS 'HI'

Scratch away the smiley surface, and this is the album's saddest song, dealing with bereavement, and how one copes. Here, the song's protagonist can't quite accept a death of a relative or close friend, so deludes him/herself that they're simply away on an extended vacation. Featuring the welcome, if brief, return of the redoubtable Carlos Alomar, it has been speculated that the song is, in fact, about George Harrison, who had died towards the end of 2001, and there's an echo of Harrison's pragmatism in the sincerity of its unpretentious lyrics.

A BETTER FUTURE

With its cheesy melody, 'A Better Future' could have come straight from *Never Let Me Down*. Its half-hearted vocal set against some very clangy mid-eighties-style synth effects, quite why this very slight and actually quite irritating song made the album at all is a puzzle.

HEATHEN (THE RAYS)

A companion piece to 'Sunday', the album's opener, the album's title track is another highlight. The faintly militaristic drum figure brings a processional imagery to the song, while the 'Warszawa'-like synthesizer ending closes the album on a desolate note. Written before 9/11, the opening lines are nevertheless quite chilling; "Steel on the skyline, sky made of glass/made for a real world/all things must pass [a further Harrison reference]." "It was quite spine-tingling to realize how close those lyrics came," Bowie told *Jam!*'s Rachel Sklar. "There are some key words in there that really just freak me out." Live, the track, if anything, gained in emotive power; closing the official set, Bowie would leave the stage, arm on Gail Ann Dorsey's shoulder, in an almost tribalistic gesture – a mixture of needing support and giving support, while the audience would clap the beat of the song's closing section as each band member left the stage.

OTHER EDITIONS:

Following its initial release, *Heathen* was repacked and re-branded as a limited edition 2CD version containing 'Sunday' (Moby Remix), 'A Better Future' (remix by Air), 'Conversation Piece' (written 1969, recorded 1970, re-recorded 2002) and 'Panic In Detroit' (outtake from a 1979 recording). An SACD 5.1 mix of the album included four bonus tracks: 'When the Boys Come Marching Home', 'Wood Jackson' (originally a bonus tack on the Japanese release of the original CD), 'Conversation Piece' and 'Safe'.

REALITY

(Original UK Issue: Columbia 5125552, Released 15 September 2003; UK chart: 3 [Total weeks in chart: 4]; US CD: Sony; US chart: 29 [4])

Released just 15 months after *Heathen*, *Reality*, again co-produced by Tony Visconti, is now destined to be a diverting, sometimes compelling, but ultimately frustrating follow-up. The album lacks a big idea or central theme to hold the songs together. For Bowie, this was the whole point of the writing exercise. The man who had drawn inspiration from global culture had pushed his mind and body to the extremes; so inspired was he by travel, by an unwillingness to settle down, that his evident decision to do just that in his own patch seemed almost like another of those sudden, unexpected oblique strategies, like going soul in 1974, moving to Berlin in 1976 or forming Tim Machine in 1988. "I just wanted it to be songs that were written at home, where I live," Bowie said in 2004. "That was the only line I gave myself: 'Here I am, at home. What songs come to me, just living around town, doing what I do, going out with the family and being on the streets?' It was that kind of feel, and it was really no more complicated than that."

If Bowie was happy 'kicking around on a piece of ground in his hometown' to paraphrase Pink Floyd, he was also comfortable in the musical palette of a basically organic guitar and piano-based sound. Bowie had once said of the contributions of his studio musicians "as long as it has some sort of essential disharmony about it, it stays in!" – treasuring the offbeat, the accidental, the surprising. But this was Bowie speaking in 1976. By the time of *Reality*, everything had the feel of being perfectly played by excellent musicians.

Reality was described by its creator as 'thrusty', and the sound of the album is certainly less dense and easier to unpack that the considerably more mysterious *Heathen*. However, *Reality* sounds underwritten; of the 11 songs, a credible case for only three or four can be made as matching the standard of the previous album.

For the first time in Bowie's career, the reviews were more supportive and effusive than the record itself merited. Once again we were told that this was Bowie's best record since *Scary Monsters*; the public, however, voted with their wallets, keeping them firmly shut. Debuting at number three in the UK charts, within a month it had sunk without a trace. It did, however, sell in sufficient numbers to be certified Gold (sales of 100,000). In the USA however, *Reality* met the same fate as all his other records for the past ten years with the exception of *Heathen*, which was to be almost ignored by mainstream America.

Bowie, however, was signed up for a long world tour, with dates stretching well into the summer of 2004. "If I tell you it's a T-shirt-and-jeans-type show, believe me, that's what it is… If you like the idea of me just singing my songs, you're going to be thrilled." The *A Reality* tour was that beast Bowie had thought he had slain back in 1990; it was, in all-but-name, a greatest hits show. *Heathen* and *Reality* provided around a third of the tour's repertoire but there would be 'Let's Dance', 'All The Young Dudes', 'Rebel Rebel', 'Ashes To Ashes', 'Fame', 'Ziggy Stardust' and "Heroes" too. The David Bowie tour of 2003/2004 wasn't art; it was entertainment, and, for most, there was nothing wrong with that. "All I'm concerned about is that I continue to have fun with my profession. I enjoy playing concerts. I'm happy that I mean something to the people who come to my concerts. Of course I suspect that I will give up playing concerts as soon as my bodily functions no longer allow it."

Bowie had been experiencing chest pains for some years before a major medical event ended the *A Reality* tour in June. It is understood that he underwent a heart bypass operation. After surgery, Bowie returned to New York to be with his family and to convalesce.

From June 2004, the world knows very little indeed about David Bowie. To all intents and purposes he stopped talking to the press completely around 2006. His official website, just five years earlier a mine of chattering gossip and information, would go silent for extended periods. Bowie himself made the occasional live performance, guesting with Alicia Keyes, David Gilmour and Arcade Fire. He also took on a small role playing Nikola Tesla in *The Prestige*. He lent his voice to a character in *Spongebob Square Pants*, and appeared as himself in *Extras*, a comedy vehicle for his friend Ricky Gervias.

With no interviews, several in the media began speculating that Bowie's health was much worse than anyone had thought, with various rumours doing the rounds (rumours which, as they are rumours, will not be repeated here). When Bowie was seen, it would be at some charity event in New York, or just going about his daily business. He would be present as the proud dad at the premier of Duncan Jones' sci-fi film *Moon*. For a man now well into his sixties, Bowie looked perfectly well, still with a full head of hair, stylish, a few more wrinkles perhaps but hardly the 'dead man walking' some had portrayed.

Bowie, it seemed, was happy being a dad, doing 'normal stuff' such as the school run, popping in for a cup of coffee and generally enjoying an extended stay away from being 'David Bowie'. By 2010, with no new music for seven years, speculation mounted that

Bowie had, in *reality*, retired, a graceful departure from public life, unannounced and unheralded. Then, quite by chance, in May 2010 an email arrived in Tony Visconti's in-box. It was David Bowie. But not *just* David Bowie. It was David Bowie armed with demos. Bowie was returning.

NEW KILLER STAR

If this had been released as a single 20 years earlier, it would certainly have gone top five. But how times have changed: such was the apparent lack of confidence in breaking a new Bowie single that the song was released as a DVD single only in the UK (complete with a cover of Sigue Sigue Sputnik's 'Love Missile F 1-11'!), thus disqualifying it from the charts. Again, it's too simplistic to call this a '9/11' song. That said, the very Bowieesque cosmic imagery and punning title suggests a fictionalised account of those events. What really carries the song though is the superb riff (with what sounds like synthesised Jew's Harp sound!) – the best bit of writing on the album, and it's a great live rock song to boot.

PABLO PICASSO

(Words & Music: Jonathan Richman)

A blast of Flamenco, and Bowie's rendition of Richman's snotty, adolescent song is out of the traps. Bowie's revved up version is a fine alt-rock version of Richman's early seventies song, and, like 'Cactus' on *Heathen*, a strategic blast of left-field weirdness before the main course of songwriting is served.

NEVER GET OLD

This defiantly silly rail against the passage of time perhaps needed an even funkier sheen *à la* 'Fashion' or 'Fame' to turn it into a classic. For most of us, this was the first taste of the new album, as seen in the clip of the song used in Bowie's amusing television commercial for Vittel. In 2004, the song reached number 47 in the UK charts in a new guise, 'Rebel Never Gets Old', a mash-up with 1974's classic 'Rebel Rebel'.

THE LONELIEST GUY

Tremulous of vocal, tremolo of guitar, minor of key, and doleful of imagery, this is the first of several miscalculations on *Reality*. Not even Mike Garson's beautifully-constructed rolling piano refrain can disguise the fact that, not only is the song average, but Bowie's vocal and lyric, which strive so self-consciously for some sort of heartfeltness, yet ultimately sound so hammy, would have been better left off the album. As music writer Alex Petridis succinctly put it: 'overcooked'.

LOOKING FOR WATER

An unusual track – partly one feels not fully realised – based around a funky descending guitar riff and a Motownesque stomp. Is Bowie giving us a clue that he's falling out of love with being 'David Bowie'?: 'But I lost God in a New York minute/ Don't know about you but my heart's not in it.'

SHE'LL DRIVE THE BIG CAR

Reality rallies with this piece of domestic reportage which brings back to mind the classic 'Repetition'. The music, folksy with blasts of harmonica, is affecting, and while this is hardly classic Bowie, it has shades of the quality of *Heathen*. 'Big Shaken Car', a mash-up of the track along with *Let's Dance*'s 'Shake It', was the winner of a 2004 Bowienet Competition.

DAYS

Undoubtedly pretty, this vaguely Harrisonesque track mines a very mainstream ore. In fact, the opening sounds like an acoustic version of Bryan Ferry's 'Slave To Love'.

FALL DOG BOMBS THE MOON

When is a protest song not a protest song? When it's a David Bowie song. Like 'Fantastic Voyage' and 'Loving The Alien' before it, 'Fall Dog…'encodes obliquely a view about world politics. Written as war broke out again between the US/UK coalition and Iraq, the song's protagonist ('goddam rich', 'cruel and smart' and with 'oil on his hands') bombs the moon (Islam's crescent moon speculates Bowie writer Nicholas Pegg). The world has degraded, greed rules and the reality of life is depthless and shapeless. The resigned, one-paced, though powerful music completes the mood of a man, perhaps, willing to give it all up.

TRY SOME, BUY SOME

(Words & Music: George Harrison)
Back in May 1979, Bowie hosted Radio 1's *Star Special*, a show which gave sundry famous rockers the opportunity to play some of their faves on air for a two-hour period. Notwithstanding the fact that playing three of your own tracks might be deemed to smack ever so slightly of self-promotion, it basically proved what we all had thought: Bowie had impeccable taste. About the only clunker, though, was this song, 'Try Some Buy Some', which he played as covered by Ronnie Spector. Bowie's dreary cover is unfortunately completely inessential, and by now we're worried that pop's personality changer has got back into his TARDIS and is heading back to 1984. This really could have come from *Tonight*.

REALITY

This was apparently the first song written for the album. "The basis [of reality] is more an all-pervasive influence of contingency than a defined structure of absolutes," was Bowie's candid assessment. We get his drift, mostly – in this whacky postmodern world of ours, don't start looking for certainties, just roll with the flow of the accidental and you'll be fine. Or possibly not. This slab of hard rock may well be what Bowie had in mind when he let slip that his new album would be 'thrusty'. In fact, this is the only up-tempo song on the album, and very Tin Machinesque (but without the crucial element of strategic weirdness that is Reeves Gabrels in a kilt).

BRING ME THE DISCO KING

Originally recorded with producer Nile Rodgers for *Black Tie White Noise*, Bowie had been tinkering with this song for a decade. This slow-paced, jazzy version is actually inferior to the creepier, symphonic electronica version on the *Underworld* Soundtrack (Lakeshore Records, 2003) which features Maynard James Keenan and John Frusciante.

OTHER EDITIONS:

One of the most irritating features of *Reality* was that no sooner did we fork out £15 for one version, another slightly different version came out and had to be bought, meaning that many fans had broken the £50 mark on just one release. As a promotional strategy, it flailed because *Reality* didn't regain momentum, despite the constant gigging and promotion. Of note are the following: a Bonus Disc Edition featured the songs 'Fly', 'Queen Of All The Tarts (Overture)' and a new version of 'Rebel Rebel'. A tour edition of the album included a DVD of a live performance of *Reality*, plus a (not at all good) cover of 'Waterloo Sunset' (by the Kinks). Finally, in 2004 *Reality* was issued in Germany featuring a bonus disc containing versions of the Bowie mash-up, 'Rebel Never Gets Old' (see the entry for 'Never Get Old' for more details).

not difficult to see why. Originally a live FM radio broadcast from the Civic Auditorium, Santa Monica, on October 20, 1972, this is a must for serious Bowie collectors. Bowie and the Spiders give a fine performance and this album trashes *Ziggy Stardust: The Motion Picture* in terms of overall musicality if not historical significance. The album was originally released by Bowie's ex-management company Mainman on Trident International in 1994 before its officially-endorsed release by EMI 14 years later. The Trident version is long-since unavailable but contains what is presumably the full show; the EMI version, although beautifully packaged, edits out much of the on-mic interaction between Bowie and the audience, thus making it a less authentic document of what is now widely regarded as one of Bowie's best live albums.

Full track listing: 'Introduction', 'Hang On To Yourself', 'Ziggy Stardust', 'Changes', 'The Supermen', 'Life On Mars?', 'Five Years', 'Space Oddity', 'Andy Warhol', 'My Death', 'The Width Of A Circle', 'Queen Bitch', 'Moonage Daydream', 'John I'm Only Dancing', 'Waiting For The Man', 'The Jean Genie', 'Suffragette City', 'Rock'n'Roll Suicide'.

SANTA MONICA '72/ LIVE SANTA MONICA '72

(Original UK CD: Trident International: Golden Years GY 002; US CD: Griffin Music 357 [Limited Edition]; Released 25 April 1994; UK chart: 74. Second UK release: EMI B001FAZYOQ. Released 30 June 2008; UK Chart: 61)

Before its official release, this was probably the most sought-after Bowie bootleg, and it's

VH1 STORYTELLERS

(UK CD:EMI B002984APW. Released 6 July 2009. UK Chart: 114)

David Bowie has been many things to many people; one of his less-discussed talents is his ability to talk. And talk. And talk a bit more. "David wants to get into people's heads a bit, and he's a talker," his friend the photographer Mick Rock said in 2003. "David would talk the fucking hind-leg off a donkey. You don't have to feed him too much to get him excited and buzzing. There are reams and reams of interviews and he always says something interesting. Most of these guys, with all due respect, are like photographers; they should get on with their fucking business and shut up."

With the possible exception of John Lennon and Pete Townshend, Bowie has given some of the best interviews in rock history. Chris Charlesworth, who would work as Bowie's press officer at RCA between 1978 and 1981, remembers interviewing Bowie for *Melody Maker* in 1976, in America. The revelation? Bowie was broke, completely brassic. "And so it went on, probably one of the best interviews I ever did and I barely needed to interrupt this flow of remarkable quotes, almost all of them worthy of headlines in themselves. No doubt about it – Bowie gives good interview."

It comes therefore as no surprise that given the chance to present a live set laced with anecdotes Bowie excels. Like an experienced after-dinner speaker his elocution is perfect, as is his timing on stories designed to raise a laugh – "Oh, the things I could tell you. You wouldn't believe the half of it!" – which they always do. We learn of the time he first met his close friend Marc Bolan painting his then manager's office, rummaging around for discarded seconds in the bins of Carnaby Street, and a hilarious anecdote from the glam period where Bowie is told by one Northern promotor that the sink doubled for the toilet: "My dear man, I'm not pissing in a sink", to which came the reply, "If it's good enough for Shirley Bassey, it's good enough for you." Bowie would also throw in more reflective recollections such a night out in Berlin when he saw a modelled recreation of the Berlin Wall torn down by tearful punks, or when Bowie's video collaborator quoted playwright David Mamet, saying: "No one going on a business trip would be missed if he never arrived." Most affecting was his retelling of his parlous mental state between 1974 and 1977, delivered with a certain

self-deprecation: "I was concerned with questions like, 'Do the dead interest themselves in the affairs of the living? Can I change the channel on my TV without using the clicker?'"

Recorded on August 23, 1999 at the Manhattan Center Studios for VH1 to a small audience of invitees and fan club members it appeared, on the surface at least, that Bowie was in the best of moods. Then 52, long of hair and wearing a grey hoody and big trainers, with a voice back to near its best. There's a shiver when he soars to hit the high notes on 'Life On Mars?' Songs from his then new album *hours…* are given faithful treatments. There is a storming version of Bowie's first solo single, 'Can' Help Thinking About Me'. Most of the songs are redesigned for the intimate setting with added acoustic guitar shadings, none more successfully than Bowie's icy neo-Ballardian tale of near suicide that was *Low*'s 'Always Crashing In The Same Car'.

The only moment of near discord comes when a throwaway remark about Tin Machine lyrics ("We won't even look at Tin Machine lyrics!") is met with a slightly frosty retort by fellow Tin Machiner Reeves Gabrels, "We can look at who wrote them". Gabrels left Bowie's band four days later and with that knowledge, one can feel a certain tension.

So, as a live album it's perfectly enjoyable, albeit without the vampyric edge of *David Live*, or the art-rock wildness of *Stage*. For the completists, it would be interesting to know how many 'Bowiedotes' were in fact edited out of the official release. A setlist included in the accompanying booklet indicates that a final song, 'The Pretty Things Are Going To Hell' was also due to be performed.

From today's perspective, it is a stark reminder of a time when Bowie was visible, talking and communicating, as happy to chat to fans online as to Chris Evans or Jonathan Ross. The only downside? Was Bowie demystifying himself? His subsequent decade-long absence from the media may suggest that he thought he was.

Tracklisting: CD: 'Life On Mars?', 'Rebel Rebel' (Truncated), 'Thursday's Child', 'Can't Help Thinking About Me', 'China Girl', 'Seven', 'Drive In Saturday', 'Word On A Wing'.

Disc 2: DVD : 'Life On Mars?', 'Rebel Rebel' (Truncated), 'Thursday's Child', 'Can't Help Thinking About Me', 'China Girl', 'Seven', 'Drive In Saturday', 'Word On A Wing', 'Survive'. Bonus Performances: 'Survive', 'I Can't Read', 'Always Crashing In The Same Car', 'If I'm Dreaming My Life'.

A REALITY TOUR

(UK CD: EMI B002984APW. Released 25 January 2010. UK Chart: 114)

Over six years after the actual shows came a double live CD. With David Bowie it is often very difficult to know the motivation for releases of new non-studio product. Dedicated followers of Bowie would have bought several bootlegs of the tour many years before this actual release. Serious fans called for an official release of Alan Yentob's 1975 film *Cracked Actor*, *The 1980 Floor Show* filmed in London in 1973 but never broadcast in the UK, or even a professionally-recorded date from the *Heathen* tour (for more information, see the 'In The Tin Can' section).

A Reality Tour, as an audio event, also came six years after the DVD release. There seemed no logic in its appearance at all; except for the fact that perhaps Bowie was planning something and did not want to give the impression in any way of a career in the past tense; anything out there to remind us that he was an active artist would do.

Like so many live albums, this is not a faithful record of an actual event but rather culled from two performances Bowie gave at The Point, Dublin, in November 2003. The opening (and rather good) harmonica-driven music used as the band took the stage is not present (and, to my knowledge, not available legally), while the running order, although broadly faithful, is compromised by the insertion of three bonus tracks at the end of the CD. Quite why these were not allotted their proper position in the running order seems illogical and careless.

The atmosphere is one of celebration and retrospection (the CD was stickered 'David Bowie's Greatest Hits Live!'). The playing is expert as one would expect and Bowie's mood is up. There's a snatch of a Beatles impersonation during 'Afraid', a hint of the Iggy drawl on 'Sister Midnight', unperformed since 1976 when it was a Bowie song, and 'Cactus' morphs very briefly into T. Rex's 'Get It On'. The most powerful tracks are those from *Heathen* and *Reality*; both 'The Loneliest Guy' and 'Bring Me The Disco King' with Mike Garson to the fore, improve on the studio originals, and there are fine versions of 'Sunday', 'Slip Away', and 'Heathen (The Rays)'.

However, when it comes to the actual hits themselves, Bowie's faithful versions have to compete with their histories. Take 'Fame' for example. The studio original and the live renditions in the seventies fizzed with the sense of new ground broken: the playing was urgent, the words sung by a young man who seemed to mean every syllable and the music, a new, intense fusion of rock, funk and synthetics, thrilled. Now, almost 30 years on, 'Fame', along with 'All The Young Dudes', 'Changes' and 'Ziggy Stardust', sound almost like cover versions of old rock standards rather than presentations of an artist's original work.

Perhaps this is overly harsh; on the previous tour to promote *Heathen*, one did sense that Bowie was present inside his music. That tour contained many very fine versions of tracks from *Low* and the band was more versatile and synthy, while the *A Reality* band was heavily-rock orientated. It always seems that the closer Bowie steps towards the synthesiser, the more exciting and the more ground-breaking his musical world becomes.

A Reality is simply good fun; anyone at the shows were given a long set and great memories but it was entertainment, not art. And some things never change; such as Bowie's incredible gift for getting dates, times and places wrong in his career in song introductions. On *A Reality* though there is a particularly telling piece of revisionism. Introducing an almost note-for-note version of his 1970 song 'The Man Who Sold The World', he tells the audience: "I still love this song a lot. I haven't done it for years and years, not until this tour actually, I'd left it out for many years and I'm glad I'm doing it again." Bowie had, in fact, performed the song on most dates from 1995 to 1997 and had even released this radically new interpretation as an A-sided single. But this was obviously in a different musical life; one which appeared to have no place in the Bowie world of 2003.

Tracklisting: CD 1: 'Rebel Rebel', 'New Killer Star', 'Reality', 'Fame' 'Cactus', 'Sister Midnight', (Bowie, Alomar, Iggy Pop), 'Afraid',

'All The Young Dudes', 'Be My Wife', 'The Loneliest Guy', 'The Man Who Sold The World', 'Fantastic Voyage', 'Hallo Spaceboy', 'Sunday', 'Under Pressure' (Bowie, Freddie Mercury, John Deacon, Brian May, Roger Taylor), 'Life On Mars?', 'Battle For Britain (The Letter)'.
CD 2: 'Ashes To Ashes', 'The Motel', 'Loving The Alien', 'Never Get Old', 'Changes', 'I'm Afraid Of Americans', "Heroes", 'Bring Me The Disco King', 'Slip Away', 'Heathen (The Rays)', 'Five Years', 'Hang On To Yourself', 'Ziggy Stardust', 'Fall Dog Bombs The Moon', 'Breaking Glass', 'China Girl'
Tracks 14–16 are not included in the concert video.
Digital download bonus tracks (iTunes): '5:15 The Angels Have Gone', 'Days'.

THE NEXT DAY

(UK CD: Iso/SonyB00AYHK7RU.
Released 11 March 2013. UK Chart: 1
[Total weeks in chart: 29] US Chart: 2
[Total weeks in chart: 10])

When David Bowie was photographed walking near his home in New York in October 2012, it was assumed that the anonymous figure in downbeat grey with a satchel and cap was wiling away his days in happy retirement. Few were aware that his man-bag carried sheets of lyrics and ideas for songs, and that he was actually on his way to work.

In the small hours of January 8, his 66th birthday, the fruits of Bowie's clandestine recording sessions with long-term producer Tony Visconti were, finally, heard. The beauteously downbeat 'Where Are We Now?' – the lead song released from a brand new album – became his biggest hit single since 'Absolute Beginners', way back in 1986.

The arrival of the new track was kept so secret that even his band members had no inkling. "I was so shocked when I woke up on the morning of his birthday and suddenly I had all these emails and Facebook had exploded," says Gail Ann Dorsey who contributed bass and backing vocals on the album. Never has a record by a major artist been made under so much secrecy. When Bowie contacted his band members with the idea of making a new record, the email's subject line read: "schtum!" "We weren't even talking among ourselves about this because if we get a leak, it will take all the gloss off it," is how Earl Slick puts it.

Notwithstanding its slow-paced melancholia, 'Where Are We Now?' was greeted with almost universal critical praise, leading to an unusually high degree of media coverage that spoke volumes about how Bowie had been missed and, perhaps, relief that he was evidently fit and well despite rumours to the contrary. *The Guardian* had Bowie on its front page with a substantial story inside, as did other UK broadsheets. When even political journalist Andrew Neil on the late-night politics show *This Week* was moved to mention David Bowie's 'terrible dirge' you knew that Bowie's return wasn't simply the property of popular culture. It seems absolutely everybody from across the broad spectrum of human activity had to have a view.

Those with longer memories realised that its appearance, seemingly out of nowhere, on i-Tunes and on YouTube was in many ways very much in keeping with Bowie's shock tactics of old. In February 1974, he released a single, 'Rebel, Rebel', which had only been recorded six weeks earlier and which almost no one knew about until advance copies were given to radio, two weeks before its release. The return of Bowie in 2013 was completely in keeping with how Bowie had worked in the past and not so strange after

all. It was also a reminder of how exciting pop music used to be, when it could hit you from nowhere, without the endless pre-ordering, pre-pre-promotion and tiresome media campaigning leading up the big day. That all this was missing was a big story in itself, an assault on an industry that nowadays relied more on packaging and publicity than content and merit.

Another parallel went largely unnoticed. In 1975 Bowie's great friend John Lennon was finally given his 'green card' which granted him permanent residency in the US and, more importantly, permitted him to travel outside of the country and return without hindrance. Lennon then did much the same thing as Bowie had done, absenting himself from the music business so as to help rear his son (in Bowie's case it was a daughter), await the termination of various contractual obligations and live a life away from the glare of celebrity. When Lennon re-emerged five years later with a new album and single he gave interviews galore, the spotlight returning with such ferocity that it attracted the attention of a crazed assassin. This too may have weighed on Bowie's mind.

People were also intrigued by something unrelated to the music. The artwork, co-ordinated by Jonathan Barnbrook in collaboration with Bowie, reminded us all of the days when sleeve design was as important as the music. On *The Next Day*, perhaps *the* classic Bowie album cover, *"Heroes",* is 'defamed' by a block of white space and its title struck through. "There were good reasons for using the *'Heroes'* cover," says Barnbrook, "and there are good reasons for it being 'undesigned' so it's very carefully thought about. It's making people think about David, the music, his age, his legacy. I do think it's quite an intellectual cover and does what Bowie does best which is bring a concept into the mainstream which maybe people are not comfortable with. Nobody has done this before – play with their old imagery in service of the new. It doesn't play the pop star game of image or rather the conventional 'new image for new consumption' that people expect for an album cover. It had the right

(coffee) and he's off. But we had to keep things so secret. On my calendar on my computer I used a code name for when I was working on the album."

"He's old school when it comes to writing; he has his book bag, his legal pad," adds Leonard, who shares guitar duties with David Torn and Bowie veteran Slick. "He's got a great way with melodies. He's really interested in the progression of the chords and the sections. You have to work fast with David. You'd spend more time discussing a video or a book than you will when you're playing. When you're playing he wants your first thought, best thought. I remember playing the song and David's got his lyrics out and he's singing and writing the song right there on his piano, actually writing the lyrics as we're going down on tape, or ProTools as it is now. I thought, 'That's great, that's not something you see every day'. He knows what he's going for."

kind of impact. The pose also, it's forward looking, the white square is an obliterating contrast to its organic form."

The new recordings began life as a series of demos back in Autumn 2010. Visconti, along with guitarist Gerry Leonard and drummer Sterling Campbell (both retained from the *Reality* tour), began work in a tiny demo studio. Around 20 songs were routined and only on the final day was Bowie persuaded to record them. "He said, 'We have to keep this secret'," says Visconti. "We signed NDA's [non-disclosure agreements]. Then we would take a lunch break and eat at the local Italian restaurant where everyone recognised him! Someone who worked at the Italian cafe snapped a photo of us and he got up and said, 'Don't do that! We won't come back here if you do that again.' David took the demos home with him for about three months. He then called me again and said, 'I think we can start an album.'"

The next sessions took place in May 2011 at recording studio called The Magic Shop. "It's very close to where David lives," says guitarist Gerry Leonard. "I think he wanted to walk to work. He's got his book bag with all the lyrics in there, he gets his Macchiato

The album debuted at number one in the UK charts, the ninth of his career. In America it reached number two (beating his previous-highest-charting album, not as might be assumed, *Let's Dance*, but *Station To Station*), kept off the top by Bon Jovi, and in Germany it became his first-ever number one album. But still, no interviews and certainly no promotional gigs. Some speculated that this was some grand Warholian device, in an age in which there is so much comment across so many platforms, saying nothing was the loudest sound of all. The 'mythogenic' Bowie was back: we would know him only through his music and his art, not by any form of direct communication in interviews. Yet another reason for the silence may have a far more human, and humble origin; perhaps Bowie knew that the first question on every journalist's lips would be about his health, his absence, his period 'retired'. It would appear by 2013 that Bowie was tired of talking about himself, particularly having to give answers to personal questions. According to Earl Slick, there was no need to worry in any case: "Because he got quiet, everyone assumed he was definitely ill. And he's not. He's fine. He looks pretty damn good for a guy who's sick, to me. He's on his game, he's singing his ass off, he's writing great. He's David! Maybe he just needed a break... maybe he just didn't feel like it."

On *The Next Day*, there is now doubt that Bowie does "feel like it". The music is honed, crafted and brilliantly written with no week moments. In style, it is art rock in the mould of *"Heroes", Lodger* and *Scary Monsters*, yet in tone, many of the songs pick out moods and situations from other eras too. What is certain is that the ten-year wait was worth every minute.

THE NEXT DAY

The best opener to a Bowie album since 'It's No Game (Part 1)' begins with a single drum kick, like someone slamming a fist on a table, or slamming the car door in annoyance. A playful, insouciant guitar line then gives way to the appearance of Bowie, a vocal as angry as any since *Scary Monsters* starter back in 1980. Gerry Leonard's snotty riff is perfect and Bowie is in bad humour – choleric, seemingly given up for dead. 'Here I am, not quite dying!' sings Bowie defiantly, while the exhortation 'Listen!' makes the hairs on the back of your neck stand up.

DIRTY BOYS

A parping, jack-the-lad sax line, and the ghost-of-'Fame''s guitar riff announce this tale of feral, urban disorder. Bowie announces in an ominous matter-of-fact line, 'I will steal a cricket bat/smash some windows make some noise.' Two songs in, and it's clear also that Bowie has spent a lot of time crafting these songs as the lovely melody of the chorus shows.

THE STARS (ARE OUT TONIGHT)

Motown stomper-meets-Motorik, this, the second single from the album was nominated for 'Best Rock Performance' for the 2014 Grammy's. This song fairly tumbles with startling imagery and haunting lines as the stars of today – 'Brigitte, Jack and Kate and Brad' are eerily cast as vampyric alien life forms, 'soaking up our primitive world' and

who' know just what we do.' Incidentally, the mid-song guitar break sounds uncommonly like a snatch of a melody from Roxy Music's 'If There Is Something', covered, of course, by Tin Machine.

LOVE IS LOST

Never has being 22 sounded so hopeless and ridden with futility in this, a cryptic assemblage of observations about youth, outsiderdom, alienation and opportunity thrown away. A highlight of the album, the doomy, insistent beat, angry guitars from Gerry Leonard, *Low*-era-sounding drums and Bowie's soulless organ part make this a wonderfully theatrical piece, as undead and breathless as anything on *Diamond Dogs*. By now one of the features of the new Bowie album is clear; Bowie is taking delight in playing around with vocal styles and techniques, his vocals here eerily double-tracked. The moment when his own backing vocal mockingly call out 'say, hello, hello', is a moment of brilliance while the ending, 'Oh what have you done, Oh what have you done?' hints at some terrible Macbethian deed done under duress.

WHERE ARE WE NOW?

The first single, and totally unrepresentative of the album but an instant Bowie classic, 'Where Are We Now?' is perhaps the only track on the album where Bowie's vocal has not been heavily double-tracked, manipulated or augmented by various effects and as such does indeed sound like Bowie's natural singing voice. One does not get the impression that Bowie's is modulating his vocal to affect a tremulous, lonely quality as he did on 'The Loneliest Guy' for example. As such, its slight frailty is touching and human. "His voice sounds slightly less majestic, slightly older, perhaps inevitably," wrote perhaps the biggest Bowie supporter of all-time in the media, Jonathan Ross. "But that gives it a quality that suits the song magnificently." The bassist Herbie Flowers, who worked with Bowie on 'Space Oddity' in 1969, stated, "It made me cry", while another long-term Bowie-watcher, Karl Bartos (ex-Kraftwern) opined: "Oh it's good! He's locked into that time frame of his Berlin time. It sounds like Kurt Weil. You know, when he plays the piano, he is in love with strange chords. We need him badly. He's the last one."

A beautiful, poignant song, it evokes a contented time in the singer's life, when he was living in then-divided Berlin in the late seventies. Bowie is 'taking the train to Potzdammer Platz', sitting in his favourite club, buying food in the supermarket, evoking memories of a time in which he lived a normal life after the craziness of the LA years. The lines: 'Where are we now?/ The moment you know/ You know, you know' is a genius piece of writing, a meditation, through repetition, on a split-second moment of self-realisation, while the closing stanza: 'As long as there's sun/As long as there's rain/ As long as there's fire/ As long as there's me/ As long as there's you', are the most poetic, most direct and most beautiful lyrics in his entire career as songwriter – 'sun', 'rain', 'fire', 'me', 'you', the human condition encapsulated in five words.

VALENTINE'S DAY

Reportedly one of the first songs written for the album, 'Valentine's Day' is in that tradition of pop song along with 'I Don't Like Mondays' and 'The One I Love', whose title is the antithesis of its contents. A snappy beat and wonderful guitar part from Earl Slick, all twangy and earthy, announces this tale, not of love, but of violence and death, more Al Capone than Amore. Bowie is inside the mind of a killer ('tiny face', 'scrawny hands'), plotting 'who's to go', and how he longed for a time when 'all the world were under his heals'. A chill snapshot into the psychology of a mass-murderer, the significance of the song has taken on a whole new range of associations since we first heard it in 2013 given the numerous brutal assassinations and religious hate-crime attacks of our times. There's also, perhaps, a resonance with the killing of his great friend John Lennon. "I was second on his [Mark Chapman's] list," Bowie once confirmed.

IF YOU CAN SEE ME

Gail Ann Dorsey's backing vocals soar disquieting over a frantic, jarring, drum-and-bass beat before Bowie arrives, his vocal heavily treated and phased: 'If you can see me; I can see you.' This is the darkest track on the album and also the most abstract: the Bowie character is now some sort of omnipotent 'end-of-days' tyrant, in a fog of unnatural ambition and desire: 'I could wear your new blue shoes/ I should wear your old red dress.' Simultaneously evoking the spirit of 'Width Of A Circle' and *Earthling*'s 'Law (Earthlings On Fire)', it is impossible to put a time or a place on this song other than a feeling of Bosch-like ungodliness ('children swarm like thousands of bugs',) either deep in the future, or some alternative present in which the medieval mind triumphs: 'I will slaughter your kind who descend from belief/ I am the spirit of greed, a lord of theft.' This is astonishing stuff and, in the context of a very fine album, the most ground-breaking piece of music.

I'D RATHER BE HIGH

With a stately, military beat and beautiful guitar line, 'I'd Rather Be High' is an anti-war song of great power and finesse: 'I'd rather be dead or out of my head/ than training these guns on those men in the sand', and 'Cities full of generals and generals full of shit.' Like much of *The Next Day*, it is an infuriating puzzle of a song with half the pieces missing. Yet there's fun to be had trying to get into Bowie's mind to unpick the seemingly random connections. For a start, are we in the trenches or are we fighting in Helmand? Or both? Or is this a universal sentiment of war being wicked and wrong, the young dying for the rich and powerful? In a valiant (though ultimately futile) attempt by *Guardian* reviewer Alexis Petridis to unpack the mine of metaphor that includes Nabokov next to Clare and Lady Manners (Petridis points credibly to Bowie referencing the 1910s The Coeterie, the precursor to Waugh's 'Bright Young Things'), he concluded, "There's a certain cultural richness here that you just don't find in, say, the oeuvre of the Vaccines." Quite true.

BOSS OF ME
(BOWIE, GERRY LEONARD)

Although still a perfectly good song, 'Boss Of Me' seems out of place on *The Next Day*, or in the wrong place coming as it does after two such strange songs and before another one song of bluff and double-bluff. This is a brief journey into the more quotidian world of power and possession, a 'small town girl''s sexual grip over the song's narrator. Saxes honk, guitars growl and there's a cool middle eight yet 'Boss Of Me', if no miss-fire, is a miss-fit.

DANCING OUT IN SPACE

Not many people, make that, no one else in rock music, would include the lines 'Silent as Georges Rodenbach/ Mist and silhouette', in what is, on the surface, pop (the reference, apparently may be to the Symbolist's poem, 'Du Silence'). The track begins with demo-like tameness; a drum beat, a winey guitar and possibly the flimsiest handclap accompaniment in the history of rock. There is a poppy, yet airless quality to this, the most conventionally catchy track on the album, and the lyrics evoke images of a Moon-lit dance in the weightlessness of space where no one can see you: 'Something like a drowning/Dancing out in space.'

HOW DOES THE GRASS GROW?

(David Bowie/Jerry Lordan)
Obliquely, some of the work for *The Next Day* takes us way, way back to a time before even this writer was born. The Shadows had some of the best tunes in pre-Beatles popular music and Bowie takes the melody for 'Apache' for this, one of the strongest, yet least discussed tracks on the album. Lyrically, we're back in the no-man's-land wartime horror of 'I'd Rather Be High', and the two are companion pieces; 'Where do the boys lie/ Mud mud mud/ How does the grass grow/Blood blood blood.' The piece ends with a squall of Belwe-esque guitars; the bassline a slight crib of the ending of 'Boys Keep Swinging', another frankly great moment on an album with their fair share.

(YOU WILL) SET THE WORLD ON FIRE

Earl Slick owns this track; the riff is big enough to fill the most soulless air-hanger of an arena full of mischief; the only problem is that there was no tour to play it on. Visconti adds an excellent orchestration and the lyric, like 'Boss Of Me', is relatively digestible; the PR babble to the young hopeful on a quest to stardom. How different today's stardom has become when a Karaoke contest such as *The Voice* can make you a million. Imagine a young Bob Dylan turning up if the show had aired in 1962? No chance, mate.

YOU FEEL SO LONELY YOU COULD DIE

The final two songs end the album with unstoppable, if quite different forces. Here, Bowie mixes *Young Americans*-style with, again, pre-Beatles American rock'n'roll, in this song of rejection (does the song, perhaps reference Hank Williams' 'I'm So Lonesome I Could Cry' or Elvis Presley's 'Heartbreak Hotel'?). Like several songs on *The Next Day*, Bowie appears visited by unwelcome shades of the past, singing, 'I can see you as a ghost, hanging from a beam', while the line 'And people don't like you' appears so personal, so direct, the listener, hit with just five words, is twisted into a spiral of self-examination about their own lives. Both 'Rock And Roll Suicide' and 'Five Years' are quoted musically in the ending section, reinforcing the 'Spectre-Sound.'

HEAT

The parting shot is a reverie, a soliloquy as if Bowie has taken the stage to release his innermost thoughts. The sad music swirls with violin and the sort of brashly-thumbed acoustic guitar that made *Hunky Dory*, while Bowie's vocal is the most impressive of the entire album. Bowie is the seer, but also the liar, the man who tells lies but also tells or maybe sells us the truths to come. In a breath-taking piece of self-examination, Bowie concludes: 'And I tell myself, I don't know who I am.' *The Next Day*, as a piece, reaffirms this central connection between its maker and its audience; with brilliance.

OTHER EDITIONS:

Bowie might have been 'away' for ten years but in his absence, some things never change… and that was the ability of his record company to squeeze as much money from his fans as possible for product they already owned for the tease of something they didn't have. So we have *The Next Day* (Deluxe Version), *The Next Day EP, The Next Day Extra*, and *The Next Day Extra (Collector's Edition)*, a Japanese version with a bonus track different to the one you can get in the UK, not to mention the temptation of buying the thing on vinyl, or checking out the difference of the version specially mastered for I-Tunes. So, what's worth having of these extras?

THE NEXT DAY EXTRA (COLLECTOR'S EDITION)

[Limited Edition, Box set, CD+DVD] (UK CD: RCA BB00FANXZL8. Released 4 November 2013. UK Chart:89 [Total weeks in chart: 1]

CD 1: The Next Day (original album).

CD 2: 'Atomica', 'Love Is Lost (Hello Steve Reich Mix By James Murphy For The DFA)', 'Plan', 'The Informer', 'Like A Rocket Man', 'Born In A UFO', 'I'd Rather Be High (Venetian Mix)', 'I'll Take You There', 'God Bless The Girl', 'So She'.

DVD: 'Where Are We Now?' 'The Stars (Are Out Tonight)', 'The Next Day', 'Valentine's Day'.

The highlight of CD 2 is the startling new version of 'Love Is Lost', not so much a remix but a complete reinvention courtesy of James Murphy (ex-LCD Soundsystem). The track starts as homage to Steve Reich's 1972 work, *Clapping Music*. Applause gives way to a hand-clapped beat before an electronic bed deconstructs the original art rock version of the song. In another moment of inspiration, the melody from 'Ashes To Ashes' is recreated in the middle section and is matched perfectly to the lyric and melody of the original. The production is superb and makes one hunger for some more Bowie electronica. The 10-minute track was edited for single release and accompanied by one of Bowie's most effective videos, released, appropriately, on Halloween, and filmed by Bowie in Manhattan with the help of photographer Jimmy King and his PA and long-time great friend Coco Schwab. Bowie revealed that the cost of the film was the cost of saving it onto his hard drive via a memory card ($12.99). In the film, Bowie is haunted by the shades of his past (the wooden figures of The Thin White Duke and the Pierrot from 'Ashes To Ashes' which were made for the aborted 'The Pretty Things Are Going To Hell' video were here used to great effect appearing, as they do, out of darkness, while Bowie appears both as 'himself' and as a grotesque wood-cut-like figure in what looks like a black cape and capotain hat. Just how this latter effect was created without a budget remains a mystery.

Another song given the remix treatment is 'I'd Rather Be High'. Now with a rather grandiloquent faux harpsichord sound, it was the music used for Bowie's opulent appearance in an ad for Louis Vuitton's Autumn/Winter advertising campaign, shot in Venice in the summer of 2013. The fifth single off *The Next Day* (or, perhaps, more accurately, 'The Next Days' given the number of versions).

The rest of the 'new' stuff collects tracks which many fans will have already bought: 'Plan' is actually a very good instrumental, just Bowie's guitar and a thudding drum figure. It was used as the opening music in the video for 'The Stars (Are Out Tonight)' and was previously available as a download or in the Deluxe version of the album along with 'I'll Take You There', and 'So She' (which as one famous Bowie fan remarked sounded in places a bit like The Brotherhood Of Man's 'Save Your Kisses For Me'!). That Japanese-only release 'God Bless The Girl' also makes an appearance.

There are four genuinely new songs. 'Atomica', all big riffs and slap-bass teases 'Let's get this show on the road'. 'The Insider' is a doo-wop slowie with Bowie taking on the big questions about life and God (again). 'Like A Rocket Man', is a pretty pop song, while 'Born In A UFO' has a *Lodger*-esque guitar part (there was some speculation that the song dated from those very sessions).

The DVD contains four promotional videos. After stepping back from making videos in the main for *Heathen* and *Reality*, peeved that ageism prevented their widespread showing, Bowie, perhaps in the knowledge that he would be neither playing shows nor even talking to the media, was back in front of the camera. All four videos are classic pieces of Bowie.

'Where Are We Now?' gained media recognition for the footage of West Berlin, filmed, according to Tony Visconti, at the time (by whom, or when, we are left guessing). More interesting is Bowie as homunculus; a co-joined puppet, his Siamese wife, played by Oursler's real-life wife Jacqueline Humphries. The big production, and least impressive of the four videos, was the one suspects where all the money went, Tilda Swinton appears as a clone-like Bowie-wife, in the 'film' for 'The Stars (Are Out Tonight)'.

Next up was one of Bowie's funniest videos of his career. Bowie plays a Christ-like figure to Gary Oldman's corrupt Catholic priest. The action takes place in a seedy pick-up bar with Bowie, at first, the musical entertainment. Marion Cotillard is Oldman's lady of choice but their liaison is rudely interrupted by a spot

of stigmata with Cotillard collapsing to the floor, blood gushing from her wrists and selfishly splattering a nearby woman's cleavage. There's also a woman with eyelashes a foot long, severed eyeballs served on a platter, and a random self-flagellator. The video ends with the cast assembled and thanked by Bowie, before he disappears into the ether with a ping. It was at this point that it became laugh-out-loud funny. However, some people were less impressed. William Donohue, the leader of the Catholic League For Religious And Civil Rights, called Bowie 'a switch-hitting, bisexual, senior citizen from London', and so managed in just one sentence to be ageist and homophobic and unintentionally hysterical (with the 'London' bit). Others grumped that such a video could never have been made mocking Islam in such a manner.

The final video is the most simple, and the best. Shot in a disused grain warehouse in Redhook New York City, Bowie, dressed coolly in white shirt and jeans tells the tale of the killer and gives it another visual twist. It is clear that if 'The Next day' took on Catholicism, 'Valentine's Day' is facing up to the pro-gun lobby. In a series of subtle, though enduring images, first spotted by Lucy Jones in the *NME*, Bowie makes a direct attack on Charlton Heston and the National Rifle Association, raising his guitar in a direct copy of Heston triumphalistic poses with a gun. Other images include the silhouette of Bowie's guitar to resemble a sawn-off shot gun and a bullet travelling at speed through the frets of his guitar.

Unfortunately, *The Next Day Extra* does not include the promos for 'Love Is Lost (Hello Steve Reich Mix By James Murphy For The DFA)' or 'I'd Rather Be High (Venetian Mix)' which used archive wartime footage to reinforce the song's anti-war theme. Also, why a Blu-Ray option was not available is also puzzling.

PART II
COMPILATION

s

Accost any innocent bystander about David Bowie and his greatest hits, and they're quite likely to mention "Heroes", 'Ziggy Stardust' and 'Changes'. It's then that the pedantic Bowie fans (and aren't we all pedants?) will point out that the first didn't even reach the Top 20, and the second was never issued as an A-side anywhere in the world, while the third sold so poorly that it failed to even make the charts. Of course, Bowie has had dozens of bona fide hits, but many of his best-known songs never enjoyed serious chart action. It's a measure of his huge creativity, and the long-lasting power of his music, therefore, that "Heroes" is now not only Bowie's most famous song, but one of rock's most important landmarks. And it reached number 24 in the UK charts.

Bowie is also loath to give space on his 'best of' compilations to three of his most popular songs. 'The Laughing Gnome', on reissue, was a sizeable UK hit in 1973, while two songs from the Labyrinth soundtrack, 'Magic Dance' and 'As The World Falls Down', are regularly among Bowie's best-selling single-track downloads.

There are dozens of Bowie compilations on the market; some are official, Bowie-sanctioned releases, others appear to be semi-official releases by record companies with apparently little connection to Bowie's main labels; quite a few reach stupid prices for the chancers who trade on deleted material. What follows is a selection of those compilations which may appeal to a music fan interested in a particular era of Bowie's work.

For those of you with more sensible ambitions, for a career-spanning best of I would reduce the choice to just four collections. For historical importance only, Bowie's first greatest hits packages, Changesonebowie, is a lovely thing to own on vinyl, the black-and-white photo and minimal design, is a companion piece to the then current album, Station To Station, likewise a red and black world in which capital letters rule. For a pretty-damn definitive best of, EMI's 2-CD Best Of Bowie,

released in 2002, is still the standard, while a clever, and perhaps more representative selection of Bowie's music, mixing as it does the well-known, key album and live tracks, and, for the time at least, completely new material from Bowie's archive, comes in the shape of the newly re-issued box set, Sound + Vision.

Perhaps best of all comes something not made by Bowie and his 'people' at all. In just over an hour, delight in the greatest Bowie-mix ever: Dave, by Soulwax, from the electronic 'configuration' (it's so old fashioned to call people 'bands' these days) from Ghent, David and Stephen Dewaele. Unfolding with such attention to detail to charm the biggest Bowie pedant (and I am certainly one of those), with the flipping of Bowie's vinyl sleeves (as perfectly self-referential as the video for 'Ashes To Ashes') to announce each new Bowie 'moment', not only is the choice of music, the rhyming, the tempos, and the editing impeccable, but also, the visuals, put together by film maker Wim Reygaert, show a touch missing from many an official release. This is a piece of art that 'real' Bowie fans will instantly invest in; more so than most official Bowie product given Soulwax's knowing attention to detail and obvious Bowie-love. Bowie himself is played quite perfectly by Belgian model Hannelore Knuts; one can't help think this as a major influence on Bowie's own video, 'The Stars Are Out Tonight'. Soulwax do it better though.

SOUND + VISION

(UK CD: Virgin Records B00M7IR5E2)
UK Chart: 63 [weeks in chart 1] US
Chart: 97 [for 1989 Ryko edition])

The latest version of *Sound + Vision* comes in a neat box set and is the second reissue of Ryko Disc's award-winning David Bowie compilation with a fourth CD expanding the original to 1993. As an introduction to Bowie's work, it's undoubtedly the best purchase, since it avoids telling the David Bowie story through the hit singles, instead delving into the albums themselves, where many of the real gems lie. Those not in possession of the original Ryko release will also be delighted to hear the rarities on the EMI reissue (all songs previously unmentioned in the text are discussed below).

Full Tracklisting:

CD 1: 'Space Oddity' (original demo), 'The Wild-Eyed Boy From Freecloud' (rare B-side version), 'The Prettiest Star', 'London Bye Ta-Ta' (previously unreleased stereo mix), 'Black Country Rock', 'The Man Who Sold The World', 'The Bewlay Brothers', 'Changes', 'Round And Round' (alternate vocal take), 'Moonage Daydream', 'John I'm Only Dancing' (sax version), 'Drive-in Saturday', 'Panic In Detroit', 'Ziggy Stardust' (Live '73), 'Rock 'n' Roll Suicide' (Live '73), 'Anyway Anyhow, Anywhere', 'Sorrow', 'Don't Bring Me Down'.

CD 2: '1984/Dodo', 'Big Brother', 'Rebel Rebel' (US single version), 'Suffragette City' (Live '74), 'Cracked Actor' (Live '74), 'Young Americans', 'Fascination', 'After Today (*Young Americans* outtake), 'It's Hard To be A Saint In The City' (*Station To Station* outtake), 'TVC15', 'Wild Is The Wind', 'Sound And Vision', 'Be My Wife', "Helden" (German version of "Heroes" – '89 remix), 'Joe The Lion', 'Sons Of The Silent Age'.

CD 3: 'Station To Station' (Live '78), 'Warszawa' (Live '78), 'Breaking Glass' (Live '78), 'Red Sails', 'Look Back In Anger', 'Boys Keep Swinging', 'Up The Hill Backwards', 'Kingdome Come', 'Ashes To Ashes', 'Baal's Hymn', 'The Drowned Girl', 'Cat People' (Putting Out Fire)', 'China Girl', 'Ricochet', 'Modern Love' (live), 'Loving The Alien', 'Dancing With The Big Boys'.

CD 4: 'Blue Jean', 'Time Will Crawl', 'Baby Can Dance', 'Amazing', 'I Can't Read', 'Shopping For Girls', 'Goodbye Mr Ed', 'Amlapura', 'You've Been Around', 'Nite Flights' (Moodswings Back To Basics Remix Radio Edit), 'Pallas Athena' (Gone Midnight Mix), 'Jump They Say', 'Buddha Of Suburbia', 'Dead Against It', 'South Horizon', 'Pallas Athena' (Live).

The following song from *Sound + Vision* have not been dealt with earlier in this guide:

SPACE ODDITY (demo)
An interesting demo featuring Bowie's friend 'Hutch'. Note Bowie's twee piece of self-promotion at the beginning when he addresses would-be sponsors.

LONDON BYE TA-TA
The track which was ear-marked by then manager Ken Pitt as the follow-up to 'Space Oddity' but was dropped in favour of 'The Prettiest Star'.

THE PRETTIEST STAR
The original single version with Marc Bolan on lead guitar – inferior to the better-known *Aladdin Sane* version.

JOHN I'M ONLY DANCING

Gutsy, *Aladdin Sane* out-take with saxophone high in the mix and arguably superior to the 1972 single version. This version also found its way on to some initial copies of *ChangesOneBowie* (now deleted).

1984/DODO

An early, less disco-inflected version of '1984' coupled with a version of 'Dodo' and recorded fro the proposed *Diamond Dogs* stage musical at Trident Studios in November 1973. The last time Bowie worked with producer Ken Scott and the Spiders.

REBEL REBEL

(US single version)
A good, echo-laden version of the song. It was this version, not the more well-known British release, which was the blueprint for the song's live renditions in the Seventies.

AFTER TODAY

This out-take from *Young Americans* is a solid track, with a groovy piano line, but it is by no stretch of the imagination an essential item.

IT'S HARD TO BE A SAINT IN THE CITY

This frenetic cover of the early Bruce Springsteen song is from the *Young Americans* sessions.

HELDEN

(1989 remix)
The German version of "Heroes" which contains a powerful Bowie vocal, is an excellent inclusion.

BAAL's HYMN (Der Choral Vom Großen Baal)

(Brecht/Muldowney)
What an absolutely astonishing vocal performance this is. Recorded at the Hansa Studios in Berlin in September 1981 for the soundtrack EP of Bowie's appearance in BBC Television's adaptation of the Berthold Brecht play, it would be Tony Visconti's last Bowie production for two decades. Bowie sings at times full-throated, at others through gritted teeth, and his interpretation is enthralling. One of the best things Bowie ever recorded, and one of the least discussed.

THE DROWNED GIRL (Vom Ertrunkenen Mädchen)

(Brecht/Weill)
Like 'Baal's Hymn', 'The Drowned Girl' found its way onto Bowie's 'Baal EP', which reached number 29 in March 1982. On the face of it, it must be the least commercial record ever to chart in the UK Top 30. At the time, Bowie's fan base was so huge in the UK that even something as decidedly non-pop as this made the UK charts.

CAT PEOPLE (PUTTING OUT FIRE)

(Bowie/Moroder)
Italian Giorgio Moroder is one of the most important producers of all time. While based in Munich, he invented intelligent, almost symphonic, disco music, and made brave, challenging singles such as the Kraftwerkian 'I Feel Love', a number one for Donna Summer in 1977. That Bowie's collaboration with Moroder brought about just one classic single is a cause for regret. Recorded in July 1981 for the movie soundtrack to the remake of *Cat People*, this is a great, if slightly camp, rock/disco hybrid. A rockier, ballsier version can be found on *Let's Dance*, but if portentous intonation and the 'Moroder Sound' are more your cup of tea, stick to this one, a UK number 26 in the spring of 1982. The song was also revived for a younger audience in its use by Quentin Tarantino in the film *Inglorious Basterds* [2009]

BEST OF BOWIE

(UK CD: EMI 539 8212, Released 4 November 2002; UK Chart: 11 [119]; US Single CD Virgin 41929, Double CD: Virgin 41930; US Chart (single CD: 70 [3], Double CD 108 [2])

This chronological selection of classics may play it safe, but really, who cares since they are among the finest records of the last 35 years. CD 2 races through Bowie's experimental albums to concentrate on his 'dancing years' as global superstar, while CD 1 is simply peerless.

Best Of Bowie has been a solid seller, and continues to out-perform even new product. Having canvassed all the different territories, the *Best Of* content varies slightly from country to country to reflect the national popularity of certain songs. A live duet with Tina Turner on 'Tonight' for heaven's sake, finds its way onto the Dutch version! Hardcore fans will hopefully be able to resist the temptation to buy all these different versions. Oh come on now, you didn't, did you?!

UK Tracklisting:

CD 1: 'Space Oddity', 'The Man Who Sold The World', 'Oh! You Pretty Things', 'Changes', 'Life On Mars?', 'Starman', 'Ziggy Stardust', 'Suffragette City', 'John, I'm Only Dancing', 'The Jean Genie', 'Drive-In Saturday', 'Sorrow', 'Diamond Dogs', 'Rebel Rebel', 'Young Americans', 'Fame', 'Golden years', 'TVC15', 'Wild Is The Wind'.

CD 2: 'Sound & Vision', "Heroes", 'Boys Keep Swinging', 'Under Pressure' (with Queen), 'Ashes To Ashes', 'Fashion', 'Scary Monsters (& Super Creeps)', 'Let's Dance', 'China Girl', 'Modern Love', 'Blue Jean', 'This Is Not America' (with The Pat Metheny Group), 'Loving The Alien', 'Dancing In The Street' (with Mick Jagger), 'Absolute Beginners', 'Jump They Say', 'Hallo Spaceboy' (PSB Remix), 'Little Wonder', 'I'm Afraid Of Americans (V 1)', 'Slow Burn' (radio edit)

The following songs included in the Best Of Bowie packages have yet to be dealt with:

SPACE ODDITY

1969, the year of the first Apollo moon landing and Bowie, inspired by Kubrick's *2001: A Space Odyssey*, had a head full of sci-fi dreaming. Snubbed by Tony Visconti who branded it a 'cheap cash-in', this magical song was worked up as home-produced demo with Bowie's musical partner John Hutchinson. The transformation is startling. The piece was given the most intricate of productions by Gus Dudgeon and a sweeping arrangement by Paul Buckmaster (the team that defined the sound of early Elton too). The music, from the echoey handclaps, the mournful acoustic melody and the chattering, spacey ending sees Bowie take a great leap; the words, a lonely dialogue of alienation between a doomed astronaut and ground control provide a metaphor for Bowie's entire career. He's out there somewhere, but where exactly? Released in the summer of 1969, its first major exposure came when it was played through the PA before the Rolling Stones' iconic performance at Hyde Park that July. A sleeper, it took several months to chart before finally reaching number five that autumn, Bowie's first big hit. 'Space Oddity' was reissued in 1975 and became Bowie's first UK number one. Bizarrely, despite all of Bowie's brilliance in the seventies, none of his singles produced in that decade would make it to number one in the UK. A 1979 remake, sparse, intense, Lennonesque, is almost as good, and a year later Major Tom reappeared in 'Ashes To Ashes', prompting RCA to issue a 12" promo single featuring both songs back to back. In 2013, the song re-entered the public imagination in a startling literal fashion. Canadian astronaut Chris Hadfield performed the song on acoustic guitar, indeed, floating round his space craft, the International Space Station, and became a *YouTube* sensation.

UNDER PRESSURE

(David Bowie/Freddie Mercury/Roger Taylor/John Deacon/Brian May)

Recorded with Queen in 1981, and a UK number one 'Under Pressure' is a modern rock standard. At the time, many Bowie fans regarded the collaboration as something of a sell-out by Bowie. John Deacon's famously sampled bass-line (actually suggested by Bowie) holds it together, and Freddie and Bowie are both in fine fettle. An a capella version has now surfaced with just Bowie and Freddie's vocals. Bowie restored the song to the set list of his two last tours, singing it as a duet with bassist Gail Ann Dorsey (incidentally, a big Queen fan).

THIS IS NOT AMERICA

(Bowie/Mays/Metheny)

From the film *The Falcon And The Snowman* this team-up with the Pat Metheny Group is actually quite successful. Bowie sings well and Metheney's soft-focus melody is affecting. The track hit Number 14 in the UK in early 1985 and was also one of Bowie's biggest-ever sellers in Germany.

DANCING IN THE STREET

(Ivy Jo Hunter/William Stevenson/Mavin Gaye)

Without wishing to deny its significance in terms of consciousness-raising, in musical terms, Live Aid was nothing special. It did, however, present Jagger and Bowie with the excuse to record this middling cover version of the Martha Reeves & The Vandellas standard and its accompanying silly video. A UK number one, naturally.

ABSOLUTE BEGINNERS

Despite the deadeningly uninventive nature of some of his post *Let's Dance* period, Bowie could still conjure up marvellous singles. He's back to his finest form with this, the title song to the Julien Temple film of the same name. There's a wash of acoustic guitars, Rick Wakeman is back tinkling his ivories and then Don Weller's fine saxophone solo at the end. It just missed number one in early 1986.

WHEN THE WIND BLOWS

Included in the Chilean version of the album is this, the title track to Raymond Brigg's animated anti-nuke film. It features a resurgent Bowie with an insistent, darkly forboding guitar riff, great drumming, rousing orchestration and a polished vocal performance. It reached number 44 in the UK late in November 1986 but deserved far better.

THE BEST OF BOWIE 1969-1974

(UK CD: EMI 821 8492, Released 27 October 1997; UK Chart: 13 [Total weeks in chart: 17])

Tracklisting: 'The Jean Genie', 'Space Oddity', 'Starman', 'Ziggy Stardust', 'John, I'm Only Dancing', 'Rebel Rebel', 'Let's Spend The Night Together', 'Suffragette City', 'Oh! You Pretty Things', 'Velvet Goldmine', 'Drive-In Saturday', 'Diamond Dogs', 'Changes', 'Sorrow', 'The Prettiest Star', 'Life On Mars?', 'Aladdin Sane', 'The Man Who Sold The World', 'Rock 'n' Roll Suicide', 'All The Young Dudes'.

THE BEST OF BOWIE 1974-1979

(UK CD: EMI 4943002, Released 20 April1998; UK Chart: 39 [Total weeks in chart: 2])

As a taster for the 1999 batch of Bowie reissues (originally to have included bonus CDs of material in the same manner as the earlier Rykodisc editions), EMI released two *Best Of* compilations. Eschewing the strict chronological approach for once, they mixed and matched Bowie classic singles and album tracks to good effect (CD 2's opening trio of 'Sound And Vision', 'Golden Years' and 'Fame' is a perfectly-judged salvo of Bowie at his grooviest best). Both issues came with liner notes from Bowie expert Kevin Cann.

Tracklisting: 'Sound And Vision', 'Golden Years', 'Fame', 'Young Americans', 'John, I'm Only Dancing (again), 'Can You Hear Me', 'Wild Is The Wind', 'Knock On Wood', 'TVC 15', '1984', 'It's Hard To Be A Saint In The City', 'The Secret Life Of Arabia', 'DJ', 'Beauty And The Beast', 'Breaking Glass', 'Boys Keep Swinging', "Heroes".

One track, from the second hits collection, has not been included in our analysis so far:

KNOCK ON WOOD

(Floyd/Cropper)
Culled from *David Live*, this was the moment when Bowie's fans first met the new, blue-eyed soul boy on vinyl. Originally recorded by Eddie Floyd and Otis Redding in 1967, Bowie's UK number 10 version was eclipsed later in the seventies by Amii Stewart's disco re-make.

JOHN, I'M ONLY DANCING (Again)

Released as a single at the end of the Seventies, this is a totally re-worked version of the 1972 single, with David Sanborn's sax high in the mix. It reached number 12 in the UK charts.

THE BEST OF BOWIE 1980-1987

(UK CD: EMI B000LW9PYY, Released 19 March 2007; UK Chart: 34 [Total weeks in chart: 2])

The seventies might have been Bowie's most significant decade in terms of ground breaking music, but four of his five UK number ones came in the eighties. When you consider that such illustrious artists such as The Who and Bob Dylan have *never* had a UK number one single then it makes Bowie's achievement, as an *artiste*, particularly impressive. This was originally included as part of another Bowie compilation called *The Platinum Collection* which gathered together the two previous best ofs 69-74 and 74-79. This release is noteworthy for including a bonus DVD of Bowie videos and the first official appearance of the promos for 'The Drowned Girl' and 'When The Wind Blows'.

CD Tracklisting: 'Let's Dance' (Single Version), 'Ashes To Ashes' (Single Version), 'Under Pressure', 'Fashion' (Single Version) 'Modern Love' (Single Version) 'China Girl' (Single Version) 'Scary Monsters (And Super Creeps)' (Single Version), 'Up The Hill

Backwards', 'Alabama Song', 'The Drowned Girl', 'Cat People (Putting Out Fire)' (Single Version), 'This Is Not America', 'Loving The Alien', 'Absolute Beginners', (Single Version), 'When The Wind Blows', 'Blue Jean', 'Day-In Day-Out' (Single Version), 'Time Will Crawl', 'Underground' (Single Version)

BOWIE: THE SINGLES COLLECTION

(UK CD: EMI 7243 8 28099 2 0, US CD: Rykodisc RCD 10218/9; Released 8 November 1993; UK Chart: 9)

In 1993, Bowie's mini-renaissance as solo artist occasioned the release of another compilation CD. Although again the focus is on the big hits, nobody seems quite sure about what songs were actually singles. There are two similar versions of this compilation, and the Rykodisc edition available in North America shades the EMI version by taking the story up to the nineties with 'Jump They Say' and through a slightly better track selection.

This Rykodisc edition omitted five tracks: 'Rock And Roll Suicide', 'Knock On Wood', 'Alabama Song', 'Wild Is The Wind' and 'This Is Not America', but added eight: 'Oh You Pretty Things', 'Be My Wife', 'Look Back In Anger', 'Cat People (Puttin' Out Fire)', 'Loving The Alien' (single version), 'Never Let Me Down' and 'Jump They Say' (single version). The Rykodisc edition also contained a limited edition CD of Bowie's 1977 duet with Bing Crosby, 'Little Drummer Boy/Peace On Earth'.

Full track listing for the EMI version:

Disc 1: 'Space Oddity', 'Changes', 'Starman', 'Ziggy Stardust', 'Suffragette City', 'John I'm Only Dancing', 'The Jean Genie', 'Drive In Saturday', 'Life On Mars?', 'Sorrow', 'Rebel Rebel', 'Rock 'n'Roll Suicide', 'Diamond Dogs', 'Knock On Wood', 'Young Americans', 'Fame', 'Golden Years', 'TVC 15', 'Sound And Vision'

Disc 2: "Heroes", 'Beauty And The Beast', 'Boys Keep Swinging', 'DJ', 'Alabama Song', 'Ashes To Ashes', 'Fashion', 'Scary Monsters (And Super Creeps)', 'Under Pressure', 'Wild Is The Wind', 'Let's Dance', 'China Girl', 'Modern Love', 'Blue Jean', 'This Is Not America', 'Dancing In The Streets', 'Absolute Beginners', 'Day-in Day-out'.

The following track has not previously been dealt with in detail in the analysis:

LITTLE DRUMMER BOY/PEACE ON EARTH

[Bonus CD on Rykodisc version] This duet with Bing Crosby, recorded shortly before Crosby's death in 1977, is one of the most surreal moments in pop history: the 30-year-old former androgyne teaming up with the bumbling cardigan Bing, forty-four years his senior. Bowie would later remark that Bing's face looked preternaturally orange, something that the video clip of the event confirms! Reaching number three in the UK at Christmas 1982, it was kept off the number one by the delights of 'A Winter's Tale' by David Essex and Renée And Renato's 'Save Your Love'.

RARESTONE BOWIE

(UK CD: Trident International Golden Years GY 002, Released 19 June 1995, not released in US)

Another in the series of MainMan/Trident International re-issues. Containing eight live tracks and Bowie's studio version of 'All The Young Dudes' it's a little over 36 minutes long and so hardly tempts with value-for-money. That said, Bowie fans will definitely want to have it as there are some genuine rarities on offer here.

ALL THE YOUNG DUDES

A superior-quality version of this song can be heard on the *Aladdin Sane* Thirtieth Anniversary Bonus CD.

QUEEN BITCH

A live, funked-up version recorded at Long Island, New York on March 23, 1976.

SOUND AND VISION

Although then a recent hit single, Bowie only gave this Bowie-favourite one airing on the 1978 Stage tour, at Earl's Court on July 1 – and here it is.

TIME

A live version from the 1980 Floor Show recorded in October 1973.

Nothing has changed.

NOTHING HAS CHANGED: THE VERY BEST OF DAVID BOWIE

(UK CD: Deluxe Edition, Box set Parlophone: B00NES1D6 Released 17 November 2014; UK Chart: 9 [weeks in chart 11]; US Chart: 57 [weeks in chart 1])

It was, perhaps, only predictable that with Bowie back releasing music, his record company would want to exploit its asset. So, in November 2014 came yet another David Bowie best of compilation. There would be one new track 'Sue (Or In A Season Of Crime)' and its B-side, ''Tis A Pity She Was A Whore', both available as a download or on vinyl. Equally predictably, this new best of came in a variety of formats – a 3-CD, a 2-CD and a double-album vinyl edition. Named after a lyric from 2002's *Heathen* opener 'Sunday' (illogically, not included) this is a more-or-less reverse chronological presentation of Bowie's best-known work targeted at the general music fan. To cram so many tracks on 3-CDs, some of the songs were subjected to some quite severe treatment with fadeouts truncated.

The art work, again by Jonathan Barnbrook, took as its theme the Bowie gaze. There were four main striking images, one from 1972, a second from 1975 one from 1996, and the cover image itself, from 2013, saw Bowie's image reflected back into its creator's face.

BE MY WIFE

Another flashback to the 1978 tour, and again from Earl's Court, July 1. Since neither 'Be My Wife' nor 'Sound And Vision' made it on to the largely disappointing official live album of the tour, *Stage,* these two tracks are worth a listen.

FOOTSTOMPIN'/ WISH I COULD SHIMMY LIKE MY SISTER KATE

This is from the Dick Cavett Show broadcast in the US on December 4, 1974.

ZIGGY STARDUST

Live cut from Santa Monica in October 1972.

MY DEATH

Interesting version of the Jacques Brel standard, despite Bowie's warning to the audience that his voice was shot, and taken from the Ziggy show at the Carnegie Hall, New York City, September 28, 1972.

I FEEL FREE

Very early version of The Cream's 'I Feel Free' from a Ziggy gig at the Kingston Polytechnic, UK, on 6 May, 1972. Warning: this would be bog-standard quality even for a bootleg.

Nothing Has Changed was the first Bowie compilation to go back to the very beginning of his career, although it is a moot point if 'Liza Jane', for example, deserves a place on the compilation ahead of 'John, I'm Only Dancing'. Most of the tracks which were trumpeted as 'new' had, in fact, been available as downloads, on CD-singles as B-Sides, or had been leaked, unofficially, online, although the finished mastered versions of 'Let Me Sleep Beside You' and 'All The Young Dudes', were especially done for this compilation. Laudably, there is a sizeable chunk of recent material. However, given its modest sales, it would be reasonable to suspect that this was simply one Bowie best of too many, and why wasn't there just something genuinely new to tease the Bowie fan?

Tracklisting (for 3-CD deluxe edition/digital download)

CD 1: 'Sue (or In A Season Of Crime)', 'Where Are We Now?', 'Love Is Lost (Hello Steve Reich Mix by James Murphy for the DFA Edit)', 'The Stars (Are Out Tonight)', New Killer Star' (radio edit), 'Everyone Says "Hi"' (edit), 'Slow Burn' (radio edit), 'Let Me Sleep Beside You', 'Your Turn To Drive', 'Shadow Man', 'Seven' (Marius De Vries mix), 'Survive' (Marius De Vries mix), 'Thursday's Child' (radio edit), 'I'm Afraid Of Americans (V1)' (clean edit), 'Little Wonder' (edit), 'Hallo Spaceboy' (PSB Remix) (with The Pet Shop Boys), 'Heart's Filthy Lesson' (radio edit), 'Strangers When We Meet' (single version).

CD 2: 'Buddha Of Suburbia', 'Jump They Say' (radio edit), 'Time Will Crawl' (MM remix),'Absolute Beginners' (single version), 'Dancing In The Street' (with Mick Jagger), 'Loving The Alien' (single remix), 'This Is Not America' (with the Pat Metheny Group), 'Blue Jean', 'Modern Love' (single version), 'China Girl' (single version), 'Let's Dance' (single version), 'Fashion' (single version), 'Scary Monsters (And Super Creeps)' (single version), 'Ashes To Ashes' (single version), 'Under Pressure' (with Queen), 'Boys Keep Swinging', "Heroes" (single version), 'Sound And Vision', 'Golden Years' (single version), 'Wild Is The Wind' (2010 Harry Maslin Mix).

CD 3: 'Fame', 'Young Americans' (2007 Tony Visconti mix single edit), 'Diamond Dogs', 'Rebel Rebel', 'Sorrow', 'Drive-In Saturday', 'All The Young Dudes', 'The Jean Genie' (original single mix), 'Moonage Daydream', 'Ziggy Stardust', 'Starman' (original single mix), 'Life On Mars?' (2003 Ken Scott Mix), 'Oh! You Pretty Things', 'Changes', 'The Man Who Sold The World', 'Space Oddity', 'In The Heat Of The Morning', 'Silly Boy Blue', 'Can't Help Thinking About Me', 'You've Got A Habit Of Leaving', 'Liza Jane'.

SUE (OR IN A SEASON OF CRIME)

Credited to David Bowie with the Maria Schneider Orchestrahe, this track was written by Bob Bhamra, Bowie, Maria Schneider and Paul Bateman. In the same way that many regarded the compilation to be one step too far, so 'Sue', part murder ballad, part trippy jazz work out, recorded with the Maria Schneider Orchestra and co-produced once again by Tony Visconti, appears to have stretched the listening capabilities of its audience. An edited version got some play on Six Music in the UK, but the fact that the single reached number 81 is the sound of the market saying that they don't like Bowie doing jazz, however, modern, however well sung, however well played. Not that Bowie could care less of course.

'TIS A PITY SHE WAS A WHORE

Available as 'Sue's' bonkers B-Side, '..Whore', is a wonderfully liberating piece of abstract electronica, un-produced and perhaps unproduceable. The music fairly crunches along and recalls an unattributed bootleg track some Bowie fans might have heard called 'Both Guns Are Out There'. In a rare public statement Bowie told us that the piece 'acknowledges the shocking rawness of the First World War', and 'If the Vorticists wrote Rock Music it might have sounded like this'.

PART III
MISCELLANE

PETER AND THE WOLF

(Original Release 2 May 1978: RCA Red Seal. UK CD: Sony Music Classical B00FVJFF0K. US Chart: 136)

Bowie narrates Prokofiev's 1936 work *Peter And The Wolf* with Eugene Ormandy conducting the Philadelphia Orchestra. It has to be said Bowie's voice is perfect for the job and the project reaffirms, along with 'The Laughing Gnome', and Bowie's introduction to Raymond Brigg's animated short film, *The Snowman*, that had his career not taken off as a singer and performer Bowie could have made the transition to other forms of media quite smoothly. Several versions of *Peter And The Wolf* exist. The 2004 reissue on BMG/Victor paired the work with Benjamin Britten's *Young Person's Guide To The Orchestra*, and Camille Saint-Saëns' *Carnival Of The Animals,* whilst a more recent edition on the Sony Music Classical imprint has *Peter And The Wolf* with the Britten piece and Tchaikovsky's *Nutcracker Suite.* Although the narration was originally recorded in December 1977, both these re-mastered versions (like the original RCA album and CD) have a photo from 1976 on the cover, a picture of the coke-addled Thin White Duke chosen, no doubt, to scare the living daylights out of the under-fives.

LIVE AND WELL

Available only through David's official site, Bowienet, this album is worth a footnote in the Bowie annals in that it provides an interesting snapshot of the *1.Outside* and *Earthling* material in a live context. Denuded of its original power, 'I'm Deranged' comes to us in an extended drum'n'bass form which sounds a tad flimsy. However, 'Little Wonder' and particularly 'The Heart's Filthy Lesson' (now with an apostrophe!) are powerful live versions.

Disc 1: 'I'm Afraid Of Americans', 'The Heart's Filthy Lesson', 'I'm Deranged', 'Hallo Spaceboy', 'Telling Lies', 'The Motel', 'The Voyeur Of Utter Destruction', 'Battle For Britain', 'Seven Years In Tibet', 'Little Wonder'.

Disc 2: 'Fun' (Dillinja Mix), 'Little Wonder' (Danny Saber Dance Mix), 'Dead Man Walking (Moby Mix), 'Telling Lies' (Paradox Mix).

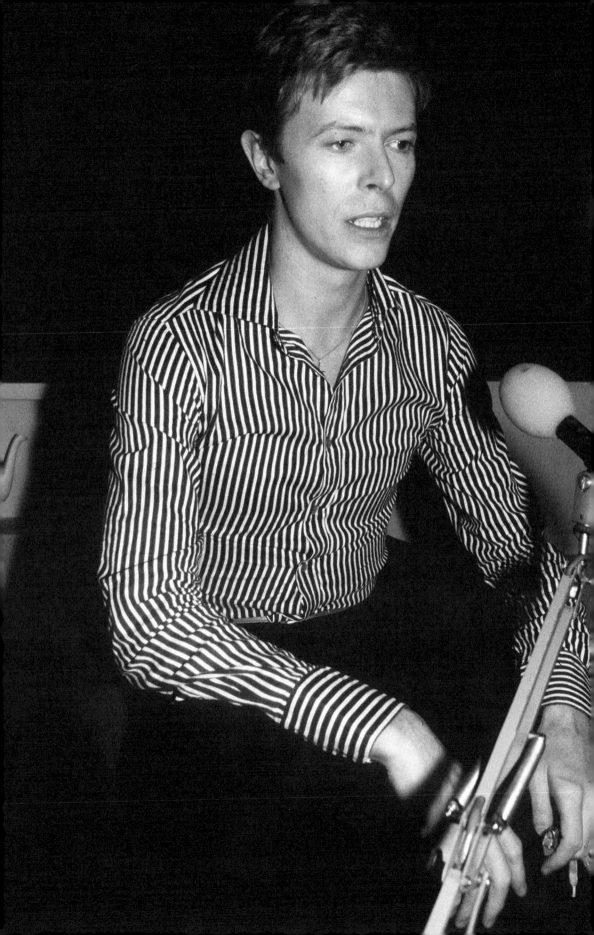

CHRISTIANE F: WIR KINDER VOM BAHNHOF ZOO – ORIGINAL SOUNDTRACK

(UK CD: 533 0932: Released 6 August 2001)

The soundtrack to a disturbing film about the plight of drug-addicted children in Berlin is a valid and moving collection, which draws on Bowie's rightly lauded mid-to-late Seventies work. "Heroes/Helden" is a magnificent full-length version of the song sung in both English and German, while 'Look Back In Anger' gives us the opportunity to enjoy Carlos Alomar's wondrous 30-second, mid-song guitar solo. For completists there's 'Station To Station', the live version from *Stage*, and the rare single edit of 'Stay'. *Christiane F* is a really fine album, and a perfect primer for those coming to Bowie's experimental work for the first time. Neatly re-packaged it boasts sleeve notes by renowned music writer Sylvie Simmons, and track commentary by the webmaster of Bowie's official site, Mark Adams. Enjoy…

Tracklisting: 'V-2 Schneider', 'TVC 15', "Heroes/Helden", 'Boys Keep Swinging', 'Sense Of Doubt', 'Station To Station', 'Look Back In Anger', 'Stay', 'Warszawa'.

THE RYKO REISSUES

Although now deleted, the Ryko versions of Bowie's catalogue, from *Space Oddity* to *Scary Monsters* (but excluding *Aladdin Sane*), contained some interesting additional tracks, some of which have not reappeared in EMI's reissue programme.

Space Oddity (UK CD: EMI EMC 3571; US CD: Rykodisc RCD 10131) – contains the whimsical 'Conversation Piece', while 'Memory Of A Free Festival Part 1' and 'Memory Of A Free Festival Part 2' are essential tracks.

The Man Who Sold The World (UK CD: EMI EMC 3573; US CD: Rykodisc RCD 10132) – bonus tracks are the folksy 'Lightning Frightening', a Spiders-era version of 'Holy Holy', and the Arnold Corns versions of 'Moonage Daydream' and 'Hang On To Yoursel'. These two tracks (later re-worked and massively improved for the *Ziggy Stardust* album) were released as a single in 1971 under the name Arnold Corns, essentially a Bowie-centred project. In true Warholian style, clothes designer and friend Freddie Burretti was the band's front-person despite contributing almost nothing to the music save some vocals on another Bowie song, 'Man In The Middle'. This was not part of the Rykodisc re-issues but released with 'Looking For A Friend' and 'Hang On To Yourself' on vinyl in 1985 on the Krazy Kat label.

Hunky Dory (UK CD: EMI EMC 3572; US CD: Rykodisc C 10133) – additional tracks are the twee 'Bombers', 'The Supermen' (alternative version), a demo of 'Quicksand', and an 'alterative' version of 'The Bewlay Brothers'.

The Rise And Fall Of Ziggy Stardust And The Spiders From Mars (UK CD: EMI EMC 3577; US CD: Rykodisc RCD 10134) – bonus tracks are 'John I'm Only Dancing', 'Velvet Goldmine', 'Sweet Head' and demos of 'Ziggy Stardust' and 'Lady Stardust'.

Pin-Ups (UK CD: EMI EMC 3580; US CD: Rykodisc RCD 10136) – bonus tracks are 'Growin' Up', now to be found on the Thirtieth Anniversary Edition of *Diamond Dogs*, and 'Port Of Amsterdam'.

Diamond Dogs (UK CD: EMI EMC 3584; US CD: Rykodisc RCD 10137) – 'Dodo' and 'Candidate' (demo version), the extra tracks on the Ryko release, can now be found on the Thirtieth Anniversary Edition of *Diamond Dogs*.

David Live (UK CD: EMI DBLD 1; US CD: Rykodisc RCD 1038/39) contained 'Band Intro', 'Here Today, Gone Tomorrow' and 'Time'.

Young Americans (UK CD: EMI EMD 1021; US CD: Rykodisc RCD 10140) – any EMI reissue of the album as a special thirtieth anniversary edition is likely to include some, if not all, of these Ryko bonus tracks: two strong ballads – 'Who Can I Be Now?' and 'It's Gonna Be Me' – and 'John, I'm Only Dancing (Again)'.

Station To Station (UK CD: EMI EMD 1020; US CD: Rykodisc RCD 10141) – the two bonus songs are live versions of 'Word On A Wing' and 'Stay', recorded at the Nassau Coliseum, Long Island, USA on March 23, 1976.

Low (UK CD: EMI EMD 1027; US CD: Rykodisc RCD 10142) – a brace of excellent and essential Bowie originals were added to the Ryko reissue. 'Some Are', co-written with Eno, sees Bowie's vocal high in the mix, yet the words are mainly incomprehensible, breathed out against a haunting piano line with what sounds like the chatter of a half-remembered schoolyard as ambient material. 'All Saints' can now be found on the instrumental CD of the same name (see earlier entry). Also included is the less-essential 1991 remix of 'Sound And Vision'

"Heroes" (UK CD: EMI EMD 1025; US CD: Rykodisc RCD 10143) – includes the instrumental 'Abdulmajid' (see entry for *All Saints*) and a superfluous remix of 'Joe The Lion'.

Stage (UK CD: EMI EMD 1030; US CD: Rykodisc RCD 10144/45) – the bonus track is, 'Alabama Song'.

Lodger (UK CD: EMI EMD 1026, US CD: Rykodisc RCD 10146) – the Ryko edition included the outtake 'I Pray, Ole', an excellent cut, and an equally intriguing remake of 'Look Back In Anger dating from 1988. The latter, recorded for Bowie's triumphant performance with La La La Human Steps at the ICA, was his first collaboration with Reeves Gabrels.

Scary Monsters (And Super Creeps) (US CD: Rykodisc RCD 20147) – four excellent bonus tracks can be found on the Ryko reissue. Firstly, a radical remake of 'Space Oddity'. On New Year's Eve 1979, Bowie bade farewell to what many critics point out as being his decade. His performance on *The Kenny Everett Video Show*, featured a new video co-directed by David Mallet. Next up is a 1979 remake of 'Panic In Detroit' which later surfaced on CD 2 of the limited-edition version of *Heathen* (see earlier entry). Then there's 'Crystal Japan' (see entry for *All Saints* above), and Bowie's version of the Kurt Weill/Berthold Brecht classic, 'Alabama Song'. Recorded in Montreux in 1978, it was released as a single in 1980 and surprisingly reached as high as number 23 in the UK Charts, backed by the re-recorded version of 'Space Oddity'. Bowie is in fine thespian fettle, though it will hardly appeal to the casual fan.

PART IV
SELECTED
COLLABORAT

ONS

In a 51-year-long career and counting, David Bowie has appeared on stage and in the studio as producer, writer, collaborator, backing vocalist, musician, guest star and muse to some of the most significant artists of the rock era. Many, including John Lennon, Mick Jagger and Pete Townshend, have already been cited herein, but a few others unmentioned elsewhere are worthy of note.

Mott The Hoople

Originally Bowie saw himself not so much as a performer, as a songwriter for other acts. 'All The Young Dudes', one of the classics of the glam era, was written specifically for Mott The Hoople and revitalised their sluggish career. At the time, Bowie himself was hitless for almost three years. Bowie also produced the parent album. The band rejected Bowie's second attempt to write for them, 'Drive-In Saturday', which went on to become one of Bowie's own biggest UK hits.

Lou Reed

Much has been made of the influence of Lou Reed on Bowie, and whilst that might be true in part, Bowie's influence on Lou Reed was, for a time, as great. Lou Reed circa 72-74 would take the stage in makeup and leathers and on *Transformer*, co-produced by Bowie, Mick Ronson and Ken Scott, Lou Reed is very much Bowie's creature. With tracks such as 'Satellite Of Love', 'Vicious' and 'Perfect Day' – not to mention 'Walk On The Wild Side', his only hit single – it is Lou Reed's best-ever solo album.

Iggy Pop

In the seventies and eighties, David and Jim were close friends. Bowie helped sign the Stooges to his management company Mainman and record label RCA and mixed their album, *Raw Power*. In 1976 and 1977, Bowie co-wrote for Pop's *Idiot* and *Lust For Life* albums, sessions which produced classics such as 'Nightclubbing', 'China Girl' and 'Lust For Life', and also toured with Iggy in early 1970 as keyboardist. Although critically less well-regarded, the 1986 album, *Blah, Blah, Blah*, contained some strong songs co-written with Bowie such as 'Shades', 'Baby It Can't Fall' and 'Isolation',

three songs that were stronger than almost anything on Bowie's own next album, *Never Let Me Down*.

Lulu

Bowie befriended Lulu in 1973 and made good on a promise to record her with sessions in France during the making of *Pin-Ups*. Bowie gave her two existing songs, 'Watch That Man' and 'The Man Who Sold The World'. The latter, with Bowie on backing vocals and saxophone, is an excellent cover version. Lulu would appear like a Bowie clone on *Top Of The Pops* and the song reached number three in the UK Charts.

Mick Ronson

'Bowie fuels Ronson' was the front page of a January 1974 edition of rock weekly *Melody Maker*, and while Ronson was no longer needed as Bowie's sideman on stage and in the studio, Bowie did co-write three songs for his first solo album, *Slaughter On 10th Avenue*, 'Growing Up And I'm Fine', 'Music Is Lethal' and 'Hey Ma Get Papa'. Ronson's final album, *Heaven And Hull*, included a version of Dylan's 'Like A Rolling Stone', with Bowie on vocals.

Reeves Gabrels

Bowie appears as vocalist on two songs from Gabrels' 1995 album, *The Sacred Squall Of Now* ('You've Been Around', 'The King Of Stamford Hill') and one on the 1999 album, 1999 *Ulysses (Della Notte)* ('Jewel').

Earl Slick

'Isn't It Evening' from guitarist Earl Slick's *Zig Zag* (Sanctuary, 2004) features a telling Bowie vocal, and a fine Mark Plati production reminiscent of the *Earthling/hours…* period.

Placebo

Bowie was an early champion of the band, and Placebo's debut album showed an obvious Bowie influence. The band opened for Bowie on selected dates on the Outside tour. At the 1999 Brit Awards Bowie joined Placebo for a live version of the T.Rex classic, 'Twentieth Century Boy', and also recorded a duet for the single, 'Without You I'm Nothing'.

David Gilmour

In 2006, Bowie made a surprise appearance on stage with Pink Floyd's David Gilmour and guested on two Floyd songs, 'Arnold Layne' and Comfortably Numb'. The Bowie/Gilmour version, together with a live version from the tour featuring Richard Wright on vocals was released as a single and reached number 19 in the UK singles chart in January 2007.

Arcade Fire

David Bowie was the first prominent musician to spot the potential of Canadian outfit Arcade Fire. As it had done with Kraftwerk 30 years earlier, Bowie's 'official endorsement' meant that the world started listening. In 2005, he made his first live performance since his heart problems in September 2005 with Arcade Fire for the charity fundraiser *Fashion Rocks* in New York, performing 'Life On Mars?', Arcade Fire's 'Wake Up' and 'Five Years'. This was released as an *iTunes* download EP.

Bowie also found himself in the studio while the band was making the *Reflektor* album. On hearing the incomplete title track, Bowie is reported to have jokingly told the band to finish it quickly before he took it! 'Reflektor' is indeed, a piece highly-influenced by Bowie who, although taking no part in the actual composition, lends some vocals to this excellent song mid-way in.

PART V
DVD

Up until the release of *Bowie: The Video Collection* in 1993, Bowie fans were incredibly short-changed when it came to seeing their man on video. This was indeed a crazy situation given Bowie's photogenic stage shows and music videos, and even now there are many gaps to be filled. There is no extended official footage available from any of his seventies concerts, bar the 1973 Hammersmith Odeon gig, or from the visually innovative *Sound + Vision* 1990 tour. Bowie's many excellent appearances on television, and the best documentary on Bowie ever – Omnibus' *Cracked Actor*, originally screened in 1975 – is still officially unavailable.

This brief tour around available product, listed in chronological order of release, is not meant to be at all-exhaustive, but rather points the first-time buyer towards interesting avenues of exploration.

THE CONCERT FOR NEW YORK CITY

(Sony Music Entertainment B00005V1WV, Released 29 January 2002)

Of interest to Bowie collectors is *The Concert For New York City,* recorded on October 20, 2001 at Madison Square Garden to benefit the Robin Hood Relief Fund after the events of 9/11. Bowie opens the concert brilliantly with the brave choice of Simon & Garfunkel's 'America', singing the song solo, sat cross-legged centre stage, accompanying himself on the Suzuki Omnichord. It is one of Bowie's finest-ever cover versions and it can be found on *The Concert for New York City*

double CD (Sony/BMG, released 10 December 2011). Then Bowie follows with an emotional version of 'Heroes'. Other featured artists include Bon Jovi, Billy Joel, Elton John and The Who.

BEST OF BOWIE

(DVD EMI: 490 1039, 11 November 2002)

Bowie's legendary power as a pop icon was based as much on the way he looked and packaged himself as on the music itself. This DVD, covering Bowie from his earliest proto-Ziggy days right up to the giddy promo for 'Survive', provides the vision as well as the sound. Again, there are some grouses: where, for example, are Bowie's television appearances for 'Fame' and 'Golden Years' which have long since masqueraded as promos for the singles?

But this is somewhat churlish in view of the brilliance contained herein. Bowie's vision of glam beauty that is his performance of 'Drive-In Saturday' on *The Russell Harty Show* led producer Ken Scott to comment in *Strange Fascination*: "I saw him being made up… and I remember looking at his reflection in the mirror and thinking, this is the most beautiful man I've ever seen." On Mick Rock's 'Life On Mars?' the stark white backdrop frames the carrot-topped rocker perfectly. An exquisitely weird Bowie performs 'Be My Wife', contorting his face to clownish, devilish, unnatural poses. After then the videos get slicker and Bowie begins to move away from simple performance videos (with the exception of the only real disappointment,

'Modern Love') to take on bigger themes such as colonial politics on 'Let's Dance' and urban American low-life on 'Day-In Day Out'. 'Ashes To Ashes' is still a stunning clip, filmed in part on location at Beachy Head, and featuring Bowie as astronaut, asylum inmate and Pierrot respectively. However, the famous drag video for 'Boys Keep Swinging' is more radical and 'Fashion', 'DJ' and 'Look Back In Anger' just as cool. Once past his creative drought of the late eighties, Bowie hits top form again with 'Jump They Say', and its neo-Hitchcockian themes, and arty cinematography. But the real gem is the Sam Bayer-directed sepia-tone hell that is 'Heart's Filthy Lesson'. Like Nine Inch Nail's clip for 'Closer' (which it strongly resembles) it wallows in the disgusting and the abject and is possibly Bowie's finest promo, if little seen. There were packs of posing performance artists, the Minotaur's head, a drum-playing puppet and Bowie, dripping paint like alien primal fluid. Finally, there's 'Thursday's Child's' poetic rumination on the whole process of ageing, as Bowie confronts an image of his younger self in the bathroom mirror, and 'Survive', which sees him levitate round the room.

This absolutely essential DVD contains hidden videos and interviews – 'Easter Eggs' – amongst which is 'Jazzin' For Blue Jean', a 20-minute, Julien Temple-directed extended pop promo dating from 1984 in its entirety. The video tells the story of Vic (played by Bowie), a cockney nerd, and his attempt to win over his love by taking her to a concert by Screaming Lord Byron, Vic's outlandish doppelganger (also played by Bowie). A piss-take of the preciousness of pop megalomania in general, and Bowie's in particular, the video itself is well worth looking out for.

Disc 1: 'Oh! You Pretty Thing', 'Queen Bitch', 'Five Years', 'Starman', 'John I'm Only Dancing', 'The Jean Genie', 'Space Oddity', 'Drive-In Saturday', Ziggy Stardust', 'Life On Mars?', 'Rebel Rebel', 'Young Americans', 'Be My Wife', ,"Heroes"', 'Boys Keep Swinging', 'DJ', 'Look Back In Anger', 'Ashes To Ashes', 'Fashion', 'Wild Is The Wind', 'Let's Dance', 'China Girl', 'Modern Love',

'Cat People (Putting Out Fire)', 'Blue Jean', 'Loving The Alien', 'Dancing In The Street'.

Disc 2: 'Absolute Beginners', 'Underground', 'As The World Falls Down', 'Day-In Day-Out', 'Time Will Crawl', 'Never Let Me Down', 'Fame '90', 'Jump They Say', 'Black Tie White Noise', 'Miracle Goodnight', 'Buddha Of Suburbia', 'The Heart's Filthy Lesson', 'Strangers When We Meet', 'Hallo Spaceboy', 'Little Wonder', 'Dead Man Walking', 'Seven Years In Tibet', 'I'm Afraid Of Americans', 'Thursday's Child', 'Survive'.

Easter Eggs: 'Oh! You Pretty Things' (*The Old Grey Whistle Test* - take 2), 'Interview with David Bowie and Russell Harty (before 'Drive-In Saturday'), Screen ad for the then forthcoming *Ziggy Stardust: The Motion Picture* DVD release (Hammersmith Odeon 1973), 'Jazzin For Blue Jean' (complete short-film length promotional video), 'Blue Jean' (recorded at The Wag Club, Soho, London), 'Day In Day Out' (Extended Mix), 'Miracle Goodnight' (Remix), 'Seven Years In Tibet' (Mandarin version), 'Survive' (Live in Paris).

ZIGGY STARDUST AND THE SPIDERS FROM MARS: THE MOTION PICTURE

(DVD: EMI 492 9879, 24 March 2003)

30th Anniversary DVD Special Edition, remixed and remastered featuring new stereo and 5.1 surround sound mixes. The D.A. Pennebaker film of the famous Ziggy retirement gig at the Hammersmith Odeon on July 3, 1973 has never been a totally satisfying visual experience. Its rather grainy texture does not do justice to either the serene Kabuki-styled Bowie or Mick Ronson's trousers, whilst some of the cinematography, with its blurry shots and jumpy pans, isn't really what we expect. There's still plenty of fun, including Bowie doing his best Lindsay Kemp on 'A Width Of A Circle', and the blistering opening of 'Hang On To Yourself' and 'Ziggy Stardust'. Unfortunately, 'Jean Genie'/'Love Me Do' and 'Round And Round' (which featured guitarist Jeff Beck) are still excluded at Beck's request. However, the overall packaging by EMI is excellent, and with extras including commentary by director Pennebaker and music producer Tony Visconti, it has to take pride of place in any Bowie collection.

Tracks: 'Opening Credits/Intro', 'Hang On To Yourself', 'Ziggy Stardust', 'Watch That Man', 'Wild Eyed Boy From Freecloud', 'All The Young Dudes', 'Oh! You Pretty Things', 'Moonage Daydream', 'Changes', 'Space Oddity', 'My Death', Cracked Actor', 'Time', 'The Width Of A Circle', 'Band Introduction', 'Let's Spend The Night Together', 'Suffragette City', 'White Light/White Heat', 'Farewell Speech', 'Rock 'n' Roll Suicide', 'End Credits'.

A REALITY TOUR

(DVD: SMV B0002TB2XI, 18 October 2004)

Culled from two concerts at the Point, Dublin, Bowie performs a near-greatest hits concert to an audience that needs no convincing. At the time, the LED screen

behind the stage was the biggest ever made for a rock concert. Fine performances abound, although the tension and risk taking of the mid-nineties tours is gone.

Tracks: 'Rebel Rebel', 'New Killer Star', 'Reality', 'Fame', 'Cactus', 'Sister Midnight', (Bowie, Alomar, Iggy Pop), 'Afraid', 'All the Young Dudes', 'Be My Wife', 'The Loneliest Guy', 'The Man Who Sold the World', 'Fantastic Voyage', 'Hallo Spaceboy', 'Sunday', 'Under Pressure' (Bowie, Freddie Mercury, John Deacon, Brian May, Roger Taylor), 'Life On Mars?', 'Battle For Britain (The Letter)', 'Ashes To Ashes', 'The Motel', 'Loving The Alien', 'Never Get Old', 'Changes', 'I'm Afraid Of Americans', '"Heroes"', 'Bring Me The Disco King', 'Slip Away', 'Heathen (The Rays)', 'Five Years', 'Hang On To Yourself', 'Ziggy Stardust'.

LOVE YOU TILL TUESDAY

(Universal B00064WC887, 7 February 2005)

Love You Till Tuesday was essentially a promotional showcase for Bowie conceived by his then manager Ken Pitt and features an early version of 'Space Oddity'. This filmed version of 'Space Oddity' was used on *Top Of The Pops* when the single re-charted in 1975, a strange move considering Bowie had recorded a more up-to-date video with Mick Rock for the 1972 US re-issue. Paired with this is *The Looking Glass Murders*, made for Grampian Television in 1970 and now for the first time officially available. This is the television version of *Pierrot In Turquoise*, a production by the Lindsay Kemp Mime Troop. Bowie plays Cloud and provides the music in a film that offers a stark reminder that Bowie was no ordinary rock star.

Tracklisting for *Love You Till Tuesday*: 'Love You Till Tuesday', 'Sell Me A Coat', 'When I'm Five', 'Rubber Band', 'The Mask (A Mime)', 'Let Me Sleep Beside You', 'Ching-a-Ling', 'Space Oddity', 'When I Live My Dream'.

SERIOUS MOONLIGHT

(DVD: EMI Catalogue B000E6UXXY, 13 March 2006)

For fans of a certain vintage, 1983 was the most exciting year in Bowie's career. No one expected the avalanche of applications for tickets when Bowie announced his first world tour since 1978. The entire UK arena dates sold out within hours and the overspill of applications was catered for by large outdoor concerts, notably at Milton Keynes Bowl, where the author first saw David Bowie live.

This live show was filmed in Vancouver on September 12 of that year. We should get the disappointments out of the way first; the picture quality on DVD is not that much improved from the eighties video releases and it is still not a full concert; the final five songs of the concert, 'TVC15', 'Star', 'Stay', 'The Jean Genie' and 'Modern Love' are still left out. One could understand that the format constrictions of presenting shows on video meant that there simply wasn't space for everything but there's no excuse now. Highlights include the segue between 'Fashion' and 'Let's Dance', a resurrected 'Cracked Actor', complete with skull and cloak as props, and an extended version of 'Fame'. Bowie's hair, backcombed and lacquered into a frenzy is a marvellous thing to behold.

Tracks: 'Introduction', 'Look Back In Anger', '"Heroes"', 'What In The World', 'Golden Years', 'Fashion', 'Let's Dance', 'Breaking Glass', 'Life On Mars?', 'Sorrow', 'Cat People (Putting Out Fire)', 'China Girl', 'Scary

BLACK TIE WHITE NOISE

(EMI B0006TNAEI, 7 March 2005)

In order to try and make amends for the decision not to tour in 1993 Bowie decided to release this, a video companion piece for the *Black Tie White Noise* album, consisting of an interview, six 'live' tracks recorded that May in the Hollywood Center Studios in LA, and the three video clips for 'Miracle Goodnight', 'Jump They Say' and 'Black Tie White Noise'. The interview material is mildly interesting but the 'live' tracks, in actuality mimed performances directed by David Mallet, are mostly plain boring and look a bit cheaply done. Bowie redeems himself however with two of his very best promo clips. 'Miracle Goodnight' is a carousel of harlequinesque images while 'Jump They Say', which sees Bowie tottering on the edge of a skyscraper before falling to his death, rivals 'Ashes To Ashes' for sheer power and invention. The videos are now available on the *Best Of Bowie* DVD, whilst the lavishly repackaged 3-CD set for the reissue of *Black Tie White Noise* (see entry above) contains the interview and 'live' performances.

Monsters (And Super Creeps), 'Rebel Rebel', 'White Light/White Heat', 'Station To Station', 'Cracked Actor', 'Ashes To Ashes', 'Space Oddity/Band Introduction', 'Young American', 'Fame/End Credits'.

Extras: RICOCHET-DOCUMENTARY. Also from the *Serious Moonlight* tour, this film contains some concert footage with some staged, though interesting, shots of Bowie going about his daily business in the Far East (in hotel rooms, on escalators, in a taxi, visiting a Buddhist shrine). There's also a distracting and weak story line intercut with material about a young fan trying to raise the dosh for a Bowie ticket.

GLASS SPIDER

(EMI Catalogue, 25 June 2007)

There is something tragically endearing about *Glass Spider*. Watched by more people than *Serious Moonlight*, it was, in turns, both thrilling and excruciating. The bad bits all came from outreach and Bowie's miscalculations. The supporting album, *Never Let Me Down*, although nowhere near the car-crash some have portrayed it, was not strong enough to build a tour around and each single underperformed, despite the world tour. Fans had seen Bowie imperious and a huge star in '83, but now the general public were pulling out (despite what you may read on Bowie message boards, and for no apparent reason than a nerdish attachment and will for Bowie to win, chart placings for Bowie albums and singles really did matter for many of his fans).

In interviews around this time, Bowie was referencing performance artists La La La Human Steps and Pina Bausch as inspirations; but *Glass Spider* was a strange mixture of the artful and the artless, veering from stadium rock poses to moments of sheer brilliance, often within one song. The *Glass Spider tour* was critically mauled at the time and it is plain to see that Bowie had overstretched himself (probably literally!), abseiling from the top of 60-foot spiders one minute, strangled by ropes the next. But there are such delights as 'Absolute Beginners' and 'Time' along the way. The *Sound + Vision* tour of 1990 did it all much better, but remains undocumented on video.

Like *Serious Moonlight*, *Glass Spider* is also substandard in terms of its DVD quality with very little discernible difference between the new version and the original video release. The original video was filmed on November 7 & 9, 1987, at the Sydney Entertainment Center and by this point the original concept for the tour had changed, probably due to critical and audience pressure. By this time, several hits had found their way into the set such as 'Young Americans', 'Rebel Rebel' and 'The Jean Genie' whilst others such as a brilliant reworking of 'All The Madmen', and several songs from *Never Let Me Down*, plus 'Dancing With The Big Boys' from *Tonight*, were dropped. Their removal makes an already confused on-stage narrative essentially meaningless.

The 2007 edition contains a bonus double CD recorded on August 30 at the Stade Olympique in Montreal and is a full, 26-song setlist. It's a very fine performance and makes the purchase of the DVD/audio combination genuinely attractive.

Tracks: (2007 release): 'Intro/Up The Hill Backwards', 'Glass Spider', 'Day-In Day-Out', 'Bang Bang', 'Absolute Beginners', 'Loving The Alien', 'China Girl', 'Rebel Rebel', 'Fashion', 'Never Let Me Down', 'Heroes', 'Sons Of The Silent Age', 'Band Introduction', 'Young Americans', 'The Jean Genie', 'Let's Dance', 'Time', 'Fame', 'Blue Jean', 'I Wanna Be Your Dog' (Alexander, Asheton, Asheton, Pop), 'White Light/White Heat', 'Modern Love'.

IN THE TIN CAN: OFFICIALLY UNRELEASED or CRYPTO BOWIE?

A favourite pastime for Bowie fans is to speculate over whether rumoured tracks actually exist, why concerts which have been known to have been filmed are not given an official release, and whether Bowie's record company are hanging back with a career-spanning Bowie Anthology because Bowie is still active musically and that would, perhaps, appear to bring closure.

SOUND

There are hundreds of bootlegs of varying quality of Bowie concerts which are being sold and traded but more often simply shared by Bowie fans around the world. We take it that Bowie himself is quite easy about this. In 1999 he said, "They've been taking my music and bootlegging my shows for ages. I know all the sites that have my bootlegs and all my MP3s. Actually, I don't give a flying fuck." What nobody liked were those few fans who would produce piss-poor quality live bootlegs for extortionate prices. Sharing music in the spirit of friendly discourse is one thing; making it an exploitative living is bad for both fan and artist. Thankfully, those particular vultures now appear to have almost died out.

However, there have been dozens of Bowie concerts which have been professionally recorded for radio over the last four decades and which many Bowie fans would be happy to buy. To take just one example, the second show on the *Sound + Vision* tour at the Milton Keynes Bowl was recorded and broadcast by Radio 1. Thousands of fans would have heard if not copied this performance but with decaying tape and knackered cassettes, it might not be that easy to relive the moment.

But what about those actual songs whose titles have been bandied around, the demos, the rumoured completed tracks? Only those who have worked directly with Bowie's

archive will know definitively what actually exists and of course Bowie, as the artist, has every right to veto any release if he thinks the work to be substandard either in terms of artistic or audio standard.

The largest cache of unreleased music would almost certainly appear to be from the first sessions for *Outside* in 1994. Bowie himself revealed: "I think you underestimate the amount of work that we put in. We have almost 27 hours of tapes. Work that out into CDs – something like 24 CDs. And I'm having trouble putting the second one together... No rest for the wicked." However, perhaps the most intriguing from the vaults release would be the work done with Paul Buckmaster in 1975 for the soundtrack for *The Man Who Fell To Earth*. Paul told me in an interview for *Mojo*: "Basically there were a couple of medium-tempo rock instrumental pieces, with simple motifs and riffy kind of

grooves, with a line-up of David's rhythm section [Carlos Alomar, et al] plus J. Peter Robinson on Rhodes-Fender piano, and me on cello and some synth overdubs, using Arp Odyssey and Solina [string machine]. There were some more slow and spacey cues [any section of music appearing in a movie] with synth, Rhodes, cello, and a couple of somewhat 'weirder' atonalish cues using synths and percussion. There was also a piece I wrote and performed using some beautifully made mbiras [an African thumb-piano] I had purchased earlier that year, plus cello, all done by multiple overdubbing. Also, there was a song which David wrote, played and sang, called 'Wheels', which had a gentle sort of melancholy mood to it. The title referred to the alien train from Newton's home world." The music was never released and a tape remains in Buckmaster's archive. On the question of whether it could ever be released, Paul told me: "Only if David were to call for a total re-recording of every piece, played by the very best musicians."

Another much-speculated area of 'lost' music is 'The Sigma Reel' from August 1974. Bowie had started (and many on the sessions thought had completed) the album which would be called *Young Americans*, in an intense three-week recording spree that summer. In 2009, snippets of unreleased songs appeared online, including different takes of 'Young Americans', and 'After Today', and two completely unreleased songs: 'I Am A Laser' (sometimes, simply 'Laser') and 'Shilling The Rubes'. Both songs sound as strong as other cuts from the session while 'I Am A Laser' – whose chorus would provide the melody for 1980's 'Scream Like A Baby' on 1980's *Scary Monsters (And Super Creeps)* – exhorts 'Let's hear it for the Gouster.'

There are other unreleased tracks dating from the pre-Ziggy Stardust period such as 'Rupert The Riley', 'Miss Peculiar' (AKA 'How Lucky You Are'), 'Shadowman' (later to be re-recorded and officially released), 'Tired Of My Life' (whose melody was reused for 'It's No Game' on *Scary Monsters*). There might be better news for Tin Machine fans, as Reeves Gabrels revealed to me for *Mojo* recently: "There are several labels interested in a Tin Machine box set. There are eight to ten tracks that have never been released including an alternate version of 'Heaven's In Here'." Whilst another Bowie song, written in 1992, 'Bring Me The Disco King', which eventually appeared on *Reality* was originally recorded for *Black Tie White Noise* and during the *Earthling* sessions, the final officially released version being at least Bowie's third studio attempt.

There are dozens of other Bowie song titles in circulation without any music available to back up their claims for authenticity. 'Black Hole Kids', from the *Ziggy* sessions, 'God Only Knows', 'I Feel Free' and 'Ladytron' from *Pin-Ups*, 'Cyclops' and 'The Ballad Of Ira Hayes' from *Diamond Dogs*, 'Moving On' and 'Sister Midnight' from *Station To Station* and 'I Feel Free' (again) on *Scary Monsters*, not to mention a version of 'Ashes To Ashes' with extra verse/verses. While other tracks *do* exist but are in such poor state as to be possibly unreleasable such as 'Zion', an instrumental demo which dates from around the *Aladdin Sane* period, 'Sleeping Next To You', a collaboration with Marc Bolan, and 'Velvet Couch'/'Piano-La', with John Cale. Of the Bolan and Cale recordings, Bowie said, "As far as I know, these have always just been bootleg songs. Unfortunately, there is nothing at a higher quality to release. I would grab those bootlegs when you see them. Don't say you heard it from me."

VISION

It is undoubtedly true that certain key moments in Bowie's career are not available officially. The most glaring omission from the official canon is *Cracked Actor*, filmed by the BBC in 1974 and produced by Alan Yentob. Whether it is a problem of securing rights (unlikely) or perhaps more to do with the intensely uncomfortable nature of many of the scenes within the film, this essential part of Bowie history remains unreleased (although available, of course, through other platforms).

There are numerous other Bowie highlights from TV which are also either very difficult to get legally, or have simply gone missing. The Jeff Beck appearance at Hammersmith Odeon in July 1973 is still missing from the film. Bowie's strange performance on *The Dick Cavett Show* in December 1974 should include 'Can You Hear Me?' which was recorded live but was edited from the final transmission. Can it be true that Bowie, his then record company or his ex-managers have absolutely no footage of either the Diamond Dogs or *Station To Station* (Isolar 1) tours? Moving on to 1978 and David Hemmings shot an entire Bowie concert at Earls Court which remains unreleased apart from the odd clip. There are also live performances from the tour which were officially and professionally recorded (such as Musikladen and Tokyo Budokan) which again are unavailable to buy.

From 1979 to 1982, Bowie was off the road but certainly visible on TV. Performances on *The Kenny Everett Video Show* (performing 'Boys Keep Swinging', with Klaus Nomi and Joey Arias, on *Saturday Night Live* (one of Bowie's best-ever performances), a live section in 1980 on the *Johnny Carson Show*, not to mention his staring-role performance in the BBC's adaptation of *Baal*, are all either extremely difficult to buy or unavailable legally.

In 1983, a fascinating short film, *South Of Watford*, took Bowie's appearances at the Milton Keynes Bowl as its focus and includes rare footage of the shows, along with an interview with Michael Watts, *Melody Maker*'s original Bowie champion. In 1986, Bowie gave one of his best-ever interviews for *Video Jukebox,* BBC 2's expansive history of the pop promo. Bowie would also be interviewed in the eighties for *The Tube*, *Nationwide*, *Newsnight* and many other regional TV shows and all these moments contain sections of unique material, either live or interview. Again, although most if not all of these are available to Bowie fans online, it is not the same as having them officially. These short television appearances, not to mention interviews on radio appearances, helped form the Bowie narrative for many fans at the time.

In the late eighties and nineties, many Bowie concerts were professionally filmed for TV. No official DVD of the *Sound + Vison* tour was ever released, despite one planned, so fans have had to make do with footage from the Tokyo Dome in less-than-perfect quality. Fans of Tin Machine have seen the live *Oy Vey Baby* video fail to even reach DVD, whilst none of the promotional videos are available to buy. One of Bowie's best-ever performances were in June 1996 at *Rockpalast* and broadcast on German television. The opener, 'Look Back In Anger', sees Bowie at his weird and cheekiest best, pulling faces and throwing shapes behind Gabrels during the mid-song solo. Into the 2000s, and whilst Bowie's *A Reality* tour is available to buy, there is sadly nothing from the rather better *Heathen* tour. Again, concerts were filmed and TV broadcasts made.

Finally comes the promos and videos. There is a film for 'Rock 'n' Roll Suicide' which uses footage filmed by Mick Rock, whilst excerpted rushes for the 1977 'Heroes' video are online, along with a film for 'Sense Of Doubt' which shows Bowie recreating through mime the 'Heroes' cover shot. Into the late nineties, and a video was started, but never completed for 'The Pretty Things Are Going To Hell'. Made with video producers Dom and Nick, it had puppets of past personae attacking their creator. An unfinished version of the video has appeared online. In a webchat, Bowie confirmed: "It was abandoned after we found that the puppets ended up looking like puppets. What I mean is it didn't have the east European darkness that Dom and Nick had wanted to achieve. Some of it is downright funny and I'm sure it will make its way onto a video compilation one of these days. To be a source of endless amusement to you all and another form of Chinese torture for myself."

PART VI
BOWIE IS

2013 was a vintage year for Bowie fans. There was his first studio album for a decade. There was also the BBC 2 documentary *Five Years* directed by Francis Whately, only the second major British TV documentary about Bowie. Focusing on five pivotal years in Bowie's career (there was a bit of license taken here as a year was often taken to be essentially two years!) and with some really excellent interviews with Bowie associates past and present such as Earl Slick, Carlos Alomar, Dennis Davis, Robert Fripp and Candy Clark, plus some either rare or unseen film footage, it was, in the main, a treat. The only quibbles would be the fact the documentary ended when it did, in 1983, and that the narrative tended to confirm what is, at best, a contested history that Bowie 'cleaned up' in Berlin (yes, he got better, but, as the man himself would confirm, there would be lapses). But what *Five Years* did was to remind not just the Bowie fans but everyone else watching, that he was such a major player, with brilliance across a whole wide range of expertise.

Bowie Is, an exhibition at London's Victoria & Albert Museum, was the perfect confirmation of Bowie's tireless work, diversity of thinking and brilliance as a singer, writer, concert performer and actor. It would be hard to think of any other figure in music over the last 40 years who could produce such startling material for a major exhibition and it pulled in the crowds, and not simply Bowienuts.

Curated by Victoria Broackes and Geoffrey Marsh, over 300,000 attended the exhibition during its run from March to August. Some 67,000 tickets were sold prior to the opening. The exhibition begins chronologically with an examination of the pre-fame Bowie then explodes thematically into specially arranged Bowiecloves of delight. A state-of-the art sound system from Sennheiser meant that different commentary and music could be fed as one moved from zone to zone. There was a video wall, a Berlin room, an array of original lyrics with crossings out, amendments and re-writes, and a large

section devoted to his on-stage costuming from which we learnt that Bowie's waist for the *Aladdin Sane* tour was a mere 26 and a half inches, and no doubt every woman there would have been delighted to be able to squeeze into these clothes. Towards the end was a dazzling outfit labelled 'Ziggy Stardust day wear' – did he really eat his breakfast in that? The final area featured projections of classic performances, including 'Rock'n'Roll Suicide' from the Hammersmith Odeon and 'Heroes' from Live Aid.

Even the biggest Bowie fan would have found something he or she didn't know. *Bowie Is* also confirmed what an astonishing pace of work Bowie kept up, particularly in the seventies, and that so much more was started, yet remained unrealised. For example, we get to see some of Bowie's work for the never realised *Diamond Dogs* film from 1975. We also find out that the original stage design for the 1976 'White Light' tour appeared to originally include huge ghost-like figurines at the back of the stage, while the original plan for the *Serious Moonlight* tour was an Escher-like stage design (although the idea would be used a few years later in *Labyrinth*).

Since its London stint, *Bowie Is* has done something Bowie the man hasn't done for a decade; gone on tour to Sao Paulo, Berlin, Chicago, Paris, and later in 2015 to Melbourne and Groninger. A book was published for the original opening by the V&A, including essays by Jon Savage, Camilia Paglia and Howard Goodall among others, while a film of the exhibition was released in November 2014. The only worry is that Bowie, in the public imagination, will become institutionalised, fixed, a memory, an artefact, rather than a still living, breathing and working artist. "Shouldn't this exhibition have taken place after he had died," one journalist asked me. "Maybe… But let's hope that isn't for at least another 30 years," was my reply.

PART VII

DAVID BOWIE IN 50 BITS: THE ESSENTIAL BOWIE TO DOWNLOAD

Having got this far, I hope you are now suitably primed, ready to either catch-up on missed pieces of Bowie brilliance, revisit those you already cherish, and to compile an essential mix-tape to prove to yourself and, hopefully, many others, just how brilliant Bowie was and is. So, here it is: the (ahem, sorry, my) definitive Bowie Top 50 to download and bother the kids with. I have imposed a few conditions on my selection. To stop myself from picking seven tracks from *Low*, I have decided to limit my choices to three per album. To keep the numbers down and the selection both affordable and listenable in one session, I have also not included any live tracks or cover versions (so, sadly, no room for 'Sorrow', 'Criminal World' or 'Nite Flights), although Tin Machine songs are allowed, and three make the cut. Ask me next week for my Top 50 and I am sure at least half a dozen of my choices might be different, and I am no respecter of reputation as the omission of some Bowie 'classics' will prove but here goes…

To be played at maximum volume, of course…

'SPACE ODDITY'
'THE MAN WHO SOLD THE WORLD'
'A WIDTH OF A CIRCLE'
'SAVIOUR MACHINE'
'CHANGES'
'LIFE ON MARS?'
'THE BEWLAY BROTHERS'
'STARMAN'
'FIVE YEARS'
'MOONAGE DAYDREAM'
'PANIC IN DETROIT'
'ALADDIN SANE'
'TIME'
'ALTERNATIVE CANDIDATE'
'SWEET THING/CANDIDATE/SWEET THING (REPRISE)'
'1984'
'BIG BROTHER AND THE CHANT OF THE EVER-CIRCLING SKELETAL FAMILY'
'WIN'
'FAME'
'GOLDEN YEARS'
'STATION TO STATION'
'WORD ON A WING'
'SOUND AND VISION'
'SPEED OF LIFE'
'A NEW CAREER IN A NEW TOWN'
'"HEROES"'
'THE SECRET LIFE OF ARABIA'
'NEUKOLN'
'LOOK BACK IN ANGER'
'MOVE ON'
'RED SAILS'
'ASHES TO ASHES'
'FASHION'
'IT'S NO GAME (Part 1)'
'LET'S DANCE'
'BLUE JEAN'
'LOVING THE ALIEN'
'ABSOLOUTE BEGINNERS'
'I CAN'T READ'
'AMAZING'
'GOODBYE MR ED'
'JUMP THEY SAY'
'UNTITLED NUMBER 1'
'HEART'S FILTHY LESSON'
'OUTSIDE'
'LOOKING FOR SATELLITES'
'SUNDAY'
'SLIP AWAY'
'WHERE ARE WE NOW?'
'THE NEXT DAY'
'LOVE IS LOST'